Names and Nunavut

NAMES AND NUNAVUT

CULTURE AND IDENTITY IN ARCTIC CANADA

Valerie Alia

Berghahn Books
New York • Oxford

First published in 2007 by

Berghahn Books
www.berghahnbooks.com

© 2007, 2009 Valerie Alia
First paperback edition published in 2009

Library of Congress Cataloging-in-Publication Data
Alia, Valerie, 1942-
   Names and Nunavut : culture and identity in Arctic Canada / Valerie Alia.
      p. cm.
   Includes bibliographical references and index.
   ISBN 978-1-84545-165-1 (hbk.) -- 978-1-84545-413-5 (pbk)
   1. Names, Inuit--Nunavut. 2. Names, Inuit--Political aspects--Nunavut.
   3. Inuit--Nunavut--Social life and customs. 4. Names, Inuit--Nunavut--
   Government relations. 5. Names, Geographical--Nunavut. 6. Names,
   Ethnological--Nunavut. 7. Nunavut--Social life and customs. I. Title.

PM50.Z9N863 2006
305.897'120795--dc22

                                                    2006018116

British Library Cataloguing in Publication Data

A catalogue record for this book is available from
the British Library.

Printed in the United States on acid-free paper

ISBN 978-1-84545-165-3 hardback, 978-1-84545-413-5 paperback

Dedication

For Dan and Dave, my darling Pete,
Mary Margaret Zahara,

and the people of Nunavut:
long may they and their names survive

CONTENTS

LIST OF FIGURES

PREFACE

It is late September and my first trip north is ending. The men are coming back from caribou hunting; the women are still gathering blueberries. Suddenly, a rainbow appears. Hypnotised, I watch, oblivious of the hour. My host rushes over, saying there is no time to walk. He captures an ATV (all-terrain vehicle, three-wheeled motorbike) 'taxi' and whizzes to the airport, arriving just before take-off. I watch the fading rainbow as we fly, and remember the beginning …

On a warmish day at summer's end, I board a plane in Toronto. Destination: Baffin Island, north of the Northern Lights and south of the Pole. The year is 1985. It has taken more than a year to organise funds, time, child care (at the time, I am the lone parent of two school-aged boys) and health (I have just undergone surgery). Friends say I should stay home; there is no way I am going to stay home. When the plane touches down to refuel in Fort Chimo (now called Kuujjuaq) at the edge of the Northern Québec (Nunavik) tree line, all the passengers scramble down the ladder into the sunshine. There are only a few moments to catch the sun, and we aim to make the most of them.

Airline personnel dress for the realities of work and weather in layers of garments with heavily hooded parkas and sturdy boots. There are no formalities of either dress or address and, in communities with only occasional flights, no rigid schedules. The flight attendant watches us cavort and then runs out of patience. She keeps calling us for take-off until, like recalcitrant schoolchildren, we dawdle and shuffle up the stairs and back to our seats …

My first glimpse of Baffin Island: Frobisher Bay (soon to be given an official Inuktitut name, Iqaluit) is cold, grey, damp and windy. At 2,400 (a figure now more than doubled – about 6,000 in 2006), the largest community in the Eastern Arctic is a centre for airline, medical and government services (Bell 2004). We have arrived 'Up Here' and up here I am from 'Outside' – the South – anywhere below the 60th parallel. That designation rapidly changes the perspective of one for whom 'south' once meant that part of the United States below the Mason–Dixon Line known as 'Dixie'. I struggle to get my bearings and turn from the thrilling air and landscape to research. Soon I will learn that the landscape is an inseparable part of the research, that identities and names of places and people are intricately intertwined. The airport sits on the edge of town, a short walk from everywhere. To southern eyes, the Frobisher Inn looks less like an inn than a warehouse. Across Nunavut, in the Northwest Territories and Yukon, I find that many of the buildings are like geodes. Outside, they are characterless and practical, made to withstand wildly shifting weather; inside, they are often beautiful.

En route to my temporary home in the Frobisher Inn, I cross the schoolyard and encounter a cluster of children. A small boy calls out, 'Can you picture me? Can you picture me?' he repeats, pointing to the camera. As I move to 'picture' him, one, two, three friends jump into line, pose, giggle, then return to their game of hide-and-seek. Years later, the pictures remain vivid. But pictures can only hint at the power of the Baffin rocks. They can not record the joy of tea, homemade bread and good talk at Rosie Veevee's house or the pungent smell of seal that permeates the home of Etoangat, sculptor, hunter and oldest man in Pangnirtung, who has 'never taken a white man's name'. Or the delight in meeting three young girls who visit the home where I am billeted several times a week and guilelessly shift from singing Inuktitut 'country northern' songs to Bruce Springsteen's 'Born in the USA'. Or the first breath-wrenching glimpse of Pangnirtung as the sturdy little Hawker Siddely (with its Rolls Royce engine and utilitarian interior) scoots between mountain walls, out of the expanse of Cumberland Sound into the deep green-blue of Pangnirtung Fiord. Or the sense of welcome as half the population surrounds our landing on the tiny dirt runway that bisects the community. Or the harsh wind and soft snow that herald freeze-up in Cape Dorset. Or the blue-green white-capped water and the ice-white frosting on Kinngait's humpbacked hills. Or, in the saddest moment, high above Igloolik, my first sight of Elise's garlanded grave. Pictures ... but I have come to learn. Studying the political meanings of names has led me here, where Project Surname once covered the Arctic and permanently changed the cultural terrain.

I had no idea this would become a lifelong project. I was teaching and writing on politics of the family and thought it would be interesting to include information about naming. To my surprise, the literature I was looking for did not exist. I found clues and titbits in many literatures and interviewed immigrants about how they negotiated naming and name changes in Canada. Then, I learned about Inuit experiences of reidentification. Decades later, most of the academic literature still considers naming only as marginal, or secondary to other areas of study. The more I learn, the more I am convinced that naming is 'the main event'.

Names are the cornerstones of cultures. They identify individuals, represent life, express and embody power. For more than twenty years, I

Kinngait (Cape Dorset).
Photograph by Valerie Alia.

have looked at the changing patterns of naming and renaming as Inuit and Qallunaat encountered each other, and the effects of interventions such as disc number identification, missionary-given baptismal names, and the government programme known as Project Surname.

The experience of Inuit in Canada is both unique and universal. Project Surname came out of uniquely Canadian conditions and affected uniquely Inuit cultural traditions. Yet there are similar reidentification programmes everywhere. I have not found a country or a culture without a history of renaming. Much can be learned from separate struggles and kindred experiences. Naming clarifies – and represents – structures of status, class and gender. When power is unequal and people are colonised at one level or another, naming is manipulated from the outside. In the Canadian North, the most blatant example of this manipulation is the long history of interference by visitors with the ways Inuit named themselves and their land.

This book looks at Inuit ways of naming and chronicles the stages in the evolution of naming and identity politics, focusing on relations between Inuit and Outsiders in the Canadian Eastern Arctic that was part of the Northwest Territories when the study began, and now is Nunavut Territory. In a period of about two years, virtually all Inuit in Canada received new names, based on a Qallunaaq (non-Inuit, Euro-Canadian)

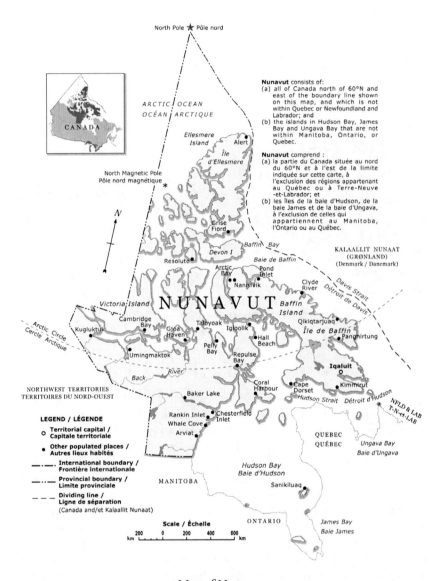

Map of Nunavut.

Source: This map was taken from The Atlas of Canada http://www.atlas.gc.ca/ © 2005. Produced under licence from Her Majesty the Queen in Right of Canada, with Permission of Natural Resources Canada.

model of surnaming. At the time the population was about 17,000. Today it has nearly doubled to about 30,000. Completed in 1972, Project Surname marked a turning point in the history of government efforts to reidentify Inuit. Its history is important to explore. The effects are still felt more than thirty years later. The research began in 1984 and included work at Inuit Tapirisat of Canada (ITC, now ITK – Inuit Tapiriit Kanatami), Tungavik Federation of Nunavut, Prince of Wales Northern Heritage Centre in Yellowknife, the Inuit Circumpolar Conference and its General Assemblies, the National Archives and Library of Canada, the library of the Department of Indian and Northern Affairs, and the library of the Scott Polar Research Institute at the University of Cambridge. Inuit and Qallunaat from Baffin communities, Igloolik, Yellowknife, Arviat (Eskimo Point), Ottawa, Toronto, Quebec City, Montreal, Yellowknife, Nunavik (Northern Quebec), Vancouver and other locations were interviewed between 1984 and 2006. These were years in which the importance of names was increasingly acknowledged, years of rapid change which at one point caused me to reassess my earlier findings:

> This New Year, January 1987, an Arctic town is being renamed. Frobisher Bay officially becomes Iqaluit. Will Canada's mapmakers rush to press, just to record this one small change on charts of our giant land? Probably not. But the change is nevertheless a dramatic and historic one … a symbol of a profound shift in attitudes … a recognition of the right of native people to name their homeland. That right has not always been apparent to those who govern Inuit. For the entire history of white presence in the Arctic, Inuit references have taken second place to the names newcomers used to identify the features of this land. But more subtly and dangerously, Euro-Canadians have always assumed their right to impose names on the people themselves. (Alia 1987: 12)

A decade after the official changeover, some (unofficial) maps still called Nunavut's capital 'Frobisher Bay'. Even today, many travel agents and journalists still can not find (or spell) Iqaluit. In 1993, I asked my university's travel agent to help book a flight; she told me: 'Frobisher Bay seems to be the nearest airport to Iqaluit'. Like the outdated maps, colonial attitudes also remain. The page from the website of Natural Resources Canada indicates the government's formal encouragement of the creation – or restoration – of Aboriginal place names on official maps.

Straightening the Record

Northern records are sparse, documents hard to find. Many of them came from people's private files. The interviews were based on a double 'snowball sample', a variation on the standard 'snowball' using two networks (Inuit and Qallunaat) with the paths occasionally crossing. The

ABORIGINAL PLACE NAMES
CHARTING OUR HERITAGE

HONOURING OUR PAST

"Canada" is not the only familiar place name that comes from an Aboriginal word — Lake Athabasca, Saskatchewan River, Kuujjuaq and Toronto are some others. And yet, there are many more names used within Aboriginal communities that do not appear on maps or road signs.

DOCUMENTING OUR HERITAGE

A growing number of communities and geographical features across Canada are being named or renamed to reflect local usage and traditions.

For example, residents of Frobisher Bay voted to change the name of their community to Iqaluit, the Inuktitut word for "place of fish." A lake in Northern Alberta has been named Atihk Sakahikun, which means "Elk Lake" in Cree.

People are collecting traditional names to suggest for approval by the Geographical Names Board of Canada. Names must be approved by the Board to be used on federal maps for mining, forestry, fishing, tourism, and search and rescue. Other uses are road signs, postal addresses and administrative documents.

By making traditional geographical names official, we can help value and preserve our Aboriginal heritage.

GETTING INVOLVED

If you or your organization want to suggest a name, the first step is to call or write to your provincial or territorial member of the Geographical Names Board of Canada. The names of board members and the procedures to follow are on our Web site at **http://geonames.NRCan.gc.ca/** or you can contact us at the address below.

Geographical Names Section
Natural Resources Canada
615 Booth Street
Ottawa ON K1A 0E9
Tel.: 1-800-465-6277 or (613) 992-3892
Fax: (613) 943-8282
E-mail: **geonames@NRCan.gc.ca**
Web site: **http://geonames.NRCan.gc.ca/**

 Natural Resources   Ressources naturelles
Canada   Canada

Canada

Aboriginal place names figure prominently on
the website of Natural Resources Canada.

qualitative (ethnographic) research featured participant observation in northern communities and Inuit organisations in Ottawa, and open-ended interviews with about 120 Inuit and Qallunaat. Most interviews were conducted in confidence. To protect privacy, some people are quoted anonymously or given fictional names. Where necessary, the community is disguised. It is not easy to maintain anonymity. The North is a huge 'small town'. Communities are small (usually between 1,000 and 2,000 people), with few Qallunaat. Diane Bell writes of the moral dilemma faced by researchers who are entrusted with secret material; she takes care to omit material that could compromise people's privacy and belief system (Bell 1983: 2, 3). Following her lead, I have withheld information that might violate the privacy of its sharers. Some material is included in ways that detach it from the person it represents; other information – even when willingly given – was left out if I thought it might harm the giver.

I originally set out to co-author a book with Elise Attagutaluk, whose Inuktitut name was Qunngaatalluriktuq, about Inuit experiences of names and naming. In 1986, we had just begun to make plans for me to stay with her family and work with her in Igloolik, when she was killed. Her tragic and premature death at the hands of her husband is the subject of continuing anguish and at least one documentary, *The Story of Joe and Elise* (Kuchmij 1995). Her name is alive in Igloolik and across Nunavut. Her disappearance from this project changed its direction. Saddened by the loss, and frustrated by my own limitations, I abandoned it for several years. Finally, it seemed more respectful of Elise's commitment to the project to take it forward in whatever way I could, while accepting and continually interrogating the limits of my Qallunaaq/Outsider/visitor perspective. The result is that this is not an inside view of how it felt to experience Inuit naming traditions, religious and government interventions, Project Surname or the early years of Nunavut. Without Elise's collaboration, it is no longer an Inuk-Qallunaaq joint project, but the work of a Qallunaaq who visits the North, sometimes staying for a few months, and returns to work Outside. I have listened carefully to the stories of Inuit and Qallunat and have tried to report their knowledge, feelings and opinions faithfully. The interpretations and perspective are my own, grounded in my broader work in the politics of naming.

ACKNOWLEDGEMENTS

My first debt is to Qunngaatalluriktuq (Elise Attagutaluk). Peter Irniq, Commissioner of Nunavut, has worked for decades to ensure that cultural continuity and naming traditions live not only in memories but in current policies and practice. Alexina Kublu taught me about the depth and power of names and her sister's legacy.

At Leeds Metropolitan University, I thank Simon Lee for placing ethics front and centre and for creating the 'running stream' professorships and philosophy; Mary Heycock for artful leadership infused with humour and respect; Gavin Fairbairn, Simon Gunn, Sheila Scraton, and Dave Webb for collegial support of many kinds.

Mark Nuttall's thoughtful and provocatively helpful reading of the manuscript is much appreciated, as were readings of earlier versions by Keith Crowe, David V.J. Bell and Cheris Kramarae. Michael Neill introduced me to Project Surname; Gail Valaskakis mentored and sketched the bigger picture. The research was informed by encounters with Gunther Abramson, Nancy Anilniliak, Lynda Chambers, Andrew Dialla, Nancy Doubleday, Martha Flaherty, Frederick Fletcher, Bruce Gillies, Jack Hicks, Sadie Hill, Bernadette Immaroitok, Rhoda Inukshuk, Helen Kerfoot, Meeka Kilabuk, Peter Kulchyski, John MacDonald, Mick Mallon, Ludger Müller-Wille, Bertie Neethling, R.A.J. Phillips, Robert Pilot, Lorna Roth, Graham Rowley, Bent Sivertz, William Taylor and Linna Weber. At the Scott Polar Research Institute, Michael Bravo, William Mills and Shirley Sawtell offered valuable reference materials and ideas. Alison Moss, Bernie Lucht, Lorne Tulk and their colleagues at CBC 'Ideas' gave memorable lessons in what radio can be. Itesh Sachdev, Heather Norris-Nicholson, Michael Hellyer, Jodie Robson and other Canadian Studies colleagues; Vivien Hughes and William Lawton of the Canadian High Commission comprise an invaluable support system.

As always, I thank Pete – resident humourist, terrifying editor, loving partner; the amazing Dave and Dan; Susan, Daneet and Sivan; Rachel, Bill and Peggy Jane; Mary Margaret Zahara and all her names. Margaret Burns brings kindness, humour and order to our sometimes chaotic lives. The lives, work and friendship of Pamela Bruder-Freeman, Valerie

Constantino, Patricia Johanson, Arle Sklar-Weinstein and Jenny Wells Vincent continue to inspire and sustain me.

In the course of this project, several very special people died. The life of my father, Julius Graber, was ended cruelly and far too soon; what remains alive is his wit and love of people, travel, music, dance, words and gardens. My mother, Bertha Graber, taught me (perhaps unintentionally) the centrality of names; I doubt that she realised how often she mentioned the anger and sadness of being renamed at Ellis Island.

Elise had a fierce sense of her names and right to self-identification, and a deep understanding of the importance of names for her community's future. Her efforts to improve the lives of others touched many people. Eleanor Leacock's generosity and humility, in a field filled with inflated egos, will be long remembered. Abe Okpik gave generously of his time, memories and experiences, though not all of my telling of the story was as he would have wished. Annie Okalik's warmth and humour were a treasure; her experiences as a midwife made me rethink medical and social policy as well as naming. When we met in 1985, I had no idea that her son, Paul, would become Nunavut's first Premier.

Portions of the research were funded by York University, the American Association of University Women, the Canadian Broadcasting Corporation, Canada's Department of Indian Affairs and Northern Development, the Social Sciences and Humanities Research Council of Canada, the U.S. National Science Foundation and Leeds Metropolitan University.

Valerie Alia

NOTES ON SPELLING, TRANSLATION AND TRANSLITERATION

Wherever possible, names are spelled according to people's instructions. I have adopted Peter Irniq's respelled name, with references to its earlier spelling, Ernerk. In Canada, the Inuktitut language is written using a system of syllabic orthography developed in the James Bay region of northern Quebec (now Nunavik) in the 1850s, by John Horden and Edwin Arthur Watkins of the Church Missionary Society. They adapted the earlier system developed by James Evans for the Cree language. The syllabic orthography was further developed and disseminated in Inuit communities of the Nunavut region by the Anglican Reverend Edmund James Peck, who translated the Gospels into Inuktitut and transliterated them into syllabics (Harper 2001: 9).

Because they are transliterated from syllabics into Roman orthography, Inuktitut words have many possible spellings when rendered in English and other languages. I chose Qallunaaq from an array of alternatives, capitalised it to parallel *Inuk*, and pluralised it as Qallunaat, following the house style of the Nunavut newspaper, *Nunatsiaq News*. Some place names are still in transition. In Nunavut, Cape Dorset is generally known by its Inuktitut name of Kinngait. The Qallunaaq spelling of Pangnirtung is often revised as Panniqtuuq, to more accurately reflect its proper pronunciation.

Where a word is quoted from other texts, the spelling may differ from the standard spelling I have adopted. In some cases I have referred to an individual in what may look like an inappropriate way. For example, calling Abraham Okpik 'Abe' reflects his own preference, as well as a difference between conventions of Inuit and Qallunaat usage. Like many other Inuit, he found the standard European reference ('Okpik') offensive. For those acquainted with Inuktitut but not with Abe, please note that his name was indeed Okpik (willow) rather than the more familiar (and in his case, sometimes misused) Ookpik (owl). I should add that an error perpetrated by the novelist Mordecai Richler in 1994 made its way into other texts, and the minds of many readers. He developed a whole discussion about the meaning of the name 'Moses' and his service to 'his people' – based on a misidentification of Abe – Abraham – Okpik. Richler called him 'an Inuit named Moses' (Richler 1994). Apparently the editors of the *Times Literary Supplement* were too uninformed to question not only Richler's facts, but his grammar. One person is *Inuk*; two are *Inuuk*, and *Inuit* means more than three. For a fuller discussion of such problems, see the section on 'Authoritative Texts' in Chapter 5. To compound the problems, Justin Kaplan and Anne Bernays also failed to check the accuracy of Richler's comments and Inuktitut grammar before appropriating his (mis)information for their book on names, which relies heavily on second-hand scholarship and includes numerous errors and half-truths (ibid.: 227). In addition to repeating Richler's misuse of Inuit as singular, they use the invented plural, 'Inuits' (ibid.: 30). Given the abundant scholarly and media coverage of Project Surname and Abe Okpik's role in it, it is surprising that Richler misnamed him in the first place, and doubly surprising that others have followed suit.

I have sometimes used the name Elise Attagutaluk, instead of her true Inuktitut name, Qunngaatalluriktuq, because she introduced herself to me and other Qallunaat as Elise. However, her real name should be noted here. Because of the way she died, and because of her outrage at receiving it on a 'birth certificate', it feels wrong to use Attagutaluk, which – though Inuktitut – was her husband's name (and after Project Surname, her married name).

LIST OF ABBREVIATIONS

AINA   Arctic Institute of North America

APTN   Aboriginal People's Television Network

CBC   Canadian Broadcasting Corporation

HBC   Hudson's Bay Company (known colloquially in Nunavut as 'Here before Christ')

IBC   Inuit Broadcasting Corporation

ICC   Inuit Circumpolar Conference, the international organisation of Inuit (includes official delegations from Canada, Greenland, Alaska and Siberia; Sámi and others participate but do not have official representation)

IQ   Inuit Qaujimajatuqangit, an Inuit epistemology that has been incorporated into Nunavut policy and programmes.

ITC   Inuit Tapirisat of Canada, founded in 1971, the national organisation of Inuit in Canada

ITK   New name of the ITC, Inuit Tapiriit Kanatami

NIC   Nunavut Implementation Commission

NWT   Northwest Territories

RCMP   Royal Canadian Mounted Police

TFN   Tungavik Federation of Nunavut (the Inuit land claim organisation)

TVNC   Television Northern Canada

Introduction

TOWARDS A THEORY OF
POLITICAL ONOMASTICS — Study of origin, history, and use of proper names.

A Personal Reflection

Immigrants

All those names mangled on Ellis Island …

…

… cut, stitched, and … remade as Mann … Carpenter or Leary.

…

Others, more secretive or radical,
made up new names …

(Carole Satyamurti in Satyamurti 2005: 25)

June 30, 1992. (The morning after my mother died)

They took away your name
at the border

Forsaking borders,
You gave away your names.

Rebecca Rivke not yours to give
Bertha not yours to take

Surnames   middlenames
Hungarianised   Jewish names
Yiddishised   Hungarian names
Unnamed   renamed
remained

My mother
who shall remain
nameless
would not name
my children
did not know
her daughter's name
mis-naming me,
un-named herself.

Cruel and unusual punishment
inflicted on
daughters
grandsons
granddaughter ...
even the chosen ones injured
by unreasoned distinction

child
after child
after child
abuses of
body
mind
trust

The cycle of trust
begun again
in sisters
sisters' children
children's hope.

What was lost:
    mothering and
    motherlove
    acceptance and
    resolution
    kindness and
    peace

What we have:
    names
    our own names
    our owned names
    love
    and hope
    and children.

(Valerie Alia 1996: 77)

As the child of European-Jewish (Ashkenazi) immigrants to North America, I grew up hearing naming stories. I knew I was named Valerie for a place called Valeria where my parents met, and Lee to commemorate a relative named Leah. I knew I was a giver as well as a receiver of names when, at age six, my parents invited me to help name my sister. I also knew the limits to my power, as my original choice of Susannah (which I thought 'fancier' and prettier) was shortened to my parents' preference of Susan.

My next name-giving experience was as a mother. My sons David and Daniel Restivo (who now call themselves Dave and Dan) were named to commemorate the different families and cultures they inherited (Italian-Catholic, Hungarian-Jewish). Dave's middle name, Owen, commemorates a residence hall at Michigan State University, where his parents met. Dan's middle name, Olam, is a Hebrew word meaning 'world', 'universe' and 'humanity', suggested by a friend when we ran out of ideas for another 'O' name. The middle 'O' that creates my sons' shared monogram (DOR) itself has several private meanings. It is a beautiful and untranslatable word in Romanian, which I was studying when Dave was born. In French, *dor* means 'of gold'; in Hebrew, 'generation'.

My daughter-in-law, Peggy Jane, shares a name with her mother and maternal grandmother. The naming of my granddaughter, Mary Margaret, whose Hebrew name, Zahara, means 'to shine' and who is nicknamed 'MMZ', is more complicated. In an account reminiscent of Inuit naming stories, her father recalls how she 'named herself' a few days after she was born:

> She picked her own name, from a series of names that each of us liked. All the names were written four times and she was given four opportunities to pick randomly. That is the name she picked every single time, and the only name anyone else got when they tried. So I guess she knew who she was! (Restivo 2004)

The name Margaret follows her mother's family custom of giving that name to a girl in each generation. That lovely tradition is in direct conflict with her father's Ashkenazi Jewish heritage, in which it is forbidden to name a child for a living relative. In a multicultural family there is no perfect way to resolve such differences.

Even where all members of a family share a cultural background, there are issues. Immigrants often name or rename family members to reflect the language and customs of the new country.

My father's family immigrated to the United States long before he and his siblings were born. Like many others, the family maintained a double cultural life. I knew that my father's 'American' name, Julius, was transformed in Hebrew to Yehuda in family conversations and in synagogue.

I knew that for decades he had fooled my mother into thinking his middle name was the dashingly European 'Anatol' instead of the ordinary, if biblically distinguished, Abraham. He playfully stole his adopted name from Arthur Schnitzler's eponymous play recounting the adventures of a spoiled young rake. Along with other Schnitzler works, *Anatol* (written in 1893) enjoyed New York revivals in the early years of my parents' marriage. They were Schnitzler fans, and my mother thought Anatol a charming 'coincidence'. I also knew that my father sometimes used his monogram, JAG, as a *nom de plume*. I thought it great fun to read a letter from a reader calling him 'JAG m'boy' (Graber, J.A. 1931). On rereading the cuttings of his reviews for the publication of New York's 'Ninety-second Street Y' (the YMHA, or Young Men's Hebrew Association), the *Bulletin*, I see that this was a response from 'The Notorious –O–' to his review of Eugene O'Neill's play, *Mourning Becomes Electra*, and (based on this and previous correspondence) suspect it was the playwright himself who was responding.

I knew my mother hated her name. At birth she had received a 'good name' – the Hungarian version of Rebecca. In childhood she was given a nickname meaning 'buddy', which in Hungarian also started with 'B'. As a small child arriving with her family at Ellis Island, she was crudely renamed by an immigration officer whose sensitivities (if he had any) were likely subsumed by a preoccupation with moving people swiftly through the queue. Hearing her called by her Hungarian nickname, that powerful but anonymous individual inscribed the new identity that would follow her on documents throughout her life: Bertha. It was a name she considered ugly, though she sometimes joked about 'Bertha the Sewing Machine girl', an industrious garment worker in Harold Rome's 1937 musical, *Pins and Needles*. Rome's musical was derived from an earlier play with roots in a less cheery 'dime novel' called *Bertha the Sewing Machine Girl or, Death at the Wheel*, by Frances S. Smith (1871). In the musical version – inspired and produced by members of the International Ladies' Garment Workers (ILGWU) – Bertha survives the advances of a lecherous, non-union impostor and is taught how to preserve her virtue in the song, 'It's Better with a Union Man': 'Always be upon your guard / Demand to see a union card'! (Bronski 2003). My parents loved the show; my mother continued to dislike her name, both in its original form and in her acquired nickname, Bert. The injury of renaming was compounded by poverty and loss – her mother died of puerperal fever soon after my mother was born. I could never understand why she did not change her name back to Rebecca, and reclaim her birthright.

When I left the United States and an unfortunate marriage for a new life in Canada, I took a new last name: Alia – a Hebrew and Arabic word meaning 'going up' – to new places (both geographic and sacred) and new levels of consciousness – liberation. Having discarded both 'maiden' and 'married' names for an identity of my own, I vowed never again to change my name for others. I kept that vow even when I joyfully married Pete Steffens, whose father, the great 'muckraker', Lincoln Steffens, was much admired and often quoted in my parents' home. I love, respect and treasure that name. Nevertheless, I have kept my own.

Pete's real name is Pete, not Peter, though people often get it wrong (including scholars who think that 'Peter Steffens' is a mysterious other man). Pete's father nicknamed his mother Peter (for Peter Pan) and then named him for *her*, adding the straight-laced middle name, Stanley, in case he grew up wanting to be a businessman or banker. In *The Autobiography of Lincoln Steffens* he explains the naming games.

> This girl danced. Her eyes danced, her mind, her hands, her feet danced as she ran … I was fascinated … She was not for me, of course. Too young. But I felt something which I smothered by likening her to a boy. Her name was Ella Winter, but I called her Peter.
>
> …
>
> … she had not decided which of her suitors would suit her … in short, I disapproved of all the other candidates for husband and recommended myself … We went to San Remo, took a villa, and there in the fall of 1924 my son, Pete Stanley Steffens, named after his mother, Peter, was born. (Steffens 1931: 812, 820)

Ella Winter came from an Ashkenazi Jewish family originally called Wertheimer. Branches of the family immigrating to Britain, Australia and the United States variously renamed themselves Wertham, Winton and Winter. Freda Lust and Adolph Wertheimer left Nuremberg for London and then Melbourne, where their children – Rudolph, Rosa and Eleanora (Ella) – were born. Returning to London in 1910, they encountered a climate of anti-German hatred and changed their name to Winter to disguise their German origins.

From the Wertham branch of the family came the U.S. psychiatrist and author, Fredric Wertham, whose postwar struggle to understand the roots of violence resulted in his study of the effects of violent comic books on children (Wertham 1953). From the Winton branch came the English stockbroker, Nicholas Winton, who in 1939 organised the rescue of 669 children from Nazi-occupied Czechoslovakia (BBC. 1998; CNN September 2002; CNN December 2002). From the Winter branch came the Australian-British activist and author, Ella Winter, my husband's mother (Winter 1968; Winter and Shapiro 1962). An outsider would be hard pressed to trace the family line through all the changes of names and countries. It is reminiscent of a well-known joke. Two immigrants meet. One says, 'What's your name?' The other tells his name, to which the first person replies by asking, 'What was it *before*?'

Pete's daughters were named by their Israeli mother. Daneet is the feminine form of Dan, which in Hebrew means 'judge'. Sivan is an early summer month in the Hebrew calendar – chosen for its sound rather than its meaning, as Sivan was born in January.

Despite the vast cultural and geographical differences between Jewish Europe and North America and Inuit-dominated Nunavut in the Canadian Arctic, my experience of names and naming provided me with excellent preparation for the encounters with Inuit and their ways of naming. Like Ashkenazim (European Jews), Inuit prefer commemorative naming, treasure and honour the namesake connection, and when naming their children, usually choose names of relatives who are no longer living. The proscription against a living namesake is stronger for Ashkenazim – there are some Inuit (usually elders) who give their names to favoured people during their own lifetimes. Like Inuit, Ashkenazim see namesake relationships as a way of continuing people's lives. I have heard stories of survivors naming children for each relative who was killed in the Holocaust, not resting until every name was sent on its new life's journey. However, Inuit have taken the namesake relationship farther, to a sometimes literal version of reincarnation.

The parallels and similarities suggest why I may have felt so much at home on landing in a culture and country entirely unfamiliar. Before my first trip to what is now Nunavut I had never been to an Arctic or sub-Arctic place, or met Inuit, or learned more than a few words of Inuktitut (the dominant language in Nunavut). Certainly, it was a shock to feel comfortable among people who spoke an unfamiliar language, who lived in a region remote from Europe, southern Canada and the United States, and who on the surface had nothing in common with my own ancestry. But it was not only naming that brought us together. Even when specific comments had to be translated by an interpreter, the Inuit style of humour, laughter and body language felt like home.

Language, Names and Power

The sociologist, Pierre Bourdieu, says: 'There is no social agent who does not aspire … to have the power to name and to create the world through naming' (Bourdieu 1991: 105). He calls 'official' naming 'a symbolic act of imposition [that makes] the state the holder of the monopoly of legitimate symbolic violence' (ibid.: 239).

On the surface, naming is simply part of the process by which people classify their environment. The essential premise of this enquiry is that it is much more – that naming people and places is a political activity of universal significance. Naming has been studied primarily by psychologists, linguists and philosophers. The *politics of naming* has never been defined as such, but has existed between the lines of many disciplines. Anthropology, linguistics, political science, sociology and cultural studies provide the foundation for political onomastics, the politics of naming. Onomasticians, also called onomatologists, increasingly address questions of power relations, though such questions remain on the margins of most work in onomastics. In some cases (e.g., Junghare 1975; Rennick 1969) issues of power are implied but not identified. Since the early 1980s, I have sought to move this inquiry forward, towards an understanding of naming cross-culturally as it embodies and creates relations of privilege and power. The research into archives and experiences – of Inuit and of immigrants in Canadian, U.S. and European diasporas – contributes to an understanding of the role of naming in political behaviour and political structures, and supports my contention that naming is inseparable from other political phenomena and is an important key to analysing power relations.

The Place of Names in Language

The word 'name' appears in some form in all Indo-European languages. Considered more broadly, names themselves 'are universal in language' (Kramarae and Treichler 1988: 290). For Vygotsky, the moment at which a child discovers names for things is the turning point at which 'speech begins to serve intellect' (Vygotsky 1962: 43). Vygotsky saw words the way we now see DNA cells – as receptacles for the whole of information, with nuclei of names. As he put it, 'A word is a microcosm of human consciousness' (ibid.: 153). Nomenclature – the bestowing of names on individuals – has a long history. Pliny claimed that some ancient tribes were *anonymi* and Hook (1982: 8) considers it 'barely possible that a few *anonymi* may still exist in remote corners of the world'. As we will see, there are instances in which names are withheld, in special circumstances or life stages. Such conjectures and instances notwithstanding, personal names appear in every known culture.

Claude Lévi-Strauss views names as both universal and elemental. 'To say that a name is perceived as a proper name is to say that it is assigned to a level beyond which no classification is necessary ... [proper names] always remain on the margin of classification' and represent the *quanta of signification* below which one no longer does any thing but point' (Lévi-Strauss 1966: 215). He suggests a continuum between 'the act of signifying' and that of 'pointing', with each culture expressing and maintaining its own acceptable thresholds. Lévi-Strauss calls space 'a society of named places' and people 'landmarks within the group' (ibid.: 168) and discovers that personal and place names are interchangeable in some societies. His term 'personified geography' covers systems like that of the Yurok in California, in which place names sometimes replace personal names in daily use. The discussion of Inuit naming takes the matter further.

W.F.H. Nicolaïsen suggests that names embody at least the following levels of meaning: lexical – dictionary meaning; associative – the explanation for using the particular lexical or onomastic items in the naming process; and onomastic – the 'meaning of a denotative name as a name' (Nicolaïsen 1974: 104). Using this 'threefold semantic tier', Nicolaïsen calls naming 'the process by which words become names by association' (ibid.). John Algeo sees names as simply words used to call someone or something by. If, like Algeo, we understand names as mere linguistic artefacts minus any social, psychological or political context, a 'strong' or predictive theory is hard to come by. 'Such onomastic theory as we can reasonably hope for is not likely to be a predictive theory', but rather the 'unscientific sort ... that offers a view of the field for onomatologists to work within' (Algeo 1985: 142). This theoretical restriction relies on Algeo's insistence on a shaky dichotomy between 'science' and 'non-science' and on his assumption that onomastics is no more than 'a part of linguistics, albeit a part generally ignored by linguists'. Adhering to an archaic perception of 'pure' language, he fails to account for such fields as sociolinguistics and its offshoot of political linguistics. At the same time, he acknowledges that names may relate more closely to performance or speech action than do other aspects of language. He calls for an onomastic theory that can connect name invention and name use to other aspects of life, and help us to discover 'such universals of naming as may exist' (ibid.: 144).

It is my conviction that once names are placed in sociopolitical context, as speech *acts*, a predictive theory is possible. My own work concentrates on *naming* rather than *names* – the sociopolitical process rather than the linguistic product. The following chapters include material on place names, but aim primarily at understanding the political implications of personal names and naming practices through the case study of Inuit experiences in pre- and postcolonial Nunavut. As will be seen, especially in the material on Inuit naming, personal and place names are not always separable, nor is such separation always desirable. In many instances, especially in the case of colonisation-caused and liberation-caused name changes, personal and place name changes occur simultaneously.

My initial fascination with naming led to the discovery of a fierce interface between names and power which emerged even from politically 'innocent' data. This relationship is only marginally acknowledged in the disciplinary literatures. It resides in what Edwin and Shirley Ardener (Ardener 1977) call 'p-structures' and 's-structures' – adaptations of Lévi-Strauss's terms, 'syntagmatic' (ordinary language observable on the surface of everyday life) and 'paradigmatic' (sacred language that is buried under layers of meaning and practice) (Lévi-Strauss 1966: 211). 'S-structures' – surface structures – are most easily observable; 'p-structures' are what others have called 'deep' structure – a level at which ideas that form a society's foundation may be concealed by ritual, custom and everyday practice. In any society, dominance can be measured by the relative discrepancy between p- and s-structures. Naming practices can shed new light on the overt and covert uses of power, and the relationships between dominant and subordinate (or what Shirley and Edwin Ardener call 'muted') groups (Ardener 1977).

Within the international onomastics community, a small but growing number of scholars are looking at ways in which naming reflects societal changes. Robert R.K. Herbert (1996) calls this extension of sociolinguistics 'dynamic onomastics', while Bertie (S.J.) Neethling calls it 'dynamic socio-onomastics' (Neethling 2005: 3). Because I am most interested in the link between naming and power relations, I call it 'political onomastics'.

Names and Power Relations

In more than twenty years of interdisciplinary and international exploration, I have identified several propositions concerning names and power relations:

- Naming is universal. While it is true that unnamed places do exist, virtually all people are named or are in some way linked to the naming process. Even where a name is deliberately withheld, naming is central to the development of a person's conception of self.
- Name avoidance is a key expression of power relations and in some form or other appears to be common to all societies (Alia 1989). Avoidance taboos help to illuminate degrees of dominance and subordination. At the extreme, rules of avoidance can represent denial of power and symbolic death. An ostracised person whose name goes unspoken becomes a non-person. Conversely, a member of a subordinate group may be expected to show deference by avoiding the attention-getting device of using someone's name.
- Negative naming – the giving of 'ugly' or otherwise low-priority names – is a deliberate strategy for protecting a child or adult from harm and is often seen as a way of fooling evil spirits into leaving the person alone.
- Secret naming is also used protectively, especially where a culture is threatened or there are more direct threats of violence to individuals who resist absorption or assimilation into the dominant society. 'Underground naming' is a form of secret naming.
- Renaming during illness or danger occurs in many regions and cultures where dangers are rampant and life is fragile; Inuit use this practice extensively.
- Considering personal and place names, personal names are the most charged with power. This upholds, and is supported by, Lévi-Strauss's

observation that individuation is the 'final level of classification' (Lévi-Strauss 1966: 172)

- Renaming for personal or political change: any substantial regime change or change of dominance and power is inevitably accompanied by changes to personal and place names. Taking control of naming is an important component of the process of assuming political power and is a fundamental part of social and political change. This kind of renaming can indicate either subjugation or liberation.
- The power to name is a politically charged power. The right to bestow names is a right which signifies that the namer has power. That said, it is not always the case that individuals who are given the right to bestow names are those most powerful in more general terms, across society. For example, women may be the namers and men the politicians or owners of property.

Would a Rose by Any Other Name Smell at All?

Whether names are seen as mere labels, as *representations* of people, or as *people*, they are always central in defining identity. Along with a multitude of psychologists, Kenneth L. Dion (1983: 245), Muzafer Sherif and Hadley Cantril (1947) emphasise the link between name and sense of self. Gordon Allport (1961) goes so far as to call the name the focal point for the organisation of self-identity. The poet Goethe goes even farther to say that one's name equals one's self. 'A man's name is not like a cloak that merely hangs around him ... It's a perfectly fitting garment. It grows over him like his very skin. One cannot scrape and scratch at it without injuring the man himself' (Goethe, in Zabeeh 1968: 5). Whitney, on the other hand, lowers naming to a *classification* and *identification* convention. 'When a human being is born into the world, custom, founded in convenience, requires that he have a name; and those who are responsible for his existence furnish the required adjunct, according to their individual tastes, which are virtually a reflection of the community in which they live' (Whitney 1979: 135).

Bentham takes a similar approach to name-as-identifier. But his distress at the ramifications of naming hints at a naming-politics far deeper than he will admit.

> ... wherever a man sees a NAME he is led to figure to himself a corresponding object, of the reality of which the NAME is accepted by him, as it were of course, in the character of a CERTIFICATE. From this delusion, endless is the confusion, the error, the dissension, the hostility, that has been derived. (Bentham, in Bolinger 1980: 59)

Others see naming as an act of gaining *power over* something or someone, or of giving power *to* a person or an object. In the Old Testament, naming is very important to the Creation story. God creates man in His image, to be master over other creatures. 'And God said "Let us make man in our image, after our likeness; and let them have dominion over the fish of the sea, and over the fowl of the air, and over the cattle, and over all the earth …"' (Genesis 1: 24). Adam's likeness to God includes his role as namer, a symbolic part of Creation. 'And out of the ground the Lord God formed every beast … and brought them unto the man to see what he would call them; and whatsoever the man would call every living creature, that was to be the name thereof' (Genesis 1: 24). Genesis clarifies man's power over woman by having Adam name Eve. 'And the man called his wife's name Eve; because she was the mother of all living' (Genesis 3: 15). As in the case of Eve, individuals gain as well as lose power through names. A child knows that her name distinguishes her from others; often, it is the first word she learns to spell or write. The child owns the name and, for a time, is likely to believe it is hers alone (Miller and Swift 1977: 2–3). Lévi-Strauss' extensive look at ethnographic naming literature (1966) is limited by his insistence on a name-as-classification bias. While class differences in naming systems are noted, he does not consider linking them to power relations or political structures. Thus, Lévi-Strauss is able to call personal and species names 'class indicators' as though 'class' had no connection to equality or inequality but existed only within a context of apolitical and cultural relativity. He is interested in the personality and the social role-related characteristics that accrue to totemic names, but not in the problem of who holds what kind of power.

All of these views suggest the difficulty of answering the question, 'Would a rose by any other name smell at all?' The proponents of *naming-as-creation* must answer in the negative, for how could an object recreated retain its former properties? The *classifiers* might find the rose's aroma subdued, limited or generalised to a vague sweetness identifiable only as odour of *flower*. The *name-as-power* thinkers might refer to the namer's right to own the rose's odour or alter it at will; or they might focus on the rose's right to assert its roseness, a power received from human namers.

The most extreme positions are held by P. Ziff and John Stuart Mill. Ziff insists that 'there is nothing in a proper name. It has information content but even so, it is all sound and if the sound is changed the name is changed' (Ziff, in Zabeeh 1968: 24). Ziff's assumption that language is *audible* ignores the existence and import of written language and the considerable abilities of deaf and non-speaking people to use language. If we follow his view to its logical conclusion, people who are hearing- or speaking-impaired would have no names, or would be 'owned' by those able to hear and speak. Alternatively, Mill sees personal and place names as 'meaningless marks' meant simply to distinguish people and things from each other. As Ziff errs on the side of spoken and heard language, Mill errs on the side of inscription and ignores the existence of spoken language. Both ignore the language of gesture and the significance of naming behaviour. Zabeeh understands names and naming by observing uses and functions of proper names in comparison with other linguistic expressions, basing this on the Austin–Searle hypothesis that speech is action (Austin 1962; Searle 1970). The 'speech acts' principle is: 'to *say* something is to *do* something (Austin 1962: 12). 'I name' is one of Austin's exemplary 'performatives' – utterances that indicate action (ibid.: 56). The range and complexity of perspectives, which this summary only begins to sketch, indicates both the importance attached to names and the challenges to understanding naming across countries, regions, times and cultures.

Language, Name and Power

Children discover their world with the help of naming: as soon as concepts are articulated, words identify objects. Other parts of speech, such as adjectives and verbs, apparently come later. In an ego-centred universe, proper nouns are all-important. The importance attached to naming is exemplified by familiar expressions:

> *She has a name.* (She is famous.)
> It is important to have a good name. (It is important to be virtuous.)
> *He will carry on the family name.* (Children – most often males – provide continuity for family or clan through the symbol of the surname.)
> *They named names.* (They revealed who was responsible, usually for something thought to be bad or shameful.)
> *She made a name for herself.* (She transcended the limits of class or status to achieve something important or prestigious in the world.)
> *They called him names.* (He was ridiculed or insultingly nicknamed).

Paolo Freire follows the Old Testament story of Adam's discovery with a secularised version: 'to exist, humanly, is to *name* the world, to change it …' (Freire, in Bell 1975: xii). Similarly, Dale Spender (1980: 163) considers naming a way of manipulating the world, while Goethe's view that to injure the name is to injure the person has echoes in many locations and cultural traditions.

The formal and informal rules of naming help to clarify the ways in which political reality is shaped in a given society. The tendency to deny or ignore the naming mores within one's own society is partly due to the taking-for-granted of daily life, but it also amounts to a kind of avoidance taboo. In a surge of political idealism Nancy Parrot Hickerson, a linguistic anthropologist, declares that everyone in the United States 'can claim an inalienable right to freedom of choice in naming the baby' (Hickerson 1980: 131). Farther out on the same limb, she says that in North America, names are chosen with no restrictions of any kind, most often on the basis of 'personal taste'. To make this claim she must ignore an array of formal and informal rules that govern the selection of appropriate names and avoidance of inappropriate names in Canada and the U.S.A., nationally and additionally in the various Canadian provinces and American states. Her own observation that Americans select from a very limited name repertoire contradicts her position – she finds that about a dozen men's and about twenty women's names predominate, with about six million 'Johns' and four million 'Marys' (ibid.: 131). In fact, there is no evidence to support Hickerson's thesis. North Americans follow many naming rules, some of them specified by law and others by custom. While the attitude is not set out formally in law, there are strong undercurrents to support the widespread, cross-culturally observable view that naming a child and giving the child life are closely connected.

In many cultures a child is not considered human or alive until named, and often is not named until expected to survive.

> At birth a child is nothing – neither Tsimihety, nor kinsman, nor human being. Its only identity is male or female, and an 'event' marked by an arbitrary name such as place of birth if this was unusual, or an object present at the birth … If the child dies during the period between birth and the cutting of the first tooth 'it is buried without ceremony somewhere in the bush', without having received a permanent name. (Wilson, in Skinner 1973: 267)

The Imbonggu of New Guinea do not name a child for several months after birth. It is referred to and addressed as *wambiri*, meaning 'child' or 'infant'. The child demonstrates its humanity at six to eight months, by showing that it 'knows people', and the father then bestows the first personal name (Wormsley 1980: 184). Thus, while the Imbonggu consider a newborn child human, it is placed in a generic category, more 'flower' than 'rose'. Among the North Australian Tiwi, naming is even more directly linked to survival.

> Some fathers gave the first name when the infant sat up by itself, and still others waited until the day when the infant stood or even walked. In the words of one informant, 'If I name him before, he might die and name no good'. (Goodale 1971: 32)

The avoidance of early naming is by no means universal. In some cultures a child must have a name, *especially* if it is expected to die. In this instance, the child must be named in order to be protected from dying soulless. In one study, nurses in a hospital in Toronto, Canada reported a long-standing tradition of naming fragile infants so that they would not die nameless (Embleton 1983).

In some instances adoption is an occasion to rename a child, with the birth name seen as only a temporary stopgap. In John Irving's novel, *The Cider House Rules*, the orphans who find permanent homes are renamed to signify their rebirth and express respect for their adoptive families.

> Dr Larch made it a firm policy that the orphans' adoptive families *not* be informed of the names the nurses gave with such zeal. The feeling at St. Cloud's was that a child, upon leaving the orphanage, should know the thrill of a fresh start ... (Irving 1985: 2)

Some Inuit report a similar kind of name-changing when a child is 'adopted out', a term used to refer to what Inuit call 'custom adoption' to distinguish it from state-sponsored legal adoption (1984–2006). According to Inuit custom, adoptions are part of everyday life. They often have less to do with need than with the view that a family is complete only with children. Adults of any age are 'given' children and it is not uncommon for elders to parent young children. Unlike government-sponsored legal adoption, Inuit 'custom adoption' is transparent in all directions, with children not only aware of their birth parents, but free to move fluidly between their birth and adoptive families in their daily lives.

Renaming occurs not only in cases of adoption, but in numerous other instances. It is important on many levels, in every culture I have studied. Where a new name cancels the old, the child (or adult) effectively becomes a new person. The adoptee gains both new status and new life. The American orphan who (like Irving's protagonist Homer Wells) must keep his nurse-given name throughout life, is doomed to live outside the normative family structure. Homer Wells gets a chance to demonstrate that such an individual may also transcend status limitations. Although Homer keeps his orphanage name, he also *makes* a name for *himself*. 'Whether a name is self-chosen or bestowed at birth, making it one's own is an act of self-definition' (Miller and Swift 1977). While names contribute to, or create self-definition, they do not universally designate or represent gender. We see this most clearly in the naming practices of Inuit, where the Inuktitut language provides neither gendered names nor pronouns. In New Guinea, native North America and Polynesia, gender-anomalous individuals are culturally recognised and sometimes accorded special honours. Some cultures designate several sexes (Ortner and Whitehead 1981). Even where 'male' and 'female' are clearly delineated categories, naming does not necessarily follow those categories. Again, this is the case in Inuit society, in which many kinds of gender roles are sharply identified but naming does not follow the gendered categories.

The Political Onomastics of Shakespeare

In Shakespeare's Verona, as in many other societies, a person's name immediately identified friend or foe. Loyalties were kinship clear, biologically based and socially enforced. Shakespeare is one of the most articulate challengers of the ethic of the family feud, a mini-war whose clearest symbol is the name. *Romeo and Juliet* opens on 'two households, both alike in dignity'. Montagues and Capulets fight for names' sake only, having long since lost the reasons for their feuding. "'Deny thy father and refuse thy name', says Juliet; 'Ties but thy name that is my enemy. Thou art thyself ...'" She sees at least the clan or family name as extraneous, but never suggests that Romeo give up his given name – his deeper sense of self. Shakespeare has a keen sense of a cross-culturally observable pattern. Clues to how a person is to be perceived and treated often come from names, and sometimes survival itself depends on concealing or changing them. Cultural and political changes go hand in hand. Like the Veronese, Americans have sometimes rejected German, Japanese, Russian and other names simply because of the 'enemy' categories they represented. Names have been rejected or devalued (and people with them) because they sounded 'Jewish'. Often the label is mistakenly applied to 'Jewish-sounding' names. An Oregon court case concerning discrimination against entrepreneurs with 'Jewish-sounding' names indicates that the problem still exists (Graber 1986).

> Living with a pet name and a good name, in a place where such distinctions do not exist – surely that was emblematic of the greatest confusion of all ... (Lahiri 2004: 118)

Immigrants with 'different' (long, non-English or otherwise unusual) names sometimes change them. The study of Inuit in Nunavut provides a prime example of layers of name-changing under social and political pressure. The ultimate naming nightmare is expressed in F.M. Esfandiary's novel *Identity Card* (Esfandiary 1966). Protagonist Daryoush Aryana loses his official card in his native Iran, and is denied identity by the state. However he *says* his name, he is granted no existence without the document. He remains without a country, trapped *inside* his country. What a person is called affects more than the sense of self. It can cause, create or control a world view. It can dictate whom to love or marry, who not to love, marry or associate with. And as Shakespeare so poignantly demonstrates, it can lead the individual from personal concerns to family feud, war and death.

Names can control relationships, work and the ability to integrate one's personal history into present and future. The politics of naming is not merely a politics on the psychological level, expressing personality and power in the smaller social order. It is a macro-politics affecting legal structures and the operations of governments and transgovernmental agencies. I have failed to locate a nation that has not passed formal legislation to regulate its citizens' naming practices. This exploration of political onomastics, or politics of naming, concentrates on the impact of large-scale politics and policy, with a focus on the experience of one cultural community – the Inuit of the Canadian Eastern Arctic who reside in what, since 1999, has been called Nunavut Territory. The research is aimed at developing an integrative, interdisciplinary approach that acknowledges the enormous social and political significance of names and naming practices.

Chapter 1 explores the importance of names in Inuit culture, surveying traditional kinship and naming practices and perspectives of Inuit in Nunavut, southern Canada, Greenland, Alaska and Scotland, based on interviews conducted from 1984 to 2004. Chapter 2 looks at the history of visitors' interference with Inuit identity and considers the impact of missionaries, traders, police, government representatives, scientists, explorers and tourists. Chapter 3 surveys the mass renaming programme known as Project Surname, drawing on oral histories and interviews and historical data from public archives, private collections, Inuit and government agencies and organisations. Chapter 4 presents a brief political history of Nunavut and a compendium of contemporary perspectives on names and identity, in the light of recent and current efforts towards cultural revival in the Inuit homeland of Nunavut. Chapter 5 considers views of homeland and diaspora as they relate to name, identity and power. It examines how the Nunavut case study can inform a theory of political onomastics and looks at the Nunavut experience in the broader context of the experiences of other cultures and regions, and of international trends towards recognising cultural diversity.

Citing the work of Wassermann and Jacobs (2003), Neethling reminds us 'that identity is a journey, not a destination' (Neethling 2005: 75). And now, I invite you to join me in a journey to the Canadian Arctic.

Chapter 1

THE IMPORTANCE OF NAMES IN INUIT CULTURE

I did not start out to study Inuit names, or work in the Arctic. In the midst of pursuing early work on immigrant names and renaming experiences, a serendipitous event changed everything. Our first year in Toronto, my sons and I were invited to a Christmas Eve party at the home of our next-door neighbours. One of the guests, Michael Neill, asked what I was studying. On hearing 'the politics of naming', he perked up and said: 'You mean, like Operation Surname?' He then proceeded to describe the government renaming programme, whose official title I later learned was 'Project Surname', and his own considerable experience of working with Inuit at the famous Cape Dorset artists' cooperative. I had been searching for a case study that would demonstrate the political implications of naming. Suddenly, it was staring me in the face. Project Surname had occurred within the recent memory of thousands of people. I dropped everything and started going North – first, from the libraries and museums of southern Canada and Michael Neill's Inuit artists database (where I learned the names of artists and communities), then, in person. The experience would forever change my understanding of naming, the 'ideas' and realities of North, and the lives and identities of northern peoples.

Inuit have developed one of the deepest and most intricate naming systems in the world. Names are the heart and soul of Inuit culture. The multilayered naming system is based on *sauniq* – a powerful form of namesake commemoration that some people describe as a kind of reincarnation. The names are passed from one generation to the next regardless of gender, with the single exception of Polar Inuit, who developed separate male and female names.

Namesake and Immortality

In his study of Xhosa names in South Africa, Neethling describes a concept called *ubuntu* that could well be Inuit:

> not easily translatable, but roughly meaning 'kindness, humanity, sharing' and often used to stress the corporate nature of African society: the individual never takes precedence over the group. In Xhosa society, this is expressed as follows; *Umntu ngumntu ngabantu* (A person is a person through other people). (Neethling 2005: 8)

Minnie Aodla Freeman was born in 1936 on Cape Hope Island in James Bay, northern Quebec (now Nunavik). In her 1978 book, *Life among the Qallunaat*, she recalled the naming traditions of her childhood. Sometimes, the namesake was a living elder:

> Before I was born, my mother had to decide who would be involved at my birth ... The first person who has to be there is a mid-wife, man or woman. In my case it was my grandmother ... Also present at my birth was the person I was named after, my other grandmother. This automatically meant that I would never call her 'grandmother' nor would she call me 'grandchild'. Instead, we called each other *sauniq*, namesake, *bone-to-bone* relation ... Our belief is that no one really dies until someone is named after the dead person. So, to leave the dead in peace and to prevent their spirits from being scattered all over the community, we give their names to the newborn. The minds of the people do not rest until the dead have been renamed. (Freeman 1978: 72, 50)

This is reminiscent of the Holocaust survivors and post-Shoah generation who could not rest until each person lost had been commemorated through the naming of a living child (1984–2006). 'The name never dies ... The name which I have is the same one that was carried by my ancestors for a very long time ... (Josepi in Robbe 1981: 46) (my translation).'

In his study of naming customs and practices in Greenland, Pierre Robbe identifies three components of the Inuit individual: *timeq* (body), *tarneq* (soul) and *aleq* (name – also known as 'soul-name') (Robbe 1981: 46). In the midst of a difficult birth, a baby will be renamed until he or she seems healthier, stops crying or seems calmer. The parents, midwife and others try different names again and again until the difficulties cease and the birth takes place. People have explained this to me as a way of abandoning a name that was wrongly given in favour of finding 'the right name'. Sometimes it takes several different people and several names to find the right one, and often the child retains several of the names, with one designated as the main one. In many cultures, children and sometimes adults are renamed when they are threatened by illness or danger. Ashkenazi Jews follow this practice, and so do Inuit. In case of persistent illness, the Qiqiktamiut perform a ceremony known as *atiktasirivuk*, which means 'to take the name again' (Guemple 1969: 472). A more extreme and desperate measure was to try to sever all of the harmful connections with the original name spirit, which were seen to be causing the illness, by adopting a child out (Guemple 1979: 43). Martha Tunnuq recalls her own experience with the life-saving effects of renaming.

> When I was a little girl I was struck with a serious illness and everyone was sure I would die. My uncle, my father's younger brother, was a shaman and he named me after my grandfather, my mother's father. From then on I began to get better, and I recovered fully. (Tunnuq 1992: 26)

Bernard Irqugaqtuq describes the privations surrounding his own birth:

> Since I did not want to be born, Uquqtuq gave me a name so that I would come out more rapidly. That name is Naai. It didn't have much effect for I still did not make my entrance into the world. Papik, Arnakajak's husband, in turn gave me a name, Kapilruq, and I was born. That is why, since then, I also bear the name Kapilruq. But the name destined for me since my conception was Irqugaqtuq. (Irqugaqtuq 1977–78: 22–23)

Each of his names has a special significance (including the Christian name Bernard) but his primary name is the one tied to destiny and the passing of name, soul and self across the generations. In the complex namesake system, the *person* is inherited along with the name.

When a child is named, he or she becomes the *sauniq* or 'bone' of all those who have shared that name. The one who gives his or her name to another and the one who receives it address and refer to each other by the term *sauniq*. 'The namegiver's namegiver is called *saunitoqa* ('very old bone'). Those with the same namegiver are *atia'uaaluq* or namesharers ...' People who are linked by names are expected to help each other in time of need, and are bound together in a complex and permanent set of relationships (Guemple 1965: 326–27). Not all Inuit observe a formal naming ceremony, and the traditional way of naming may be either separated from, or connected to, a Christian baptismal naming. Lee Guemple's research reveals that the (traditional) naming ceremony was sometimes delayed if the child was frail or if the family was considering infanticide (Guemple 1969: 469).

In Inuit society souls and names are seen to be closely connected to cosmic forces. Robert Williamson considers the Inuit idea of a compound, multilayered, soul and the related naming system far more complex than the idea of soul that has been 'conceptualised by more modern religious beliefs such as Christianity ... *The name, in Eskimo belief, is the soul, and the soul is the name*' (Williamson 1974: 23–24). In his search for a way to communicate Inuit culture to his fellow Europeans, Vilhjalmur

Stefansson compared the Inuit soul-name to 'the European idea of a guardian angel', based on its role in protecting the namesakes across the generations (Stefansson 1922: 467). More recently, Hugh Brody offered his own explanation of the Inuit naming system. He tries both to make the information accessible to *Qallunaat* through comprehensible cultural parallels, and to make a careful distinction between Inuit and European traditions and practices.

> When an Inuit baby is a few days old it is given its *atiq* ... usually translated as name ... an essence or soul (*though we must imagine away the Christian connotations of these terms in order to translate with accuracy*). The *atiq* is usually a relative who has died. For the rest of its life, those who do not know the child will ask '*Kinamik atirqarpit?*', 'whom do you have as an *atiq*?'. (Brody 1987: 137, italics mine)

A child is not a complete person until he or she receives an *atiq*. From then on, the child becomes both him- or herself and a person whom the namers wish to immortalise. Bernard Saladin d'Anglure observes practices and customs which demonstrate that an individual's identity is composed of many layers:

> Inuit believe that the essential ingredient of a human being is its name. The name embodies a mystical substance which includes the personality, special skills, and basic character which the individual will exhibit in life. Without that substance the person will die. If a person exchanges his or her name for another through a ritualised renaming process, he or she becomes a different person. The name substance is induced into the body within three or four days after birth ... Often the name is that of some recently deceased community member ... Names are never exclusively held by individuals ... [several people] may bear the same name and thus be the same person in principle ... the society consists of a limited number of names each having its own social identity ... since the social identity comes to the individual fully formed, it is not something the individual or the community [can] change in any major way ... Every individual shares a community of spirit with others ... in Inuit society, that community is with those who bear the same name ... (Saladin d'Anglure 1977: 33)

As Hugh Brody puts it, 'No child is only a child. If I give my grandfather's *atiq* to my baby daughter, she *is* my grandfather. I will call her *ataatassiaq*, grandfather. She is entitled to call me 'grandson' (Brody 1987: 139).

Names, Birth and Resurrection

The Inuit soul-name is the 'symbol of the continuity of [the person's] social life on earth, and the assurance of his or her immortality' (Saladin d'Anglure 1977: 36, my translation). The moment of naming marks the 'symbolic death of the eponymous ancestor or beginning of a new cycle for the name-soul' (ibid.: 33). Birth was always a very important event among Qiqiktamiut of the Belcher Islands. Before the intervention of modern medicalised and hospitalised birthing, the process was carefully and ritually organised. At the start of labour, the mother was taken to a special birthing tent or snow house next to her home, where she was joined by four people – a (usually female) midwife,[1] a man or woman to tie the umbilical cord, a male or female name-giver, and a male or female 'ritual sponsor'. In Greenland,

> The process of separation from the womb *(illiaq)* is one in which the baby *(naalungiarsuk)* is brought to a 'state of life' *(inuuneq;* life, or literally 'the state of being a person'). There is a powerful imagery and linguistic link between the womb *(illiaq)* and a house *(illu)* ... An *illiaq* houses the *illaq*, another word for foetus, just as an *illu* houses a person ... It is only in one sense that childbirth marks the beginning of life, the foetus being already alive in another sense ... the unborn child was simply 'waiting to become a person' ... (Nuttall 1992: 64)

Regitze Søby's studies of Kullorsuaq and Upernavik district in Greenland reveal a similar pattern. The primary namesake-name is dominant, but each child is named for several people. A particular name may be bestowed on several different children. In this region, commemorative naming seems most often to follow along gender lines. When Kalaaq, a distinguished young hunter from Kullorsuaq, died in 1984, eight boys in town, and others throughout the region, were named after him. Similarly, eleven girls were named for a woman called Ane. There is a hierarchy imbedded in the system.' The first child in the line to be given the name of a dead relative – *ateqqaataa* – is considered the most important of those who are named after this relative' (Søby 1992: 3). Following the idea of reincarnation-by-naming, in this region, the recipient of a name is sometimes called *makeqqiut*, 'the resurrected'.

> ... the Kangersuatsiarmiit say 'my name is like my soul' ... identities continue when children are given the name of a deceased person, or the names of several dead people ... The name contains properties of the deceased which are ineradicable ... Once named, a new born child is both him/herself and the person(s) whose names s/he receives. (Nuttall 1992: 666–67)

Polar Inuit in North Greenland also hold the widespread belief that name and soul are linked. 'The connection between the name-soul and identity was so intimate that new names seldom developed ...' When a person died, the name was considered taboo until it had been given to a newborn child. The name avoidance rules were strong. Other people who shared this name could be called, and referred to by any of their other names, but were required to avoid this one until the name had been passed to the new baby. If the name was not passed on, it was believed 'that it would lose its power' (Gilberg 1984: 586).

His studies of naming in Nunavut led Robert Williamson to conclude that the

> whole soul complex and naming system is in fact a series of constantly-changing transcendencies and mutations. The Aivilimiut had names for a baby in the foetal stage. When the baby was born, the soul embodied in the foetus went through 'some form of death' and a new name was given to the baby. The name is almost always the name of someone important in the genealogy of the kin-group. Among many Eskimo the giving of a name to a child is something not undertaken by the parents, but more commonly by the older and wiser and more knowledgeable grandparents, and equally often in consultation with a shaman. (Williamson 1974: 24)

Throughout most of the Canadian Arctic, Inuit name-givers are deceased or near death. When a person dies, the 'name soul leaves the body and remains homeless until it is recalled to reside in the body of a new-born child'. While the first child born after the namesake's death is usually the most important, the name may go to many children. Name-sharers have special relationships, not only with their deceased namesakes but with each other. Variations on these practices occur throughout the Arctic and sub-Arctic regions. The Nunivak – Yup'ik Inuit (or Eskimos, as Alaska people sometimes prefer to be called) – live on an island in Alaska's Bering Sea. They have developed taboos that limit the use of a person's 'real name'. Lantis says she is unable to judge the extent to which name and soul are connected here, but she has observed that 'it at least represented the essential intrinsic being or a vital essence of the person' (Lantis in Damas 1984: 219).

In the Mackenzie Delta region of the western Canadian Arctic children were often (but not always) named for deceased grandparents and 'treated with the respect previously accorded their namesakes …' Here, name taboos extended to marriage. 'People who had the same name could not marry each other. Each person had several names, but only one might be in common use' (Smith 1984: 355). The Copper (Central) Inuit developed elaborate avoidance and respect relationships, which included namesake partnerships between those with the same (deceased) namesake (Damas 1984: 403). An Inuk from South Baffin told me that there are levels to the namesake relationship. In this person's experience, only a small number of name-sharers are considered really close enough to be bound by gift exchange, hunt-sharing and other customs. Other name-sharers are on the margins of the namesake constellation.

Although in most places Inuit namesakes are deceased, in the Belcher Islands the namesake was also the name-giver and was 'always a living person'. As among other Inuit, names were given at birth. A child was named only if he or she was born alive, seemed strong enough to go on living, and was not slated to be killed. If an Inuk child had not received a name, he or she was not considered human. Balikci has an interesting interpretation of the relation of these rules and practices to infanticide:

> Naming had a restrictive influence on infanticide. The Netsilik believed that a personal name had supernatural power closely associated with an individual's personality, and that the dead had a strong desire to reincarnate in newborn infants, irrespective of sex. The dead chose their new infant bodies at the time of birth. If the mother was having a difficult childbirth, she called out various names of dead people in hope of enlisting their help. The name proving the most helpful at delivery was retained, the mother believing that the spirit had entered the infant's body ... The dead chose their new infant bodies at the time of birth ... it was essential that infanticide take place prior to naming, since killing a named child might offend the spirit of the reincarnated person, and so the naming of unborn children in hopes of easing childbirth did restrain mothers from practicing infanticide. (Balikci 1970: 148–49)

In the South Baffin region – which includes Pangnirtung, Iqaluit, Cape Dorset, Broughton Island and Lake Harbour – interpersonal relationships 'cannot be understood apart from the meaning of a name and the process of naming'. Children are named only for those who have died (Kemp 1984: 470). In the 1950s Inuit were relocated from Southampton Island in northwest Hudson Bay to Grise Fiord in the High Arctic. Suddenly they were thrown together with people from different communities. Yet the groups retained 'distinct factions having separate dialects and modes of living nearly forty years after being brought together'. This was especially the case where marriage and naming were concerned, and had the effect of severely limiting the range of possible partners. At Grise Fiord, marriage between Baffin Island and Hudson Bay Inuit 'remains very rare' (Freeman 1984: 676). In this region, name sharing

> can be either planned, in which case the partners will refer to each other as *sauniq*, or accidental, whereupon they are *atikulugiit* (pl.) or *avvariit* (pl.). The exact nature of the *sauniq* relationship varies from group to group. For example, a Port Harrison family will choose an infant's *sauniq* only from among living persons, whereas at Pangnirtung the *sauniq* is always chosen from the recently deceased. This custom has remained unchanged in both groups following immigration [to Grise Fiord]. (Freeman 1984: 679–80)

Although the ways of naming described above have been recorded for more than a century, they remain current: Inuit names and namesake relationships are very much alive today, and in the early years of Nunavut there is renewed interest in maintaining them. 'I talked to Ugjuk when the Old Man died. A gentle, aging son of 70, Ugjuk spoke of his certainty that

Kavik's name will bring his spirit back to live within the bodies of newborn Inuit soon to come. He said, with quiet pride, and in solid faith ... "Kavik is dead, it is true. His life was extremely long, but his soul is not dead. Soon Kavik will come back, that is quite sure'" (Williamson 1993: 46).

The Tangled Structures of Kinship, Commemoration and Cross-gender Naming

> The kinship network involves a continual redistribution of names ... establishment and re-establishment of relationships ... (Nuttall 1992: 79)

> The naming of children for deceased relatives and community members makes the social landscape 'a memoryscape of persons. (Nuttall 1992: 59)

Mark Nuttall sees personal and place names as closely connected, and kinship as 'multifaceted, embracing genealogy, friendship, name-sharing, age-sets, birthday partners, chosen kin and name souls ... a collection of symbols highly charged with emotional energy'. While the kinship categories can have varied meanings, individuals have the 'freedom to employ them in any way they choose. It is in this sense that kinship is symbolic ...' According to Nuttall, the 'reluctance to regard kin terms and genealogy as coterminous results in an elaborate construct: a universe of realities transcending "biology". ... Kinship is ... inherently socio-cultural rather than biological' (Nuttall 1992: 93–94). According to Christopher Trott, 'Nuttall backs away from making the naming system the centre of Inuit social relations but continues to see it as an add-on to the genealogical set of relations, providing another avenue for expanding flexibility' (Trott 2005: 10). It is the premise of this book that the naming system is indeed the centre – not just of Inuit kin relations – but of all of Inuit society.

Trott suggests the need to revise dominant anthropological analyses of Inuit kinship, based on the concept of *ilagiit*, or 'kindred', based on an understanding of *tuqluraqtuq* (as it is called in North Baffin), which is linked to naming. It has 'a range of meanings including "nickname" but more precisely refers to "the term by which one calls another person"'. According to Trott, this term is absent from the literature on Inuit kinship, but is crucial because it highlights 'the importance of naming, and the naming system for Inuit understandings of their own kinship system' (Trott 2005: 1).

Inuit kinship is flexible and changeable. Ann Fienup-Riordan observes that kin relations can change over time, and from season to season, with those considered close kin in one season sometimes not considered near relations in another (Fienup-Riordan 1993). The 'cycling of people through names' links with other cycles – of

The living and the dead, the visible and the invisible, animals and humans, the reproduction of animals and the reproduction of the entire cosmos. Names provide the link between humans, animals, and the universe in a way that integrates Inuit symbolic thought into a whole and makes kinship a part of the wider symbolic world. (Trott 2005: 10)

Trott's research in Arctic Bay began with the Inuktitut question, '*kisugiviuk?*' 'What do you have so-and-so as?' Inuit told him to replace it with '*kinagiviuk?*' 'Who is so-and-so to you?' 'Inuit had shifted the entire focus of my study ... I was being told not to ask for the genealogical relationship but rather what the relationship was through the name'. (Trott 2005: 11)

While it is generally assumed that (internationally and cross-culturally) surnaming accompanies the emergence of ownership of titles, goods and lands, there are indications that traditional (surnameless) Inuit naming can have a function in relation to land use. In Arctic Bay from 1908 to 1980, Trott notes that the 'name Attagutsiaq was held by three different people ... there was always an Attagutsiaq present – sometimes a woman, sometimes a man. Ultimately, what this allowed Inuit to do was to define very precisely who belonged on what lands – a clear definition of land ownership mediated by the naming system' (Trott 2005: 16). I would replace the term 'land ownership', which seems based on Qallunaaq ideas of permanency and profit, with 'land use', which seems more in keeping with Inuit ideas of land, water and subsistence. The collective suffix -*miut*, which identifies families and communities with the spaces and places they use, is carried into contemporary political life, as *Nunavummiut* (people of Nunavut) identify more broadly with the political territory they inhabit.

Until the early 1900s, Inuit winter ceremonies culminated in a ritualised, shaman-guided spouse exchange in which women and men first stood and called out their names and birthplaces before being assigned their temporary partners. The system of arranging intercourse for the night was a way of rearticulating 'relations between people and ... land as mediated through names ...' The coupling supervised by *angakkut* [shamans] may have been a way of 'reuniting partners through their names' to recreate 'the social organization of the previous generation, for the present generation' (Trott 2005: 19).

Alexina Kublu's naming stories convey the complexity of the Inuit naming system and its link to a network of kinship reference. It is a meticulous and familiar tapestry to Inuit; to Qallunaat, an incomprehensible tangle of interwoven identities. A linguist and educator, Kublu comes from the High Arctic community of Igloolik. With an amused and challenging look, her husband and teaching colleague, Mick Mallon, explains one of their shared relationships: 'Kublu and I are fellow old men. I'm an old man because I've reached that stage all on my own. Kublu started life as an old man because she is her own great grandfather' (Alia 1995: 1). Kublu elaborates:

> I am my *paniq's atatukulu*. My paniq's my grandmother ... My grandmother is my *paniq*, which is 'daughter'. I'm her *atatukulu* because I'm named after her stepfather. Her biological father was lost out at sea when she was a baby, so she never knew her father. The only father she knew was Kublu and so to her, he was her father. My younger daughter calls me *inni* (son), and I in turn, call her *atatta* (father).
>
> Some people call me Apak and it's through Apak that she's my *atata*. And through Apak that I'm her *inni*. But first of all, I was always going to be Kublu because my *atiq* [namesake] died before I was born ... and so my family knew who I was going to be. I was born already about to be Kublu, so when I became born, so naturally I became Kublu ... My mother's midwife – the first person who held me – told my mother that she wanted her son to live with her ... My mother by name [told] my mother by birth that she wanted to have her son living with her. So that's how I became Kublu. (Alia 2005: 3)

Martha Flaherty is a well-known translator/interpreter and former president of Pauktuutit, the Inuit Women's Association. She is also the granddaughter of the filmmaker Robert Flaherty (who made *Nanook of the North*) and Alice Nuvalinga, the Inuk 'wife' he added to his existing marriage. She explains how it worked in her family:

> When my father died, there was a little boy born who was named after my father. So, everybody calls him my father: he is my father; my mother calls him husband. When he got his first seal, he gave a piece of that to my mother, gave the skin to my mother so my mother could make something for him. If he goes to the store, he'll buy sugar or tea for my mother. He calls all of us his children, according to how our father named us. (Alia 1995: 2)

The ties between an Inuk and his or her namesake are so strong that kinship terms, dress and behaviour often follow the relationship rather than the individual's biological sex. Jose Kusugak is one of Nunavut's contemporary political leaders who are working to ensure the continuity of Inuit cultural traditions along with the inevitable political and social change. He is especially committed to carrying on the names and naming traditions:

> traditionally, because I was named after a woman, I would have gotten a mark on my right thumb, a tattoo. But I was one generation too late for that, so I never got a tattoo. It would be a nice thing, I think, to bring that back: having a tattoo on the thumb to signify that, if you're a man and you have a tattoo on your right thumb, then people would know that you are named after a woman. (Alia 1995: 3)

Napatchie Akeego MacRae describes how cross-gender naming, or *sipinig*, worked in her family:

A lot of the names are about a hundred years old that I know of ... My father's sisters call me Akeego. When I was born, [a man] had just recently died ... called Napatchie ... [pronounced 'Napat-see']. Akeego was my dad's younger sister, and my middle name is named after her. I don't know how many names I've got so far. I know only about a few, but not all of them, but they are not used as often ... Napatchie was a man – the person I'm named after – his relatives call me his younger brother. One of the midwives that helped my mum was [his] mother ... my parents decided to name me after him. It's almost like reincarnation in the name's way. And that's how it works ... they feel like to respect the dead they let the name carry on for their family's sake.

Her identities are even more complicated than this first explanation would imply, because in addition to being a 'younger brother' she is also a 'younger sister':

My middle name is Akeewok, after my dad's youngest sister. All of my dad's relatives treated me like I was their little princess because I was named after their younger sister. My grandfather showed his love towards me more than towards my other siblings because I was named after his youngest daughter, and my aunts ... And my dad ... me being his first daughter, treats me with better respect than his other kids. I don't call him 'Dad' in Inuktitut; I call him 'Brother' and I call them my aunts in English but in Inuktitut I call them older [or younger] sister.

Her biological family treats her as female, but the family whose brother is her namesake treats her as male.

The older brother would ask me if I want to go hunting with him, or catch my first caribou or seal ... but the way I saw myself, I was more female, so I didn't want to do that. It's kind of hard to explain how it really works. There's some people I've noticed that had a daughter named after a boy ... they would make them grow up as if they were boys right from the birth ... A family adopted my youngest sister, and she was named after the brother of the adopted mother. They made her dress up like a boy, gave her a haircut like a boy, from the time she was old enough to get a haircut. It went on and on and on until she was old enough to decide which way she wants to dress up. If a child was named after a female it would work the same way – dress him up like a female – let him grow his hair long ... That's how it works with some people, but other people ... with me it was different 'cause I had two names [one male, one female]. It confused me for a while, but I got my mom to explain why this man was calling me his younger brother even though I'm a girl ...

The first pair of *kamiks* my little girl got from my mom were in a boy's *kamiks* style. There's two different ways of making *kamiks*, the female and the male styles. She was getting the male style ... because of her name. Once the person that is named after a person [of the] opposite sex, once they are beginning to feel that they are too old to be treated the way they were treated when they were younger ... they would grow out of it. And they would let the parents know. But it's up to the child. We would still have that name – she'll

know that. For the child's emotional or mental stability, they have got to stop
somewhere ... you have to make them understand how it really works so they
won't be confused all their lives. (Alia 2005: 5–8)

Peter Irniq is Commissioner of Nunavut and a long-time cultural
teacher and political leader. He is especially concerned with Inuit names
and naming practices, and a few years ago, changed the spelling of his
own name – from Ernerk (as recorded by various officials) to Irniq, which
more accurately reflects the correct pronunciation. Traditional naming is
strong in Peter Irniq's family:

> My brother, who died about forty years ago, was named after my grandfather.
> When my parents adopted a child ... they named him again so ... he continues
> to have this new life each time. Same person, but living. He drowned in 1968.
> In 1969 they were given a baby [by traditional or 'custom' adoption] ... They
> named him my grandfather again ... I named my grandfather in our own
> family so that he's alive in our own family ...

His mother's name was given to his daughter; his father's name was given
to his son, and so on. 'These are the names that I have carried because
these are the people who were my leaders, my role models. They
provided direction for me all my life, so they're in my family, all of them'
(1984–2006). George Quviq Qulaut comes from Igloolik. His oldest
daughter carries the name of an elder who passed away a few months
before she was born, and who was also named after George's father. Like
many Inuit, she carries the names of female and male relatives because
'all Inuktitut names are unisex ... there is no woman name or man's
name. It works well' (Alia 1984–2006).

While Polar Inuit developed separate names for men and women, in
most parts of the Arctic names and gender are not connected. For example,
naming among the Utkuhikhalingmiut (Utku) is free of gender designations
and is not marked by any dramatic events. Jean Briggs describes the
unceremonious acknowledgement of birth in one community:

> While we ate, the baby, in a manner as informal as that of her birth, received
> her first name: 'Qayaq', in memory of Allaq's loved ... brother, who had
> drowned a few years earlier. (Briggs 1970: 156)

In most communities it is quite common to name a female after a male
relative (and vice versa). The commemoration – reincarnation – of the
important person takes precedence over the gender of namesake or
recipient. In the Mackenzie Delta most names are acceptable for both
men and women (Smith 1984: 355). As we will see in the next chapters,
the combined effects of missionary and government activities gradually
brought gender-consciousness to Inuit naming practices.

Inuit are not the only people to experience the introduction of gender distinctions into a genderless naming system. In Tahiti, gender distinctions also arrived with colonisation. Earlier, most names had applied equally to males and females. Missionaries brought biblical names and, with them, the idea of gender (Levy 1973: 33). I suspect that here, and in other cultures experiencing similar cross-cultural shifts, the transition was far from smooth. In the Canadian North, when Inuit first adopted missionary-given names, they sometimes passed them down in the old way without paying attention to the sex of the child (Neill 1984–86). In doing this, they were effectively resisting what Sneja Gunew calls 'ventriloquizing "ethnicity"', in which the 'foreign name' is seen as the 'authentic' one, by representatives of the dominant culture (Gunew 2004: 74).

Saladin d'Anglure's interview with a twice-named Inuk from Igloolik provides one of the best portraits I have seen of the intricate relationship between namesake, identity and gender. Iqallijuq was originally named Savviuqtalik after her maternal grandfather,

> from whom she received simultaneously name and identity ... In a remarkable narrative, she tells her granddaughter of the time (recalled in detail) when she was 'the name-soul of the old man in his grave' ... [and when] she left the grave and entered the womb of ... her mother. She describes her life in the womb, how she changed sex before leaving for the outside world, her life as a transvestite during childhood [a practice called *sipiniq*] and finally, the acquiring of her status of womanhood at the beginning of menstruation ... (Saladin d'Anglure 1977)

Iqallijuq was interviewed along with her cousin (and until her parents chose another man, her live-in partner), Ujaraq. This was a most interesting couple: Ujaraq, too, was a transvestite. Named for a woman, he dressed and lived as female until he killed his first caribou at puberty.

Names, Kinship and 'IQ'

Name and kinship classifications create particular categories and constellations of relationships, with the result that some relationships considered inappropriate in European society are perfectly acceptable to Inuit. In 1984 a Qallunaaq in his fifties told me that one Baffin Island community had a particularly high incidence of what in Qallunaq terms would be called incest. 'A brother would marry a sister. They're blood siblings but they were brought up in two different adoptive families. It's incest to us, but they are classified as two different families; they didn't grow up in the same home' (1984–2006). Such practices present a challenge for Inuit who live in their home communities, in the newly formalised territory of Nunavut, and in Canada. There are clear cross-cultural and legal difficulties in attempting to reconcile two entirely different definitions of incest.

> Up to a certain point ... the *sauniq* system contributes to the reproduction of the kindreds from one generation to the other. The transmission of names helps to foster the identity of the kin groups, which have their own repertoires of *sauniq* and family names. On the other hand, the 'memorial' names, whose transmission transcends the kindreds' boundaries, reconstruct, so to speak, the entire community, by continually renaming all of its newborn children with the appellations formerly worn by its deceased members. In this way, the naming patterns ... support, at the same time, the personal, family, and collective identities ... (Dorais 1997: 65)

It is important to note that, while traditional naming crosses gender lines and names are not gender-specific, many kinship terms *do* specify gender. Dorais finds that until the 1960s, when most Inuit were based in communities, 'most activities were based on kinship relations'. Hunting, gathering, fishing, trapping and other activities, and the camp groups that supported them, 'were based on kinship relations' (Dorais 1997: 67). Today, kinship terms are often a mix of traditional Inuktitut terms and contemporary English or French usage. 'Many youngsters, for instance, now call their mother "mom", rather than *anaana*, the proper kinship term' (ibid.: 68)

In Nunavut, the importance of kinship relations is imbedded in the principles of *Inuit Qaujimajatuqangit*, often abbreviated as 'IQ' (Arnakak 2000):

> To me these words have almost the same ring as 'Next year in Jerusalem' does to Zionists: like Judaism, the IQ concept is a binding force for a people ... What is IQ? I've been asking myself that question since I started working for the Department of Sustainable Development in late 1998. [It] is like asking how many grains of sand there are on Baffin Island. We can never hope to count [them] ... but we can describe what a grain of sand generally looks like, and that was how we approached the issue ... (Arnakak 2000)

While the 'traditional knowledge' component is often the most prominent, IQ is much broader and deeper. It links traditional concepts and practices with contemporary realities in what Jaypetee Arnakak calls 'a living technology', using 'the traditional Inuit family-kinship model' as 'a workable management model' for Nunavut (Arnakak 2000).

With the formation of Nunavut Territory, IQ was developed into a strategy for ensuring that Inuit culture and language would be an integral part of the society, in the context of the formal constitution of Nunavut as a public government encompassing Inuit and Qallunaat citizens. Most people say there is no easy definition of IQ.

The traditional meaning, 'that which is long known by Inuit', indicates the values and practices that allowed Inuit to survive in the eastern Arctic. At the same time, IQ is also the way in which the Inuit live their lives ... [and] approach daily decisions at home, at work, and in the family. IQ is thus how an Inuk conducts his or her life ... (Henderson 2005: 1004)

According to Paul Okalik, culture 'is a defining part of any society', and Inuit culture must be visible in policies and operations of government:

In Nunavut, we call our culture Inuit Qaujimajatuqangit ... IQ refers to a way of viewing the world and the values that go along with living a proper life. It is an approach that defines Inuit. It involves many aspects, including strong values related to social harmony, mutual sharing and assistance, and honesty. When I was a boy growing up in Pangnirtung ... I remember the stories my grandmother and mother recounted of Inuit history. I remember hunting my first caribou ... This connection to my culture was vital. It gave me the foundation I needed to go back to when my life grew too confusing. The Government has made a commitment to include Inuit Qaujimajatuqangit as an integral part of government policy development. (Okalik 2001)

Each Nunavut department is developing its own IQ-based policies. The shared objective is to 'ensure that public government represents the cultural inheritance and current values of the majority culture' (Henderson 2005: 1004). Among the guiding principles identified by Nunavut's Department of Sustainable Development are *Pijitsirniq*, the principle of serving; *Aajiiqatigiingniq*, the principle of consensus decision making; *Piliriqatgiingniq*, the principle of collaboration for a common purpose; *Avatimik Kamattiarniq*, the principle of environmental stewardship; and *Qanuqtuurunnarniq*, 'being resourceful to solve problems', which Arnakak calls the closest to a 'defining factor of being Inuit' (Arnakak 2000).

He summarises IQ as an epistemology (theory of knowledge) that encompasses 'a set of teachings on practical truisms about society, human nature and experience passed on orally ... from one generation to the next ... holistic, dynamic and cumulative in its approach to knowledge, teaching and learning ...' It utilises the traditional kinship structure, not just in relation to transactions and exchange of goods and services, but as a way of disseminating 'ideas, values, knowledge and skills'. The kinship structure of *Tuqturarngniq* links individual, family and society and guides a complex set of social and familial obligations that integrate moral and ethical obligations with social and practical obligations (Arnakak 2000).

Name, Community and Health

Names do not just continue individual lives; they continue the life of the community. When the community celebrates the birth of a child, the child is treated as 'a new person', yet at the same time, people are also celebrating their awareness 'that the child is also a recently deceased person's *atsiaq*. The community is thus celebrating the return of that deceased person. In doing so, the community is celebrating itself [while] the deceased's family [celebrates] its own continuity' (Nuttall 1992: 124).

Søby describes her experience of this twofold celebration when, in 1988, she visited the family of a Kullorsuaq hunter, Juulut, who had been killed a few days before. 'When I walked into the house it was full of people who were enjoying themselves, lively music was being played on the cassette recorder and the table was set for coffee and cake. The family was celebrating a christening ... the party's main person – a little boy ... was the first to be given the name Juulut after the dead hunter' (Søby 1992: 7).

Bestowing Names

As for a name, they have decided to let Ashima's grandmother ... who has named each of her other six great-grandchildren in the world, do the honors ... Ashima's grandmother has mailed the letter herself ... [It] contains one name for a girl, one for a boy. Ashima's grandmother has revealed them to no one. (Lahiri 2004: 25)

That is just the beginning of the lifelong struggle the characters in Jumpha Lahiri's novel, *The Namesake*, endure as they try to cope with naming while bridging the space between homeland and diaspora. Distance, health, communication and custom are to cause innumerable difficulties for the grandmother, the family 'back home' and the parents and child who have settled in the United States. While looking for ways to solve their naming problems and resolve their son's identity, the young parents never lose sight of the grandmother's primacy as namer.

The right, privilege, or obligation to choose names varies considerably among cultures. The giving of names is linked to other aspects of leadership. 'Quite frequently the roles of leader and namer are synonymous ...' (Poole 1981: 154–57). In more than twenty years of interviewing and talking with Inuit from Nunavut and other regions, I have heard many different stories about who does the naming. Sometimes, it is husband and wife together, sometimes husband, wife or friend. Sometimes a shaman, priest or relative does the naming. Some families and communities are very flexible about who does the naming; others have stricter rules or traditions. The literature reveals a similar range of preference and practice.

In the Mackenzie Delta region, shamans traditionally had responsibility for naming. In the Belcher Islands, either parent had the right to name a child but it was required that the parents agree, and ideally, the name choice would be 'a consensus of the whole household'. Because the owner of the name was still living, he or she had to give permission for the child to receive the name. If the name was chosen but permission was refused, the process had to be repeated until a suitable name-donor was found. In some cases, the name-owner initiated the process and chose someone on whom to bestow the name (Smith 1984: 355).

Even where they have few other powers, women often have the right to bestow names. When the name echoes or equals the *person*, this tells us something about power that may be generally unacknowledged. Although patriliny dominated pre-twentieth century European Jewish naming, a secondary matrilineal tradition reflected the frequent position of woman as breadwinner, man as scholar. The Waneng Aiyem Ser, a cross-gender sacred figure among the Bimin-Kuskusmin of New Guinea, is both name-giver and ritual leader. As in other cultures in which women achieve high status, she is past childbearing age – considered less threatening or polluting than her fertile sisters. She has three names: female, male and sacred (Poole 1981). Among Delaware people, visionary ability was the traditional criterion. Dream- and vision-related practices culminated in an annual twelve-day Big House Ceremony. A woman or man who experienced a vision became a giver of names:

> The possessor of such revelations ... was qualified per se as a name-giver or *Way-huh-wee-huh-lahs* ('one who gives names over and over') ... the visionaries were regarded as the elite. (Weslager 1971)

In Australia a Tiwi mother may name her children, but only after the primary name has been given by the child's primary 'father'. A woman may have many partners, but only one man can 'dream' a child and he may or may not be the child's biological father (Goodale 1971). Inuit children are named by women and men, by parents, spiritual leaders, family or community members. Inuit women have been shamans and men midwives. The namesake is the crucial concern. As we have seen, although the name itself has no gender, identification with the namesake is so powerful it can affect gender identity in other ways.

Names and Dreams

Deborah Evaluardjuk describes the ways in which namesakes are able to communicate directly to the family, through dreams:

My mother had a dream that my namesake came to lie down beside her and my father. He had this great big beard, one of the few Inuit who had a great big beard (his grandfather was a whaling captain from Scotland) … One month later, when they adopted me, she knew what it meant … that my namesake wanted to come back to them, because they were very, very close to him.

A month before her daughter was born, she had a dream:

I saw my uncle, Calepee Apak, who had recently passed away with cancer, coming toward me. And he was healthy. All of a sudden I looked down in my dream and the baby came out. It was a girl, and I knew it … I looked on the sand-type ground and I saw this tree twig; and right there it spelled A-P-A-K: Apak; and I knew right then and there that that's what the baby's name was supposed to be. (Alia 1995: 3)

Alexina Kublu tells a story that, like Deborah Evaluardjuk's, shows the strength of the connections between namesake and recipient. The namesake of one of her daughters had died in a plane crash, but her daughter had not been told about it.

When my daughter was about eleven, we were flying down to Winnipeg from Rankin and it was pretty turbulent. They didn't know if we were going to land … and … [she] says, 'I was in a plane crash, wasn't I?' And I said, 'No, you weren't in a plane crash.' And she goes, 'I *know* I was in a plane crash … I keep on dreaming about it.' I said, tell me about the dream. And she goes, 'I'm in the airplane, I'm looking out the window, I know we're going to crash, we crash, I get to the door and that's it.' She said she'd had the same dream over and over again. And I'm holding her and I said, 'Yes, you were in a plane crash, but not you as you. You as your *atiq*. You were in a plane crash.' He was found at the door of the airplane, and she said every time she got to the door, everything would go black and that was it. I held her and she started crying and she said, 'That's how I died, wasn't it?' (Alia 2005)

Kublu explains why it is virtually impossible to describe Inuit relationships in terms that Qallunaat can understand. In Qallunaat society, you are a person, and a person who marries your uncle is your aunt. But that (European) system does not account for Kublu's relative, who is

my dad's uncle's wife, whom I called … cousin, but she was my sister. She was my sister because she was the sister of the person I am named after. As a child, I considered the two people who were the name – who were the mother and father of my atiq – as my parents. I honestly thought that they were my parents, that I was their child and my biological parents were just looking after me for them. I felt … at home with them. I was their child. They were my parents. Their children were my brothers and sisters. My brothers and sisters' children were my nieces and nephews. I very much felt part of the family and I'd go in there and I knew I was home …

You know before the child is born who they are going to be. My [fifteen-year-old] daughter was in a bit of a dilemma a few years ago when a little girl who was named after my sister was killed … [It] brought back … the memory of my sister's death because she was named after her … my daughter [asked], 'What am I going to do … when I have a baby? What names [will] my child … have?' … We don't have any other babies in the family, and so there's this backlog of names to be given, for us to keep, for us to have, because I have my uncle, I have my parents by name … I do not have my mother, I do not have my sister and she's going, 'Well, I have two sisters, my mother and my aunt and then there's my aunt …' 'I want them all' and she goes, 'Is my baby going to have all these names?'[I said,] 'I don't know, I think so', so we … put that on the shelf to be thought about when the time comes …'

The way we name in Igoolik is still very strong … it's part of the healing process, part of the grieving process. It gives me a lot of joy to have a little child come to me and I can put my arm around them and say … this is my mother … or the children that come up to me and say, 'Hi sis' I don't know how to describe the feeling. You know that this is not the sister that you had, but this is still your sister. And … to have people refer to my own daughters through their name … that bond … there is no biological bond, yet they're not just my child.

The sister to whom Kublu refers is Elise (Qunngaatalluriktuq). Her death affected countless Inuit and Qallunaat whose lives she touched; her life continues through the lives of the people who carry her name.

Names and Adoption

In South Baffin, a number of women have told me they are concerned that southern adoption laws may destroy or discredit the Inuit system of adoption. It is interesting to note that increasingly, Qallunaaq individuals and social service agencies are fighting the legalised, secrecy-bound single family system that has generally denied adopted children the right to know their biological families. It would seem that Inuit wisdom has superseded European-North American wisdom, as Qallunaat move closer towards a system more akin to the one Inuit developed long ago. The Inuit view of extended family and community encompasses 'custom adoption'. Such practices are facilitated by smallness. People living in clan-sized groups on the land or in communities of only a few hundred can easily maintain a fluid relationship between birth and adoptive families. In Nunavut communities, I have seen children move daily among the homes of birth and adoptive parents, relatives and friends, receiving care, food and companionship wherever they landed.

However, it is unwise to oversimplify. I have heard of Inuit families that treat adopted children as secondary (a story that is also told of some Qalunaaq adoptions). Two people said they had seen adopted children treated 'as slaves' in the adoptive household, suggesting that condition was linked to a hierarchy of power between the birth and adoptive families. In general, people say that Inuit custom adoption is more welcoming and less stigmatised than adoption among Qallunaat. I have met families in which adopted children were much loved by both their biological and adoptive parents, and certainly in these instances, the children benefit from the extended attention and affection. I have been told that adoptions are a part of everyday life and that giving a child for adoption is a way of making sure every *amauti* (or *amautik*) (the baby-carrying hood on a woman's parka) carries a child. Bernadette Driscoll underscores this in the titling of her wonderful exhibition and book, *The Inuit Amautik: I Like My Hood to Be Full* (Driscoll 1980). Keith Crowe notes that in earlier times, 'almost all families gave or received children' (Crowe 1991: 56). This practice derived not only from a sense of community but from necessity: when people lived out on the land, a family needed able-bodied workers.

When communities are small and communication is open, adopted children grow up well nurtured and loved, with two families and the freedom to travel between homes. In the Inuit custom-adoption culture the whole Qallunaaq idea of biological versus adoptive families has no relevance. To understand why, we must return to naming:

> In Inuit society children are not thought to be extensions of and therefore in some sense 'owned' by their parents. Since their identity is not inherited in the form of some substance such as 'blood' but is rather introduced into their bodies in the form of a name spirit, family members have nothing to gain or lose by the successes or failures of the child. The bond between parents and child is the bond of 'love' and the only persons whose personal sense of self worth is affected by the actions of the child are his [or her] ritual relatives, most importantly his [or her] namesakes. (Guemple 1979: 51)

In 1969, the Council of the Northwest Territories tried to move the North the other way. Councillor Robert Williamson (the anthropologist whose much-respected work on names and identity is cited in this book) introduced Bill No. 7, An Ordinance to Amend the Vital Statistics Ordinance, designed to make adoptions 'confidential' (i.e., secret) (Government of the Northwest Territories 1969: 20). Today, the trend is reversed, and custom adoptions are regaining status. I was told that many Inuit continue the practice of changing a child's name when he or she is adopted out. The name is changed privately, and maintained through daily use; it is not recorded on the person's birth certificate and is often absent from other public records.

With the coming of Christianity, Greenlandic people took Danish names and, until the cultural revival that followed home rule, generally stopped using Greenlandic names in their daily lives. In the Canadian

Eastern Arctic names were never entirely abandoned. If you scan a Greenland telephone book, the country looks Danish. If you scan the Baffin telephone book you see many Inuit names, in both syllabics and English, and get a very different impression. Things are changing; there is a trend towards 'Greenlandicising' names (for example, Daaveeraq or 'little David' or Susaat for Susan) (Nuttall 1992: 68).

Throughout the Inuit world, the giving of a name remains an act of incomparable importance for the individual and the community (Robbe 1981: 54), and is often separated from the baptismal ceremonies brought by missionaries and absorbed into Inuit lives:

> Today, the traditional ritual of name-giving remains independent from the ceremony of Christian baptism. What is primary is the giving of names according to traditional Inuit custom, at the moment of birth; the baptismal ceremony takes place several days later. (Robbe 1981: 78, my translation)[2]

Regardless of the particular characteristics, preferences and practices of a community or region, naming is a – perhaps *the* – central component of Inuit culture. It is often viewed literally as reincarnation – the embodiment of continuity from person to person and generation to generation. Because Inuit usually bestow names without regard for gender, class or title, patrilineal Western surnaming made little sense when it arrived. The following chapters examine the effects of Western visits and incursions on Inuit naming practices and the politics of identity.

Notes

1. Although most midwives are women, there are accounts of male midwives, as well as men who assist in birthing babies. Martha Greig told me that her grandfather (who was blind) was a noted and respected midwife in Northern Quebec (what today is called Nunavik). She said he was widely loved for his gentleness and skill (1984–2006).
2. Original text: 'Aujourd'hui le rituel traditionnel de dation du nom reste independant de la cérémonie du baptême chrétien. Il y a *d'abord* la dation des noms selon la coûtume traditionnelle inuit au moment de la naissance; la cérémonie du baptême a lieu quelques jours apres.'

Chapter 2

VISITING, COLONIAL STYLE: FROM EARLY DAYS OF CULTURAL INTERVENTION TO THE COLD WAR

When I first went North I had to discard countless preconceptions and learned ways of politeness and decorum. Some of the ways I was taught to behave were turned upside down. This was especially true of what I had learned about 'proper' methods of conducting research, and about the etiquette of visiting.

Visiting, Inuit Style

Having obtained funding and made elaborate personal arrangements restricted by limited funds, research time and child care, I proceeded to contact key people in Iqaluit (Frobisher Bay) and Pangnirtung, the first communities I visited, from my home base in Toronto. No one official mentioned it, but I learned by chance from another researcher that everyone conducting research in northern Canada required formal approval and a Scientific Research Licence (Figure 2.1). It was administered from Yellowknife by the Government of the Northwest Territories, as until 1999 the Eastern Arctic that is now Nunavut Territory was then the eastern part of the Northwest Territories. In those days before e-mail I set out to send letters of explanation and introduction, and make telephone calls, thinking to make appointments for interviews and consultation well in advance. It took a long time to learn how foolish and inappropriate this was. Week after week, my mailbox remained empty. There were no replies to my carefully and respectfully written letters. The letter I wrote several months in advance, to the Pangnirtung Mayor, Joanasie Maniapik, and the Hamlet Council was never answered. I later learned that, like most men in the community, the mayor was out hunting, camping on the land all summer, and would not return until the

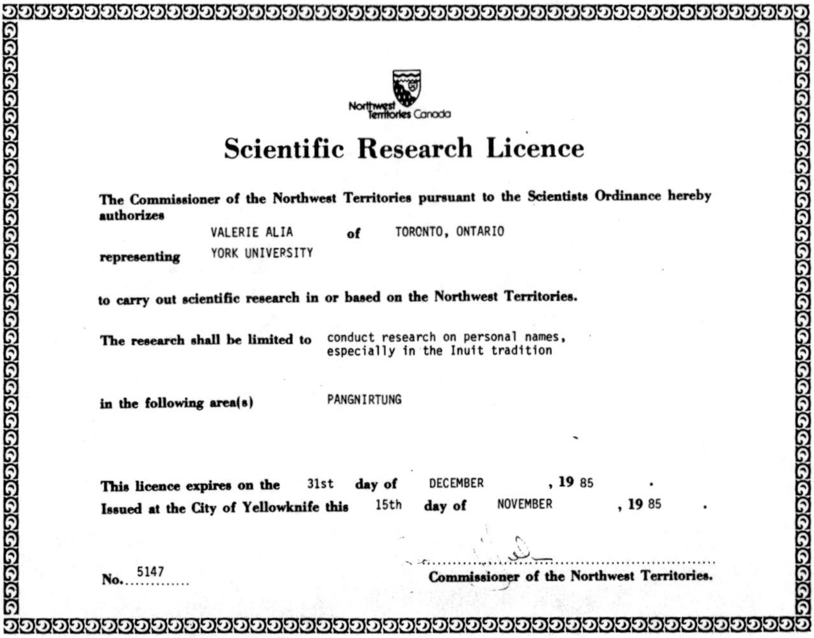

Northwest Territories Canada

Scientific Research Licence

The Commissioner of the Northwest Territories pursuant to the Scientists Ordinance hereby authorizes VALERIE ALIA **of** TORONTO, ONTARIO

representing YORK UNIVERSITY

to carry out scientific research in or based on the Northwest Territories.

The research shall be limited to conduct research on personal names, especially in the Inuit tradition

in the following area(s) PANGNIRTUNG

This licence expires on the 31st **day of** DECEMBER **, 19** 85 .

Issued at the City of Yellowknife this 15th **day of** NOVEMBER **, 19** 85 .

No. 5147

Commissioner of the Northwest Territories.

Figure 2.1 Scientific Research Licence granted to the author, 1985.

caribou season ended in early September (I was due to arrive in August). No one could make a decision about whether to allow my project, because there had been no quorum of the Hamlet Council during the entire summer. And besides, the mayor neither spoke nor read English. Only one member of the Hamlet Council did, and like everyone else, he was out on the land.

The Inuit ways of living and communicating with each other and with Outsiders were further complicated by political realities and bureaucratic structures. Within the next decade things changed, and most community management shifted to Inuit control. In the mid-1980s most community management was still in the hands of Qallunaaq Secretary-Managers. In Pangnirtung the position was held by a young southern Canadian man who processed all the mail and decided which messages and documents would be translated for the mayor and council members. What he set aside or failed to translate, they did not see. Had I known this I would have had my introductory letter translated into Inuktitut far in advance of the summer hunting season, and sent it directly to the mayor.

Not only were there no replies to letters; I soon learned that few people had telephones, those who did seldom answered them, and when they did, usually spoke Inuktitut. My vocabulary of a few words and phrases was virtually useless. I did finally reach one person with whom I could speak, Deputy Mayor Hezakaiah Oshutapik, one of the council's few English speakers. We had a very pleasant conversation. I discussed the proposed project, admitting I had not yet obtained the requisite licence and explaining that my university, children and resources all required that I make the trip at the time planned. He listened carefully and replied kindly but firmly: 'I cannot give you approval. You will have to come and make a presentation to the Hamlet Council. They will decide whether to allow this research. You are very welcome to come here as a visitor.' Frustrated, unprepared and stunned, I stuttered, 'But I don't know what to do. I tried to reach people in advance but nobody replied. My flight is booked. What should I do?' Kindly, patiently and firmly he replied: 'You are welcome to visit. You will have to make a presentation to the Hamlet Council' after you arrive.'

I had just twenty-four hours to decide whether to go ahead without official consent or cancel and try to reschedule the entire project. There was more than convenience at stake. There were ethical considerations as well. I could not afford an Arctic holiday. From the university's and funding agency's perspective, it was a research trip. Would I have to give back the funding if I went as a visitor and was refused permission to conduct the research? It was a double bind: I could not go to Pangnirtung without research permission; I could not obtain permission without first going to Pangnirtung. I went, knowing that research was contingent on official approval and I might end up with only a visit. Luckily, it turned out to be the right decision. I landed in Pangnirtung in that odd and transitional season, in time for several important events: the annual 'sealift' of supplies (brought in from Quebec by ship) and the all-night, community-wide process of welcoming and unloading the ship; the return of the men from caribou hunting; the start of the school year; and the delightful exchange between the community and Canada's first astronaut, Marc Garneau, whose visit coincided with mine.

It was fortunate that permission was not required to visit Iqaluit (Frobisher Bay) to interview Abraham (Abe) Okpik and others. Abe, who almost single-handedly conducted Project Surname for the Government of the Northwest Territories, was fluent in English and had agreed in advance to be interviewed. In the years that followed we had several other interviews and exchanges as he considered and reconsidered his problematic role. In Iqaluit and also in Yellowknife, Ottawa, Montreal and elsewhere, I interviewed as many English-speaking Inuit as possible, both for the ease of interpreter-free communication and to learn how more acculturated individuals perceived the issues. The first visit to Iqaluit was both eye-opening and rewarding. There were people to visit who were friends of colleagues and friends; personal introductions always help. There were also impromptu visits and encounters, and I often learned the most from the encounters that were least expected. Here is an excerpt from the diary I kept during the first trip North:

In the schoolyard, jungle-gym enthusiasts ask what will become the most familiar question: 'Can we visit?' Visiting is not casual or occasional, it is an institution. Saying I've only a hotel room fails to deter my new friends. 'We'll come with you' says the oldest girl, bravest and most proficient in English. And they do. Laughing, we jump puddles in the near-freezing August drizzle, en route to the Frobisher Inn. Later, it's off to the home of friends' friends, instructed in rules of visiting light-years from those in Toronto. 'Just come in. The door's open. The living room is upstairs', I am told after we have set an approximate time. Time is always approximate. If I were a member of the community, time would be irrelevant and scheduling unnecessary.

'You don't have to *do* anything', says a friend who has lived in the North. There are no invitations, and my learned rules of politeness are thrown out the window. The host does not invite people to visit. Visiting is an outside-in process: it is the visitor's responsibility to go out and see people. Hosting is unprogrammed and can happen at any time. Things are even more flexible in Pangnirtung, with its (then) population of about 800, than in Iqaluit. At first, whenever someone shows up I start rummaging in the kitchen looking for food and drink to prepare and serve. But this is not expected. Visitors of all ages arrive at all times. Sometimes we bake together; sometimes no food is shared. I am billeted with a well-liked and welcoming educator whose home is a popular place to come and whose collection of recorded music is known and appreciated widely. I am often there alone, and tend to use the evenings for writing and quiet reflection – at least, that was the initial plan. In reality there are many quiet evenings but few opportunities for solitude, except as Inuit understand and respect it. I have been told that people able to respect privacy while visiting, and will not 'see' someone who is concentrating on work or family, or is incompletely dressed. People walk in and respond appropriately to whom and what they find.

Teenaged 'regulars' show up and immediately make a beeline for their favourite albums. One evening, a young man arrives, puts his favourite music on the stereo and, without a word, quietly stretches out on the sofa for a nap. On another occasion a trio of laughing, chattering pre-teenaged girls come visiting. They, too, go straight to the stereo, put on a Bruce Springsteen tape and then proceed to grill me about my relationship to the host. There are numerous risqué jokes and instructions on Inuktitut words for various body parts. There are requests to photograph our visit; turns are taken with the camera to get everyone into the picture. Then they go off and 'case' the house to confirm the (separate!) sleeping arrangements, giggling and teasing all the while. I have hired an interpreter from the community, Andrew Dialla. One evening my host comes home from work and suggests we go to see Andrew, his partner and their new baby. My Qallunaaq sense of propriety resists. I think we must phone ahead and warn the young parents of the impending visit. We do no such thing, and have a lovely visit. Not to visit would be rude; arriving unannounced is not.

It is not only visiting I must learn to re-understand. 'Appointments' also have new meaning. Andrew never contacts the people we plan to see, although – perhaps to accommodate my southern habits – he often promises to phone ahead and 'make an appointment'. What he really does is make appointments with me – give or take an hour or two – and take me to people's homes when he expects them to be there (they always are). Other 'appointments' and 'interviews' are equally ad hoc (though the concept of ad hoc is distinctly Qallunaaq). There are two (dirt) roads in Pangnirtung, one on each side of the (dirt) landing strip. I walk the hamlet's paths several times a day, play with children, stop at the co-op and Hudson's Bay store and the hotel. This affords at least superficial contact with a large proportion of the resident and transient populations. Some of the most important information is learned on those walks. By accident or design, people suddenly show up and join me, stop at the hotel for tea or invite me to go visiting with them. One person tells me Qallunaat usually keep to themselves and Qallunaat teachers always walk in pairs. Walking alone renders me available and visible, and sensitises me to the seemingly slower and less structured pace of 'northern time'.

Receiving Permission

At the beginning of the second week in Pangnirtung I was told, '*if* there is a council meeting' I might attend and present my case. I kept asking people and finally, just before it started, learned when the meeting would be. I attended and was invited to make a brief statement. I said I had been told that some people were not happy with the naming programmes and might have suggestions about improving them, and promised to share information with the community. I spoke in English; the Council secretary interpreted. The response from council members ranged from polite acceptance to warm encouragement. I received approval to proceed, and began the promised information-sharing process by writing a short item for the community newsletter, explaining the project. I wrote another item in response to a question asked by one of the informants. The mayor promised a letter of acceptance – which would enable me to formally apply to the Territorial Science Institute in Yellowknife for the 'required' Research Licence. The mayor's letter and the research licence arrived at my Toronto home some months after my return, with a November start date for my August arrival (see Figure 2.1).

People were extremely generous with hospitality, opinions, experiences and information. Once the 'application' process had been ritually observed (I cannot say 'completed' for the reasons described above) I was able to undertake formal interviews – though most would not be counted 'formal' in Western scientific terms. People invariably became more open when they learned I was a student and mother with no links to government, corporations or large research teams. Children, women and men were happy to hear I was a mother; that I was a 'single mother' was irrelevant (except when one male elder offered to find me 'a good husband'!). Because Inuit society places no negative sanctions on non-marriage or single parenthood it is not out of the ordinary, and is not stigmatised.

The transcultural accommodation went both ways. I had been told by academic 'experts' that Inuit dislike being asked questions. Assuming this to be a constant, I tried to tone down my way of talking and keep questions to a minimum. During one interview with a distinguished elder, in which I kept avoiding asking, he suddenly smiled mischievously and said, 'Why don't you ask me some questions?' Whether the intent was to adapt to *my* culture or simply to get through a conversational impasse, he forced me to reassess the facile assumptions. Either way, he was a gracious host. The very openness of Inuit visiting customs has left Inuit open to the excesses of visitors' interventions.

Visiting, Qallunaat Style

In one community, I meet a journalist from a prominent U.S. publication. He clutches a Ken Kesey novel and speaks with the self assurance of one who has in three days become an expert. The jokes about this are so rampant it's hard to believe he hasn't heard them. He tells me he will write about the beauty of his hike and 'the lifestyle changes of the Inuit people'. He rejects the offer of contact names. 'I don't need to talk to anyone else, I'm leaving tomorrow. I had two Inuit guides on the hike; I've already talked to two of the native people ...' Two men for a portrait of 'the Inuit lifestyle'. Never mind women, children, other men, other generations. Having hiked outside the community, he has returned to wall himself into a building and watch movies. 'I've met two natives', he says again. (Alia 1985b)

Over the years visitors to Nunavut have studied and observed, praised and criticised, confused and distorted, regulated and registered, revised and amended Inuit social structures, families, identities and names. In the 1920s Anglican, Catholic, Moravian and other religious missionaries brought Christian names, which Inuit added to their existing Inuktitut names. In the 1940s the government brought in 'disc numbers'. In the 1950s people were moved (or encouraged to move) into communities. In the 1960s 'Project Surname' was organised to make Inuit 'like other Canadians', as a way of celebrating the 1970 centennial of the Northwest Territories.

A few years ago, I sat in an Iqaluit apartment having tea with a young family. We talked for a while about the ways Inuit had been identified by visitors. Suddenly my host got up from the table, went to a cupboard and took out a small, flat, pressed-fibre circle of ugly reddish-brown. He slapped it down and with a bitter tone, said 'That was my name'. On the back were the words 'Eskimo Identification Canada'. On the front was a number. 'That was my name: E6 ...' he said (see Figure 2.4). Disc numbers were not the first encounter with renaming. Reidentification of Inuit had been encouraged or imposed by visitors for generations.

Hugh Brody traces Canada's intention to establish ownership of the Arctic back to the turn of the twentieth century. By the 1920s 'the three southern institutions' of missionaries, policemen and traders were well established. Members of these institutions discovered 'Eskimos who were "in need" – of Christianity, trading posts and enforcement of Canadian law' (Brody 1975: 18–19).

Missionary Naming

It is the nature of the missionary's 'mission' to change people's lives. It is not my place to judge the relative merits of different values and belief systems. What must be said, to understand the effect of missionary work on Inuit naming, is that Inuit had complex and deeply meaningful spiritual traditions which had evolved over centuries before the missionaries of various faiths arrived. To understand cultural change and avoid ethnocentrism we must view the missionaries' arrival as a meeting

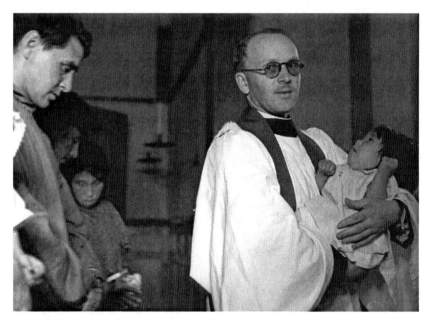

Figure 2.2 Missionary Naming. Reverend Trevor Jones holds an Inuit baby during a baptism ceremony at the Anglican church. Aklavik, Northwest Territories, 1939. *Source*: Finnie/NWT Archives/N-1979-063:0070. Northwest Territories Archives.

of different cultures and beliefs – which should have equal validity and equal power for the people to whom they belong. It is neither fair nor accurate to pretend that Inuit beliefs about names, souls and spiritual lives are inferior to those of European or North American Qallunaat, regardless of the particular nations or faiths they represent.

Qallunaat had to learn enough of Inuit ways to survive in the northern climate. For their part, missionaries brought far more than religion to the North. They brought a writing system, education and often, improved health care. In the best instances these complemented rather than replaced traditional ways of learning and promoting health. The missionaries also brought new names and new ways to bestow and celebrate old ones. They brought baptism – of Inuit, French, German, Danish, Russian or English names. However we view the particular and general aspects of missionary work among Inuit, the essential premise of missionary work is to replace one set of beliefs with another, or to extend or reinterpret those beliefs through the new system.

> Although the missionaries were sure that they were doing the right thing, their actions sometimes brought confusion and sorrow. Those who stopped the drum dancing, forbade the Coppermine Inuit to wear lip ornaments, and christened children with foreign names were little by little helping to destroy independence and pride ... The greatest fault of the missionaries, however, was, and still is in places, their private 'war' for power. (Crowe 1991: 148–49)

> Every living Belcher Island Eskimo has two names: a Christian first name, usually of Biblical origin and suffixed by the ending *-ii* ... and an Eskimo name, usually the term for some act, attribute or natural phenomenon. The first is of recent origin, having been introduced into the Islands after the turn of the century by missionaries. (Guemple 1965: 323)

Roberts thought the new names 'were no problem to the Inuit who, in most cases, continued to use a second (Eskimo) one anyway'. Dr A.G. MacKinnon, Pangnirtung Medical Officer, wrote that in 1936, the local missionary, Mr Turner, had the greatest influence of the Qallunaat in the community on the naming of children. He was uncertain as to whether it was the desire of government to 'have the Eskimo adopt the Biblical names in place of their own' or the desire 'of the Eskimo or the local Missionaries ...' He did notice that the duplication of names – which Qallunaat seemed to find so distressing – not only was failing to disappear, it 'seems to be increasing with the adoption of biblical names' (Roberts 1975: 7–8). Greenlandic people found their own ways to maintain cultural continuity while complying with missionary preferences for biblical, or Danish, names. 'Long after the introduction of Christian baptism, Greenlanders continued to give their children, along with a Christian name, a Greenlandic name' (Kleivan 1984: 612).

Figure 2.3 Inuit at Mission House in Pangnirtung. The original caption: 'Pangnirtung natives, at Mission House, Baffin Island, NWT, ca. 1927'. Child on right is thought to be 'Malaiya' (Kudlu Pitseolak) (see figure 2.5).
Source: PA-102462/Pangnirtung natives at Mission House, Baffin Island, NWT, ca. 1927. Northwest Territories Archives.

Class and gender distinctions that permeate English naming were even more difficult than pronunciation. Inuit names and personal pronouns never specify gender or class, and there is no such thing as a title. I told someone I had met Mayor Maniapik and he replied, 'you mean Joanasie?' Confusion and ambiguity accompanied the arrival of baptismal naming. Some changes rendered the originals almost undetectable. There is no 'r' in Inuktitut. A name like 'Mary' might be spelled 'Imellie'. Many names are neither English nor Inuktitut but a fusion of the two. The Pangnirtung surname Dialla (a reconstruction of Taylor) is an example (Crowe 1984–96). It is often impossible to determine an individual's gender from his or her name. Even Christian names have sometimes been bestowed in traditional Inuit fashion without regard for the person's biological sex. The missionaries were not universally welcomed. The Pangnirtung elder, hunter and sculptor Etoangat, recalled the slow progress of Christianity during his youth on Blacklead Island in Cumberland Sound. 'There were a lot of people opposing Christianity and wanting to stay with shamanism', he told me (1984–2006). While most Inuit converted to Christianity the persistence of distinctly Inuit naming practices, non-legal marriages and non-legal adoption suggests that Christianity was applied selectively, if not superficially.

'We call you as you are', Nancy Anilniliak said with a smile. Inuit use no titles or qualifying pronouns. The word *Inuk* can refer to a male or female, child or adult. In general, once gender, class and pronunciation problems were dealt with, there is little indication that introduction of baptismal names per se caused significant difficulty or concern. I suspect this is because (a) they were added to an individual's accumulated given names in a manner not entirely inconsistent with Inuit tradition; (b) they did not replace Inuktitut names; Inuit were able to continue traditional naming practices and usage; (c) the new names facilitated communication with Qallunaat who had trouble pronouncing Inuktitut names. The lack of reciprocity in adapting English names to Inuktitut indicates the nature of power relations in the North: only Qallunaat who worked quite closely with Inuit were (openly) given Inuktitut names (although some apparently received covert, not always flattering, nicknames).

In East Greenland modifications to the traditional naming system accompanied the arrival of Christianity. The three basic 'solutions' to cross-cultural problems were (1) to give a traditional name as a baptismal/certificate name when the infant's sex differs from that of the namesake (and therefore, his or her Christian name); (2) to give one of the namesake's other names that does correspond to the infant's sex; (3) to feminise or masculinise the namesake's name to fit the infant's sex. In 1980 Gilberg found that '[in] spite of the influence of Christianity', traditional naming practices (including namesake-naming and taboos) continued among Polar Inuit (Gilberg 1984: 586).

Fingerprints and Numbers

The missionary naming programmes did not solve everyone's 'problems'. Traders, police, doctors, explorers and other Qallunaat 'were stumped by the absence of surnames and either unable or unwilling to learn the distinguishing name …' (Roberts 1975: 2). So long as Inuit owned no property in the southern sense, and continued to live on the land, there was no need for surnames or other identification. An array of services evolved out of the growing relationship between government administrators and Inuit, who were increasingly encouraged (and sometimes prodded) to live in settlements. Requests for new identification procedures began to come into government headquarters from various newcomers to the North.

In 1929 Royal Canadian Mounted Police (RCMP) Sergeant O.G. Petty suggested that the Canadian government standardise the spelling of Inuit names. Apparently no action was taken. In 1932 Major D.L. McKeand of the Department of the Interior proposed that Ottawa establish a separate file for each Inuk, with his or her name in both English and syllabics, and also including the person's fingerprints. He was not worried about the ethics of opening police files on people who had not broken the law – an unprecedented concept.

'[If] all the Eskimo were finger printed it would be a start in the right direction,' McKeand said in 1933 after returning from his expedition to the Eastern Arctic (Nunavut). He could see no reason not to proceed. The Chairman of the Dominion Lands Boards thought the idea was harmless, appropriate and efficient:

> The only possible objection to finger printing the Eskimo would be from those who are strongly opposed to the system of finger printing. They seem to think that there is some connection between criminals and finger prints and there might be questions asked in Parliament concerning it. However, very few Eskimo can read or write and the finger prints would serve as his [sic] mark. (Roberts 1975: 3)

At the outset no objections were heard, and fingerprinting was begun in the Eastern Arctic. McKeand reported 'unqualified success' and said Registrars of Vital Statistics (who then were RCMP officers) would handle fingerprinting when children could be fingerprinted at age eight or nine. The fingerprinting programme would probably have continued had protests not emerged. Dr J.A. Bildfell, the medical officer who had accompanied the 1933 Eastern Arctic Expedition, found fingerprinting unacceptable, objecting on both administrative and humanitarian grounds.

> As regards the value of fingerprinting ... in my opinion the procedure hardly justified itself. The matter caused overcrowding of already cramped examination quarters, and in many cases frightened the natives quite noticeably. I further believe that it requires an expert to interpret the prints, and he is stationed in Ottawa. As a means of identification it is, unquestionably, infallible, but is hardly adaptable, in my opinion, to the North. (Roberts 1975)

Fingerprinting soon went out of fashion without having become standard practice. In a continuing dialogue missionaries, traders, police and government continued to tackle the identification 'problem'. The next undertaking was to give Inuit identification numbers.

Disc Numbers

In May 1935 Dr. MacKinnon wrote to the Department of the Interior to protest the difficulty of following individuals from one part of Pangnirtung to another. 'There are five divisions to the settlement and I think that if left to get the names from the natives each has a different spelling for each name' (MacKinnon in Roberts 1975: 5). When I visited Pangnirtung in 1985, 1989 and 1995 – after several decades of intervention and reidentification – Inuit and Qallunaat complained about the same

Figure 2.4 Disc number identity tag.
Photograph by John McDonald and used with his permission.

problems reported back in 1935. Clearly, something had not worked. Early on, MacKinnon saw no improvement emerging from the missionary renaming programmes.

> It does not seem to ease our troubles any that [Inuit] have in recent years taken their names from the Bible. A good example of this is in the rather common name of Ruth. The native cannot get his sounding mechanism around the letter R at the first of the word. As a result different persons would write down the following when the native gave the child's name, Vrootee, Olootee, Alootah with other alterations along the same line. To one who does not know them personally, this makes it rather difficult when it comes to putting them in alphabetical order. (MacKinnon in Roberts 1975: 6)

In terms of cultural retention or revitalisation the Inuit response to missionary-given names was constructive. As we will see, Inuit throughout the North have found different ways to combine Inuit and Qallunaaq ways of naming. Although MacKinnon and Neill attribute these changes solely to the difficulty Inuktitut speakers have with English pronunciation, it is also true that the new names were made Inuktitut-like and were therefore perhaps easier to incorporate into the existing naming culture. In all of the literature and interviews, no one has mentioned (except as a way of justifying Qallunaaq reidentification programmes) the equivalent responsibility of Qallunaat to learn Inuktitut names. Avoidance of this responsibility underlay the 'need' for the disc number system.

> How it started was … when they were setting up the United Nations in 1945. I was sixteen years old then but I listened to it on the radio. Lester B. Pearson made a presentation … he was representing Canada at that time. He said they should

do something about the North – they were dying like muskrats or something to that effect … There was only two hospitals in the whole of the Northwest Territories, run by Anglican missions, and maybe three by Roman Catholic. There was no administration. So in 1945, when Parliament opened the family allowance and old age pension, they started the numbers. (Okpik 1985–95)

Others say the numbers began much earlier and were in place in time for the 1941 Arctic Census. Each year the RCMP updated the disc list for each settlement. Because the numbers alone were used for record keeping, no one worried much about inconsistencies in the spelling of names.

A significant factor in considering and assessing subsequent events is that this … fact of ignoring names in favour of disc numbers applied to the Eskimo people themselves. In the future evaluation of Project Surname this must be borne in mind. (Government of the Northwest Territories 1971a: 3)

In 1993, John MacDonald, Director of the Igloolik Research Centre, shared some of the delights of the disc number legacy.

The municipal authorities here allow anyone not in government housing to number their dwellings as they see fit. The result, of course, has been a wonderful parody on the whole point of numbering: instead of order you get disorder! Thus, for example, two houses side by side on the same street could be numbered respectively 62–1/2 and 3002! Igloolik would be a fine place for a cab drivers' purgatory. An interesting variation on this process is that one or two residents have taken to numbering their newly-built homes with their old disc numbers; in one particular case the numbers have been rendered with calligraphic care and emblazoned onto the side of the house … A more practical employment of disc numbers recently came to my attention. There's a man in Igloolik (for obvious reasons I won't name him!) who always uses his 'E-number' on combination locks and even on his banking access card because, as he says, it's the only number he'll remember all his life … a rather interesting irony on a system initially designed to get an administrative grasp on a 'pre-literate' society. (MacDonald 1993: 1)

We had one name. My name wasn't Abraham Okpik. Mine was registered 'Abraham'. But I still had to get a number. When the RCMP were given the opportunity to do a Census on the Inuit population we all got names. What they had was a disc number. You ever see an old disc list? RCMP used to issue them every year. There were nine districts in this area (E, the Eastern Arctic). E-1 was Eskimo Point. E-6 was Pangnirtung. Quebec was E-8 and 9. Northern health services were using it and RCMP was using it. Missions were using it. There were no communities. People weren't congregated. (Okpik 1985–95)

All this was happening in a rapidly changing policy climate. Between 1930 and 1950,

federal policy in the North shifted dramatically … from the somewhat laissez-faire attitude of the 1930s to one of active intervention … All this came about with the support of a southern electorate who were excited by the vision of a new northern frontier, yet who were also apprehensive of any major American military presence which might diminish Canada's sovereign rights or control. But by 1950, the fear of a nuclear war overrode all other concerns. (Grant 1988: xvi)

In 1934, fifty-two Inuit from Cape Dorset were relocated to Dundas Harbour on Devon Island and then to outlying areas, ostensibly to help them find food. 'After thirteen years, they returned to the mainland; the experiment had failed. In retrospect, the project appeared to be designed less as a solution to Inuit destitution, than as a way for the Hudson's Bay Company to get around the restriction of new trading posts in the game preserve, with the assertion of sovereignty as justification' (Grant 1988: 33).

Enter the disc number system, originally proposed in 1935, by MacKinnon, in typically paternalistic terms.

> My humble suggestion would be, that at each registration the child be given an identity disk on the same lines as the army identity disk and the same insistence that it be worn at all times. The novelty of it would appeal to the natives. (Roberts 1975: 6)

Except for one report of a man who wore his disc 'for good luck' and Ernie Lyall's pride in being the only Qallunaaq with an 'E-number' no one reported wearing his or her disc. For Lyall it was a sign of acceptance in the Inuit world that he was designated 'Eskimo'. An Inuk in her thirties told me she had given her disc number to Canada's National Museum of Civilization. A delegate to the 1985 Inuit Women's Association annual board meeting in Ottawa said, 'I wish we could have the disc numbers back' because that system was less complicated and offensive than the one that followed it. In the years preceding signing of the Nunavut Agreement, some Inuit said they preferred the disc system to surnaming but many, especially younger adults, expressed resentment at the numbers.

> When MacKinnon first made the recommendation in 1935 there was no action. A year later he reiterated the proposal. To strengthen his case he pointed out that 'the five southern institutions represented in Pangnirtung [the hospital, Hudson's Bay Company, missionary, RCMP and government] had five different ways of spelling and pronouncing the same Eskimo names'. (Roberts 1975: 6)

Again, his request for action received no response and the matter rested for several years, until it was raised in 1940 by Major McKeand. Again there was no action. In a letter of 9 May 1940 to Roy A. Gibson, Assistant Deputy Minister of the Department of Mines and Resources, McKeand wrote, 'The suggestion that metal discs be worn either around the neck or wrist has not met with favour, because – (a) Indians do not wear them;

(b) Misunderstandings might easily arise if Eskimos wore chains; and (c) So far as we know, wards of other Dominions do not wear identification discs' (Roberts 1975: 8). He softened his proposal to a 'small identification card (linen) enclosed in celophane [sic]' like an oil company credit card,' and added:

> Eskimos as a race are instinctively careful of their belongings because of the limited resources of the country. I venture the opinion that the idea of an identification card would appeal to them generally, and the loss of their card would be looked upon as a calamity. (Roberts 1975: 9)

He said the identity cards (which would be unique to Inuit, among Canada's inhabitants) would help to teach Inuit 'conservation' and help them 'realize that the Arctic regions are their own and they will be responsible for their development' (Roberts 1975: 9). Given the history of Qallunaat resource use, especially in relation to the history of the resource use of indigenous peoples, the assertion is preposterous. Apart from history, it is hard to follow the leap of logic that got him from identity cards to resource conservation! The identity card proposal was rejected, but R.A. Gibson, Deputy Commissioner of the Northwest Territories, returned to the idea of disc numbers. He assigned the task of researching the project to McKeand's staff. They found that the idea of 'instituting a simple system of identifying the natives of the Northwest Territories and Northern Quebec has been under review periodically since 1929' and had been mentioned several times before 1929. They chronicled the various proposals:

July 1929	Sgt. O.G. Petty, RCMP, proposed standardized spelling.
October 1932	Major D.L. McKeand proposed a file for each 'native' and in addition, fingerprinting.
February 1935	A.E. Porsild proposed introducing 'the white man's' surname system, 'compelling the head of each family to select a common name for his family.'
May 1935	Dr. Diamond Jenness repeated Porsild's proposal to give Inuit Qallunaat-style family names.
May 1935	Dr. A.G. MacKinnon proposed issuing identification discs with "number similar to that used in the army."
December 1935	Dr. J.A. Urquhart proposed introducing disc numbers as part of the Census process.

In the Financial Post of 3 April 1943, an optimistic headline heralded the joyous consequences of the Second World War: War Unlocks Our Last Frontier: Canada's Northern Opportunity' (Grant 1988: 121). That same year, the National Film Board produced a movie (narrated by the warm, authoritative voice of Lorne Greene) titled *Look to the North*. The film 'minimized the dominant American presence, highlighted the "joint cooperation" aspect, and particularly stressed the opportunities provided for postwar development' (Grant 1988: 149). The following year (1944), the Arctic Institute of North America (AINA) was founded by a group of Canadian and American military, government and scientific specialists, and dedicated to research and dissemination of information about the North. AINA was formally incorporated in Canada, by an act of parliament, and under New York state law. In 1945, James Glen (former Speaker of the House) took over the role of Minister of Mines and Resources. In his speeches he talked about a 'northern empire' (Grant 1988: 164).

In 1946, the U.S. Congress passed a bill to establish Canadian-U.S.A. weather stations throughout the Arctic, a project grounded more in 'defence' than in monitoring meteorology (Grant 1988: 174). In 1947, Hugh Keenleyside was appointed Deputy Minister of Mines and Resources. A member of the Arctic Institute, Keenleyside was 'committed to the concept of a 'new North' (Grant 1988: 188). He undertook a major administrative reorganisation, introducing a series of ordinances addressing scientific, judicial, educational and social concerns'. By 1950, Ottawa policymakers were once again talking of a 'new North', but this time it was a military North' (Grant 1988: 212). At that time Frobisher Bay (Iqaluit) was the last community still controlled by the United States, having been built as a military base and maintained as a Cold War outpost. Shelagh Grant calls this a 'regressive' period, in terms of social reform, and attributes the downward trend partly to the appointment of Robert Winters as Minister of Resources and Development. Winters brought in 'democratic reforms' which Grant calls 'autocracy in disguise'.

> ... while Bill 189 amending the Northwest Territories Act allowed for three elected members on the council, it also gave the commissioner the authority to decide who should be allowed to vote. As a result, the Inuit were refused the right to vote in Territorial elections, despite the fact that they had been granted the federal franchise on 30 June 1950 ... The elected representatives to the Northwest Territories Council soon discovered the limitations of their hard won 'self-government', and protests arose over the procedures ... (Grant 1988: 235–36)

At the 122nd session of the Northwest Territories Council, 14 March 1941, a Dr McGill moved that 'the system of identification discs for Eskimos be approved'. The motion carried (Roberts 1975: 13). In August 1941 McKeand reported from RMS Nascopie on the Eastern Arctic Patrol: 'Census enumerators have been instructed and supplied with schedules ... Identification disc numbers have been allotted [sic] commencing at 1001 to 7400 for the Eastern Arctic. Everywhere the idea of native identification has been welcomed by all concerned' (Roberts 1975: 15). After this idealistic report, 'it soon transpired that all was not well, either with the use of the discs or their distribution' (Roberts 1975: 16). Apparently the RCMP in Pangnirtung were not completing the identification numbers for their community. And at the other end of the Territories, the RCMP in Aklavik reported it had no discs on hand. In fact Sgt. H.S. Covell of the Aklavik RCMP reported,

> It might be as well to make clear at this time that none of the Mackenzie Delta Eskimos have discs. The Census of the Delta was delegated to Dr. L.D. Livingstone, but the Police took the Census of the natives at Tuktoyaktuk, Banks Island, Baillie Island, Maitland Point, Cape Bathurst, Stanton and Bellot Point. Dr Livingstone kindly supplied the Police with 300 discs which were issued out to these natives ... Dr. Livingstone was to obtain more discs for distribution by him to the Delta natives but apparently these did not arrive. (Roberts 1975: 16–17)

The absence of discs in the Mackenzie Delta was again noted by Inspector D.J. Martin, who in 1943 issued a call to all RCMP detachments in the Eastern and Western Arctic, instructing them to submit (in triplicate) a list of names of all Inuit who had received discs to date. In future all detachments were to submit updated 'disc lists' annually. In addition to the name and number of each Inuk, the list was to indicate marital status, age and occupation and, for married women, the number of children. McKeand proposed decentralising administration of registration and other 'affairs' to fit the 'nomadic non-tribal life' of the Inuit. He saw identification as the crux of all services. 'Our knowledge of native health, aspirations, education and other particulars so necessary to the administration of their affairs depend ... on vital statistics and identification' (Roberts 1975: 19). In 1944 Census fieldworkers received new instructions which stipulated that each Inuk would receive an identification disc and each newborn child would receive one soon after birth. Identification numbers were to be used after the names of any Inuit referred to in correspondence and were to appear on all birth, marriage and death certificates. The discs issued were of pressed fibre. The Deputy Commissioner advocated changing this.

> Inasmuch as they are to be an integral part of our record, it would seem that we should make them of white metal and possibly with a dignified design on them ... It is not contemplated that the name of the Eskimo will be written on the metal disc but merely that the number stamped on the disc should be assigned to him and recorded in our Vital Statistics records here. (Roberts 1975: 23)

Taking this to be a proposal to give Inuit medals, rather than identification tags, McKeand voiced strong objection to abandoning the fibre discs already in use. Apparently he was worried that Inuit would be seen to be receiving elevated status, rather than the status of wards of a colonial government! In discussing Arctic administration, the Major was locked into a military paradigm:

> The armed forces have been using regimental numbers for identification purposes for more than forty-five years ... At the same time His Majesty awarded medals or tokens for services rendered. There is no connection between the regimental or identification number of a member of the forces and a medal for good conduct, efficiency or distinguished service. In my opinion there is no necessity whatsover [sic] for replacing the present identification disc with a medal or token of any kind. As I have been pointing out for twenty years, once the Eskimo realizes that the white man wants him to memorize an identification number and use it in all trading and other transactions, the Eskimo will fall in line (Roberts 1975: 23–24).

During this period Inuit began receiving Family Allowance and the Department of National Health and Welfare found it necessary to define 'Eskimos and Nomads'. The tautological definition is a delicious example of bureaucratic absurdity:

> 'Eskimo' means a person who is listed as an Eskimo on the roll or records of, and to whom an identification disc has been issued by, the Bureau of Northwest Territories and Yukon Affairs of the Department of Mines and Resources. (Family Allowance Act of 1944)

How, one might ask, was it known in the first place, who were the Eskimos who should receive the discs which, in turn, defined them as 'Eskimos'?

> 'Nomad' means a person of mixed Indian or Eskimo blood, residing in the Northwest Territories or the Yukon Territory, who is neither an Eskimo nor an Indian, but who follows the Indian or Eskimo mode of living. (Family Allowance Act of 1944)

Whoever authored this definition of 'nomad', which I have not seen anywhere else, consulted neither the social science literature nor the dictionary.

With the institution of Family Allowance came revision of the disc number system. The Arctic was divided into twelve districts, separated into West and East. The original discs were recalled and replaced by new ones (still fibre) with the designation 'E' (East) or 'W' (West) and numbers for district, community, family and individual. Most family members had numbers close to those of other family members. A typical disc number would be E5–2468. Major McKeand saw the discs in purely administrative terms, assuming they would help 'keep track of (a) hunting (b) trapping (c) education (d) hospitalization and (e) misdemeanors' (McKeand in Roberts

1975: 15). His list is a catalogue of Inuit-government relations at the time. Apparently, he was not known for enlightened views. When Vanast went to Ungava to learn more about Inuit health care, he found that

> Major McKeand took disturbing information about Inuit health care ... as a personal insult. He was a pompous figure, much given to retelling stories of his military career, his childhood proximity to Queen Victoria's carriage, and his adult meeting with King George. Dressed in his army regalia, he presided over the government party as it landed at northern trading posts, where he delivered a formal speech to the Inuit about the government's good intentions. Many whites who worked with him still discuss him with disdain. In interviews I conducted in 1992, several former northerners asked me to turn off the recorder and then called him 'a very stupid man'. (Vanast 1991: 64)

An Inuk in his late twenties, too young to recall the early days of disc numbers first-hand, said:

> People had to register their names with the RCMP before the government started coming up here. The original names that were given to the RCMP years ago are no longer in existence. They've got different names now. Everything's changed. Like before when they had to register with the RCMP they registered nothing but their first names. Nothing at all. And the only difference [between people with the same name] would be the number. So it would be Rosie E6–something and another Rosie would be E6–something different. That's why they ended up calling the kids numbers in school. (Alia 1984–2006).

Census and Certification: Reshaping the Inuit Family

When I was growing up it was my mother's house; it was my aunt's house, my grandmother's house. We never referred to the house as my father's house. My father made decisions about when we were going to be leaving for this camp or wherever ... but within the house, it was my mother's domain. So I would have considered my mother as 'head of household'. My grandmother was head of her household; my aunt was head of her household.

But they went around to who *they* perceived to be head of household. And they asked, 'Is your family going to keep your name? Or are you going to take your husband's name?' ... my sister, Elise, who was Kunatuloitok (*sic*) [Qunngaatalluriktuq – misspelled in the CBC transcript] ... became Attagutaluk. Oh, she was upset about that. And she was taught ... when you are married you take your husband's name. The following year we had new recruits into the school, a new teaching couple – with different last names. So she went up to them: 'Aren't you married?' 'Yes, we are'. 'So how come you have different last names?' 'Because I chose to keep my last name'. 'You *chose* to keep your last name?'

She was livid. Here she became Attagutaluk because Project Surname was getting us Inuit like the rest of Canadians – we were taking the naming system of the rest of Canadians; we were taking the rest of Canadians' customs – and then they turn around and say, 'Oh, I've decided not to change my name'. 'She was livid.' (Alia 1995; 10).

At the time it was first introduced in Nunavut, the Canadian Census was filled with inconsistencies and absurdities. Lists followed official standards for 'the Canadian family' without regard for Inuit family structure or tradition. Census takers relabelled children who were full family members in Inuit society 'boarder', 'step' or 'adopted'. They issued birth certificates with precise times and locations for births that were never recorded, for people who travelled widely and identified time and place in non-southern ways. 'You can get the year within a year, and … the season, but generally they were just made up' (Neill 1984–86). The priest, Guy-Mary Rousselière (known affectionately in Pond Inlet and across Nunavut as Father Mary – an example of Inuktitut-style cross-gender naming in Qallunaat Roman Catholic traditions!) wrote: 'The situation … is a real mess …' because whenever officials met Inuit in a particular place or community, the Inuit

Figure 2.5 Kudlu Pitseolak (Malaiya) as an elder.
Photograph by Valerie Alia.

were automatically recorded as having been born there. Even if, as is known, a large percentage of them were not born in the region they inhabit at present … we were shown two birth certificates for the same man indicating that he was born in two places quite distant from each other ([Rousselière 1972: 18)

Interviews conducted between 1985 and 2004 revealed numerous problems such as that of Kudlu Pitseolak, who, at age eighty, said her pension cheques had begun to arrive years before her older sister's.

Birth certificates portray the official image of a 'normal' family. They carve identities into the official record and convey privilege or subjugation that can last a lifetime, and beyond. Misunderstandings and errors were in evidence when birth certificates came North, and persisted during Project Surname. It was reported that Abe Okpik interviewed 'heads of families' – a concept alien to Inuit (Tukisiviksat 1971b). The author of the report found 'a total lack of understanding among the Eskimo people, about the legal, social and moral aspects of names', 'legal usage' and 'ownership of property', concepts largely irrelevant in Inuit society. In Qallunaaq record keeping, 'surname' equals 'head of household'. But the father and husband is 'not necessarily the most powerful person in an [Inuit] extended family' (Alia 1984–2006; Neill 1984–86). Each family was told to pick a name, which generally referred to the most powerful person in the previous generation. In the end, Inuit brought their own sensibilities and values to the project, undermining its objective of simplifying Qallunaat record keeping. At Baker Lake the artist Jesse Oonark chose her own name as a surname, while her children chose their own names (Figure 2.8).

The government reported that 'marriage customs have never developed in the sense of the "western civilised ethic", as the family unit had no common name tying it together' (Tukisiviksat 1971b). In this ethnocentric view *family* equals *surname*. One 'mistake' that concerns the report's author is a 'common-law wife's' legal use of her husband's surname. Marriages not sanctioned by Western law are still common, despite the energetic efforts of missionaries. Qallunaat attitudes towards indigenous families were paternalistic at best. At worst, colonisers such as the Jesuit Father Le Jeune lamented such 'problems' as 'the excessive love the Savages bear their children'. The 'Savages' refused to allow Christian educators to use corporal punishment, and the women were so outrageously independent that the 'natives' had to be instructed that man 'was the master and that in France women do not rule their husbands' (Leacock in Étienne and Leacock 1980: 26). Le Jeune was referring to the Montagnais-Naskapi (Innu) of the St Lawrence Valley, and we must take care not to confuse his views with the very different attitudes of those such as the much-loved Father Roussellière. However, such attitudes were widespread and are still in evidence. In the late 1980s a Qallunaaq health care worker in her mid-twenties expressed outrage at 'the way these people coddle their kids' and told me that such 'spoiling' led to chaos. It was 'wrong' to hold a small child's hand as he underwent an unfamiliar procedure (one, I might add, that would frighten many adults) (Alia 1984–2006).

What the Census takers seemed to miss was the Inuit's close family ties and clearly defined identities (Alia 1984–2006; Briggs 1970, 1979, 1982; Guemple 1965, 1969, 1979). As we saw from the discussion in Chapter 1, not all of these identities parallel those of Qallunaat. The Census distinction between a 'real' and a 'common-law' wife was meaningful only in non-Inuit terms. In *The Namesake*, the U.S. officials in charge of certifying names and births are equally obtuse. Several days after their baby's birth, the Bengali-American parents, Ashima and Ashoke, have still not named their son. They are waiting for a letter from his grandmother in India, telling them what name she has chosen. In the absence of a letter, the decision is postponed indefinitely. This is no affront to Bengali tradition, but it mightily troubles the American officials.

> [They] have agreed to put off the decision of what to name the baby ... ignoring the forms from the hospital about filing for a birth certificate. [The] letter ... has yet to arrive ... Names can wait. In India parents take their time. It wasn't unusual for years to pass before the right name, the best possible name, was determined. (Lahiri 2004: 25).

While the naming traditions Lahiri describes are specific to Bengali lives and customs, the situation in which her characters find themselves has resonance for my own family. Our granddaughter did not receive (or find) her names until officials in Toronto reminded her parents that the deadline for certifying her birth was fast approaching. I embroidered a blanket with all of the names they wanted, along with images representing each of her inherited cultures. Confronted with the reality of sending her out into the world of passports, driving licences and other documents with limited writing space, they settled on a way of having her choose a shorter string of names.

> The fourth day ... Mr Wilcox, compiler of hospital birth certificates, [tells them] they must choose a name for their son. For they learn that in America, a baby cannot be released from the hospital without a birth certificate. And that a birth certificate needs a name. 'But sir ... we can't possibly name him ourselves ... We are waiting for a letter ...' 'I'm afraid your only alternative is to have the certificate read "Baby Boy Ganguli." You will, of course, be required to amend the permanent record when a name is decided upon ... I don't recommend it ... You will have to appear before a judge, pay a fee. The red tape is endless ... [What] about naming him after another person? Someone you greatly admire?' (Lahiri 2004: 27)

The child is named Gogol, whose writing is linked to a favourite book and an episode in which Ashoke's life was saved. In a sense, it is a perfect solution to the cross-cultural naming dilemma – a new name, neither Bengali nor American, with meaning for the parents. 'Ashima approves, aware that the name stands not only for her son's life, but her husband's' (Lahiri 2004: 28).

Removal and Relocation: Showing the Flag

The early 1950s saw the end of Inuit isolation. Government 'moved North in a big way and soon fixed settlements, each an administrative centre, took the place of hunting camps' (Roberts 1975: 25). It was 'colonialism of the worst kind. Canada had a need to show its flag – to show its dominion' (Neill 1984–86), many people say the relocations were less voluntary than government claimed (Marcus 1992; Tester and Kulchyski 1994). In 1986 Makivik Corporation, the organisation representing Northern Quebec (Nunavik) Inuit, organised a meeting of relocated families in Iqaluit. John Amagoalik, 'the father of Nunavut', had been asking the government to make amends for many years. A restitution process begun in late 1988 is still incomplete.

One of those at the centre of the relocations, Bent Gestur Sivertz, had served in the Royal Canadian Navy and then entered External Affairs as a Foreign Service Officer. In 1953 he was appointed executive assistant to Deputy Minister of Resources and Development, Hugh Keenleyside, whose administration brought greater government involvement in the North and the controversial relocation of Inuit from Nunavik to the High Arctic. The relocations have received ample attention elsewhere (e.g., Marcus 1992; Tester and Kulchyski 1994). It is important here to note their context: the growing concern of government to establish a stronger Canadian presence in the North. In 1954 Sivertz was appointed Chief of the Arctic Division. He found a Northern Administration with no directive 'giving objectives in citizenship, health, education, language, employment, residence or anything concerning the Aboriginal people other than Indians' (Sivertz 1993a: 1). In 1963 he became Director of Northern Administration, 'with my office in a suitcase, coping with NWT and Yukon management of mining, oil and gas, water power, highway and railroad building, municipal affairs, schools, and High Arctic matters as well' (ibid.: 5). He sought greater involvement of Inuit in the Territorial Assembly. 'At my last session of the Territorial Legislature in 1966, the franchise extended for the first time to all parts of the NWT and two of the Members were Inuit. Abraham Okpik and Simonie Michael were legislators, full fledged' (ibid.: 5). The new councillors would soon become key players in the Project Surname drama.

When he spoke with me by telephone from his home in Victoria, British Columbia in 1993, Sivertz cautioned, 'I'm eighty-eight years old and don't remember things too well' (Sivertz 1993b). He could not recall having initiated the pilot surnaming project in Pangnirtung, though R.A.J. Phillips told me that Sivertz was in charge when it was organised (Alia 1984–2006). 'Surnames and discs were not a subject I found especially interesting', Sivertz said; 'discs were adopted before I was connected with administering in the North. There were many occasions when we discussed the discs.' The identification programmes were accompanied by difficulties and, sometimes, tragedies.

> When I was chief of the Arctic Division, I engaged two Inuit women, taught them English ... taught them how to ride streetcars ... sent them on hospital visits to lonely Inuit men and women [in hospital, often with tuberculosis]. The problem was deep and very cruel. When they went home ... they had new habits, using forks and spoons, washing their hands at mealtime ... people were ridiculed.
>
> There was a problem identifying people who did not have discs, or had lost them. It was difficult to assign [people who had been sent out to hospital] to a family or community without the discs. There were a lot of children who were lost because nobody bothered to send their discs with them.
>
> Then there came a lot of criticism against identifying people by number. The Northern Administration Branch recommended dropping disc numbers, not because of criticism but because of the feeling that it was insensitive for government to assign numbers. [The feeling was] 'You can assign names to people; you can even stamp their names on cards ... but not numbers'. (Sivertz 1993b)

Sivertz said, 'as far as I know, [Inuit] always used their names.' I asked why a different way of 'assigning names' was thought to be necessary in the North. He declined to answer, moving on to other subjects. Over the years Sivertz's policies and positions were complex and sometimes contradictory. In the 1990s his continued support of his role in relocating Inuit generated much controversy. He was an early advocate of devolution from Ottawa to Yellowknife (now further devolved to Iqaluit). He advocated moving administration of Dene, Métis, Inuit and Inuvialuit affairs from federal to Territorial jurisdiction. In 1966, newly retired from his post as Territorial Commissioner, Sivertz was asked to appear before the House of Commons Standing Committee on Northern Affairs and National Resources. Although he found disc numbers problematic, he did not see the contradiction between administering Qallunaat surnames and advocating Inuit cultural survival. Yet he voiced a strong commitment to egalitarian principles:

> I am one of those strong believers that separate but equal is not equal. If you have ... Indians in Canada managed by a separate agency from the agency that

manages the affairs of other people who live as their neighbours, then you are saying, in effect, these people are so different and their problems are so different that they are not really part of the human race; they have to be handled by a different agency with different principles. This, I think, is all wrong ... [You give] cheques for family allowances to every mother who is white but if she is an Eskimo you give her a grocery list that the mounted policeman makes out ... It says [to her] ... in such minor administrative matters as the handling of family allowances, the registration of births of babies, 'you are different, and moreover, you are not competent' ... (Sivertz in Badanai 1967: 907)

While I cannot agree that birth registration and family allowance are 'minor' matters, I admire Sivertz's strong and timely statement.

Photographer Wilfred Doucette praised the humanity and commitment of the 'primary architects' of Inuit relocations. His letter to the *Toronto Star* praised Alex Stevenson, Officer in Charge of the Eastern Arctic Patrol (Arctic Division, Northwest Territories Administration, Department of Resources and Development) and Inspector Henry Larsen, Officer in Charge and Commander, 'G' Division of the RCMP:

Both these individuals were noted for their great concern for the Eskimo (as the natives were known then) way of life and culture. When I first met Larsen and Stevenson I was struck by their knowledge of Eskimo language and customs. They knew many Eskimo by their names, not just by their E-numbers ... (Doucette 1991: 1)

What is striking is that Doucette considered what in society at large is basic courtesy an indication of the officials' exceptional behaviour. It is sad that he was probably right to highlight such behaviour. More problematic is his position as (freelance) 'Journalist and Photographer' who, having visited northern Quebec and Ellesmere Island during the relocation period, adopted what some would consider a government advocacy role, not to mention a paternalistic tone:

The rationale for the move was a sincere attempt to improve the standards of living of the Eskimo families involved, and to move them into areas of the High Arctic that would reduce their contact with the destructive influences of the Southern white population, and help preserve some vestiges of their traditional culture. (Doucette 1991: 2, 6)

The text is laden with assumptions. There is no awareness of differences among Inuit communities and no acknowledgement that Inuit are capable of self-direction and self-determination. Doucette carries all the old baggage, assuming it is appropriate for one group of people to move another to 'help' them. This 'well-intentioned' relocation is as insidious as the alternative of using relocation to assert sovereignty. A comparable argument would advocate relocating all Italian-Canadians to a remote region to help them preserve 'some vestiges of their traditional culture' – or perhaps relocating Mr Doucette from Toronto to Quebec, to help him maintain the cultural ties implicit in his francophone name.

'Canada Promotes Nationalism in the Arctic', read a 1969 *New York Times* headline atop a story describing Governor General Roland Michener's trip to Chesterfield Inlet, which made it clear Inuit weren't as keen as government.

> When he ventured higher into the Arctic Circle ... the Governor General found evidence of Eskimos who think of themselves as Eskimos and not Canadians ... Before an elementary class in Resolute Bay ... Mr. Michener got not one word of response when he asked the children 'Do you know who I am?' ... His visit to the Arctic ... coincided with a special effort by [Prime Minister Pierre Elliott] Trudeau to secure Canadian sovereignty in the north. (Walz 1969: 14)

In the early days of the twenty-first century, those attitudes have returned with a vengeance. The U.S.A. – which during the Second World War and the Cold War firmly established its own interests in the Inuit-dominated Canadian North – is taking a freshly proprietary look at ways of exploiting northern lands and resources. The world's dwindling oil and gas reserves and the refusal to develop substantial energy alternatives – plus Canada's history of accepting outside development – render Inuit more vulnerable, even as Nunavut brings them more dignity and control over their resources and lives.

In April 1969, on the eve of Project Surname, the *New York Times* sent a reporter to join an eighteen-stop, two-week tour of the Eastern Arctic that had all the trappings of a public relations junket. In Igloolik the reporter heard Inuit at what he called a 'town meeting' express concern 'that they are losing their own culture'. Like so many others, the reporter portrayed Inuit as 'caught between two cultures' '... his own leisurely one of hunting, socializing and living by the season and the white man's structured style of schools, jobs and living by the clock' (Walz 1969: 14). Only a person out of touch with what it takes to hunt in Arctic conditions would call the hunter's life 'leisurely'! Perhaps the reporter thought Inuit hunters worked for recreation, rather than for their family's and community's clothing and food. He found that 'Eskimos are called only by their first names', except for a few who had taken 'a second name' (presumably a surname). Apparently that was the case in much of the Eastern Arctic, before the official start of Project Surname.

Chapter 3

RENAMED OVERNIGHT:
THE HISTORY OF PROJECT SURNAME

In a period of about two years, virtually all Inuit in Canada received new names, based on a non-Inuit model of surnaming. Completed in 1972, Project Surname marked a turning point in the history of government efforts to reidentify Inuit. The effects are still felt more than thirty years later.

The Political Climate

Everyone wants a piece of the Arctic. It offers great (though sometimes dubious) riches – gold, diamonds, gas, oil, uranium. People, the richest resource, have sometimes been ignored in the process of developing land, minerals and policy. Early in the twentieth century the United States and Canada collaborated on the now outdated Distant Early Warning System – a collar of beacons set out to guard against the Cold War's perceived 'threat of Communism'. John Amagoalik has long expressed concern about its legacy, which continues in the form of ugly structures and still-undetermined levels of pollution. (Amagoalik 1993: 9)

This is a case study of *cultural* pollution. Canada's northern policy has its foundations in a gentle colonialism, what Paine calls 'welfare colonialism', in which the behaviour of visitors towards Inuit is 'solicitous rather than exploitative ... liberal rather than repressive'. However benevolent, it is based on 'two illegitimate positions: the colonisers are illegitimately privileged ... the colonized ... illegitimately devalued' (Paine 1977: 6). There are two concurrent streams of northern policy. One leads to cultural genocide or assimilation, the other to home rule, self-determination, and cultural integrity. In 1985 the Igloolik linguist Bernadette Immaroitok told me: 'you know what they say: Greenlanders have home rule, Alaskans have the bucks, and Canadian Inuit have tradition and culture' (Immaroitok 1985). That has changed; since 1999 Canadian Inuit have also had home rule.

> Life was hard in the old days, but it was good. Men had certain things to do and so did women, but they depended upon one another. That is how we survived. Everybody had things to do, and everybody got along. (Aksayook [Etoangat] et al., undated)

Inuit lives were never easy but identity crises were not among the usual problems in a world where hypothermia remains a major cause of death. As Chapter 1 explains, in Inuit society names literally create and continue life. To interfere with the names is to risk destroying a people. To respect the names is to respect a people whose sovereignty predates 'Canada's Arctic' by centuries. As noted, to conduct research in the North, one must have permission from the communities and obtain a Territorial Research Licence. In his letter answering my request, the Science Advisor for the Northwest Territories warned: 'As you are probably aware, you are treading on somewhat sensitive ground for this ... research. However, it is entirely up to the people ...' His was not the only warning about the 'sensitivity' of studying Project Surname, a position which probably had inhibited critical analysis of policies and procedures for many years. Contrary to the warning, most people were positive and supportive. I suspect that his reference to 'sensitivity' concerned Qallunaat policymakers. Others said the work was useful and graciously granted permission. In exchange, I promised to make the research public and to protect the privacy of those who spoke in confidence.

The Power of Names

> In the spring of 1937 when I was seven years old my father told my brother and me that our mother had tuberculosis. We would have to go from Cambridge Bay to the hospital in Aklavik ... When we landed at Aklavik my mother went to the hospital and my brother and I were told we would be going to a boarding school ... [at school] An Eskimo girl ... introduced me to the other girls by my Christian name – Alice. My Eskimo name was not mentioned and I did not hear my name Masak again until I went home. (French in Petrone 1988: 204)

Names may well be our most important possessions. They are so powerful that wars are fought, families feud – people are killed for names. Renaming is universal. Immigrants, people who experience 'contact', women who marry, conquered subjects may be colonised in different ways, but renaming is almost always part of their colonisation. Harold Isaacs addresses the familiar business of name changing by individuals who want ... to be more 'like' those more favoured, to [share] ... at least in name, the identity of the dominant group. In the ex-colonial world, the shift in power relations has brought about some reversal of this process. European given names were often acquired by colonial subjects by baptism, bestowal or choice ... [I]n the Philippines ... Spanish surnames ... from a Madrid directory were simply 'given' to ... people by a mid-nineteenth-century Spanish governor for the greater convenience of his tax collectors ... (Isaacs 1989: 77)

Nations, cities, topographical features and people are renamed by colonial regimes and again by liberation governments. On 1 January, 1987 the official name of Frobisher Bay was changed to Iqaluit. This was far from superficial; it reclaimed Inuit sovereignty and removed a visitor's name (explorer Martin Frobisher) from the map and the mental landscape. Approved by a three-to-two margin in a municipal election and reaffirmed by the Territorial Legislative Assembly in 1985, the name change was part of a bigger picture: the process of formalising the Inuit homeland, Nunavut ('our land'), which would not be complete until 1999. Retired Navy Captain Thomas C. Pullen is one of those who protested, and thereby underscored the political importance of name-changing:

The threat to change thousands of northern place names is disturbing ... So also is the news that responsibility for naming geographic features in the Northwest Territories has been surrendered by Ottawa. I am dismayed at the sanctioning of this assault on the history of the Arctic, our collective Northern heritage. (Curwin 1987)

Although the population of Nunavut was then 95 percent (today 85 percent) Inuit, Pullen was angry about the 'Inuk who tells us he would prefer it if they took 'all the white names off the maps ...' and hoped 'the recent renaming of Frobisher Bay does not signal the start of a regrettable trend. Frobisher Bay is Frobisher Bay, not because of the natives, but because of the development work that has gone on ...' It was indeed the start of a trend that acknowledged the centuries of Inuit civilisation that long preceded such 'development work'.

'Discovered' by seventeenth century explorers, the North has known traders, governments and religions since the early 1900s when Catholic and Anglican missionaries arrived, hot on the heels of the Hudson's Bay Company (HBC – for good reason, nicknamed 'Here Before Christ'). (Brody 1975)

The Route to Project Surname

As we saw in Chapter 2, proposals to standardise spelling go back to 1929. The first documented proposals to introduce 'the white man's'

surname system and compel 'the head of each family to select a common
name for his family' came in 1935 from A.E. Porsild and Diamond
Jenness. According to the anonymous author of the government's Project
Surname 'Summary',

> Outcry against the 'indignity' of the [disc number system] did not come from
> the Eskimo people initially. It came from missionaries, from anthropologists ...
> individuals well up in the hierarchy of the various churches ... government
> employees at the field level who were dealing directly with the people
> involved ... [not] from the bureaucratic organizations ... the cry to 'eliminate
> disc lists' and 'get rid of disc numbers' came from very few places initially ...
> [from persons] sufficiently prolific in written protest, and sufficiently well
> known to senior officials of the Territorial Government to receive a
> sympathetic hearing, and to prompt action. (Government of the Northwest
> Territories 1971a: 4)

Like many northern policies, the identification program was not
legislated, but originated in

> a decision taken for 'administrative convenience'. There is no legislation or
> policy written, requiring or authorizing a 'disc number'. With the Indian
> population ... the Indian Act specifically outlines Indian identification, band
> affiliation and specific entitlements. No such legislation or policy [of]
> identification exists for the Eskimo population. ... the term [surname] is
> meaningless. [Inuit have their] own naming process, which fits within [their]
> own traditional culture. (Government of the Northwest Territories 1971a)

But like so many others, MacKinnon assumed that Inuit were simple-
minded, and that tampering with identity had little consequence.

> As far as the Eskimo is concerned, it does seem to me that this names business
> is of no great concern to them. They have got on nicely for a long time without
> cluttering up their minds with such details. (MacKinnon in Roberts 1975: 8)

In 1967 the Northwest Territories underwent a radical administrative
change. The Territorial Council was devolved from Ottawa to Yellowknife
and two Aboriginal councillors were appointed. Dr. Lloyd I. Barber,
Councillor from Saskatoon, noted 'with considerable interest the
gathering together of all the strings of governmental activities within the
Territorial Government. My first impression when I arrived last fall was
one of hopeless administrative confusion' (Hodgson 1969: 35). Under
Stuart Hodgson's commissionership there was yet another incursion into
Inuit identity.

> Project Surname, a program directly connected with Vital Statistics, has been
> commenced as a Centennial project ... Eskimo people are being asked to
> select and register a surname, by which all members of one family will be

known. The eventual objective of this program is to eliminate Eskimo Disc Numbers, and do away with Disc Lists (Hodgson 1969: 31)

Project Surname

Stuart Hodgson had been a trade union leader in Vancouver. In 1964 he was appointed to the Northwest Territories Council and in 1967, to the position of Territorial Commissioner (Cowan 1969: 22). The person he selected for the job of renaming all the Inuit in Canada was Abraham (Abe) Okpik, disc number W3–544, who had been the government's first Inuit Area Administrator at Spence Bay and a translator and interpreter for the Department of Northern Affairs. He covered the building of the pipeline for the Canadian Broadcasting Corporation (CBC) and had worked as a counsellor at an alcohol and drug treatment centre and the Baffin Correctional Centre (Crowe 1991: 203). In 1965 he was appointed the first Aboriginal member of the Council of the Northwest Territories, followed in 1966 by the first *elected* Aboriginal councillor, Simonie Michael (Crowe 1991: 207). Abe Okpik had written and spoken of the importance of Inuit language and culture, believing Inuit "'need our language to keep us happy together ... If an Eskimo forgets his language and ways he will be nothing ...'" (Arigaktuk 1967: 4). Project Surname received a great deal of public attention.

Abe Okpik Meets the Queen

Mr. Okpik has been appointed the new Area Administrator at Spence Bay, NWT
...

The government practise of identifying members of Canada's Eskimo population by *disc numbers* will be abolished, the Northwest Territorial Legislative Council was told Monday ... Territorial Commissioner Stuart Hodgson told the Council at its 39th session that, as use of the numbers is dropped, a three-member board will travel throughout the territories in an attempt to ascertain family names and their correct spelling – for the region's 10,000 Eskimo people. (*Leader Press* June 24, 1969: 5)

The 'three-member board' apparently was collapsed into the person of Abe Okpik (figure 3.1), who received occasional assistance from others.

The idea of ascertaining family names was absurd; most Inuit families had no such thing. The Council, and the media, were told why the disc number system had to go: 'For example, Tedjuk of Cambridge Bay, NWT, would be known on government blotters as Tedjuk, E-420'. What was not mentioned was that Tedjuk was a whole name, not part of a name with a surname attached. The Commissioner strengthened his sales pitch by saying that improved orthography would, with the new surnaming,

Figure 3.1 Abe Okpik being interviewed for CBC Television at the ICC General Assembly, Sisimiut, Greenland, 1989. Photograph by Valerie Alia.

'solve, once and for all, the problem of spelling and pronouncing Eskimo names properly'. This declaration was based on so many false assumptions that the mind reels. As we saw in Chapter 1, Inuit naming traditions are very strong, and do not include surnaming. Spelling is no guarantee of 'correct' pronunciation. People in the U.S. state of Oregon distinguish themselves from Outsiders by calling their river 'Wil-LAMM-ette', not 'Wila-METTE', surely not a pronunciation guaranteed by spelling. Orthography is useless when it comes to proper names. One has to ask, listen and learn to say a name as its owner wishes; the 'same' names are pronounced differently in different regions. Bellingham is 'Belling-HAM' in Washington State and 'Bellin-JUM' in Northeast England. No one proposes to assign one 'correct' spelling and re-name every Catherine, Kathryn, Katherine and Katrina. Why Sean and Shawn, but not Pitsiulak and Pitseolaq? Another 'problem' was that different people had the same name, an excuse that looks downright silly if one scans a telephone directory. It would be hard to imagine a (government funded!) programme to rename all of the John Smiths in the U.K., Canada and the U.S.A.

In Pangnirtung, an unofficial prototype for Project Surname was organised several years before the national programme began. At the time, Keith Crowe was Settlement Manager. The 'Pangnirtung surname process took place in 1963, a few years before Project Surname. It was already done. Within two weeks … Ottawa asked us to do it (Crowe 1984–1996). The request came from Northern Program director R.A J. Phillips. 'We got the request, and assumed everybody else was doing it. Afterwards, we found out we were the only ones' (ibid.). That first surname project was carried out by Keith Crowe, 'Ross Peyton, Sid Wilkerson, Etoangat, Kilabuk, and an RCMP officer. We all had to get together on the spellings' (ibid.). There was apparently a climate of community spirit and cooperation among Inuit and Qallunaat, and there remains some ambiguity about Abe Okpik's role in Pangnirtung. Several people told me stories about his involvement in Project Surname there, and he moved there when he married a member of the community. In the 1960s Crowe found that traditional naming customs were still quite strong.

> I am reminded of a woman in Pang who told me happily that 'Sikrinerk is back', because a new baby had received that name, which had belonged to a young boy who died in Montreal. The 'new' Sikrinerk is now a leading light with the Tungavik Corporation.

In 1993, R.A.J. Phillips told me that the 'main reason for the change was to get rid of the apartheid philosophy' (Phillips 1993). For all its good intentions, the policy retained a double standard, replacing apartheid with assimilation. I asked Phillips why he chose Pangnirtung for the pilot study. 'One has to start somewhere, so you say, "There's an able northern service officer in this community", and that's where you start' (Phillips 1993). The 'able northern service officer' was Keith Crowe. As noted, Phillips was under the supervision of Stuart Hodgson's predecessor, Territorial Commissioner Bent ('Ben') Sivertz. Eventually the Northern Administration Branch recommended dropping the disc numbers. Phillips recalled that the journalist I. Norman Smith led the opposition to Project Surname. Phillips thought Smith was writing for the *Ottawa Citzen*, but G. Campbell McDonald says Smith was a columnist for the *Ottawa Journal* (McDonald 2006). ('In about 1963, we decided to discuss it; at the 1964 session, the Council of the Northwest Territories rejected the motion to bring in surnames in preference to keeping the discs. The 'Project' went forward nevertheless. In 1965 Phillips resigned as director, leaving Project Surname for others to organise (Phillips 1993).

The Project Surname Process

Although it was never legislated into existence, Project Surname was proposed, promoted and christened in the Territorial Council. Abe Okpik began work on 23 September, 1969. He had attended the residential school at Aklavik, where his father told the missionary he should become a minister, but where 'there was no opportunity whatever'. At sixteen, he hurt his leg and was hospitalised in Edmonton, where he met 'Indians from northern Alberta, southern Alberta – Crees, Saracees, Stoneys, Chippewyans ... I got along with the Cree pretty well. They were the majority. I had to learn to speak Cree. They got to be my friends' (Okpik 1985–95). He worked on the DEWline, took a correspondence course, 'didn't do bad on math', went to night school in Ottawa. 'I lived there a year and a half. It was the hardest year of my life, 1959'.

'Abe's many years of community work and dedication [are] appreciated by all. He is known as *Oikpialuk* meaning 'giant okpik' which translates into 'a man who can do so much for other people', Ann Meekitjuk Hanson wrote (Hanson 1989: 17). Not everyone sees him in this light. One Inuk expressed offence that 'Abe only talked to the men' and then gave women their husbands' names without consulting them. A Qallunaaq who was in the North at the time said, 'Abe Okpik got the job because he was one of the few people willing to go and do it. He spoke English and that went a long way in those days. He was a pompous guy' (1984–2006).

While opinions differ about Abe's personality, strengths and weaknesses, he served his community on the Iqaluit Council, was widely known (primarily for Project Surname) and appeared often in the media, though the reporting was not always accurate. The carelessness and haste that characterise southern journalism about the North also pervade some of the northern literature. Newspaper and magazine articles wrongly identify 'Operation' Surname and publish dates with serious discrepancies. In 1993 an article in a northern magazine said Abe Okpik was 'originally from Tuktoyaktuk' and 'the present surname system' was created 'when the government attempted its first Census of the North' (Robinson 1993: 17). The first error is inexcusable. The information that Abe came from near Aklavik was available first-hand from him, is widely known and was published in an earlier article for the same magazine (Alia 1986/7: 12–23). The second error is based on a misreading of history. Census and reidentification were linked for many years, and the dates can be confusing. In 1935 Dr J.A. Urquhart proposed introducing disc numbers – not surnames – as part of the Census process. Disc numbers were in active use in time for the first full Census, in 1941, nearly thirty years before the start of Project Surname.

Project Surname was discussed while Abe Okpik was still on the Territorial Council and the surnaming idea had been considered for several years. Councillor Simonie Michael

> was getting mail against the [disc] numbers. The kids who were going to school were protesting, saying 'Why do I have to call my number every morning in the roll call'? ... kids in grades 7–8 and 9. 1965 was the time of my appointment [to the council]. I remember kids from everywhere told me that they didn't like to be called a number. We thought about it in the council but

I never really pushed it. Simonie Michael was the one. His number was E7–551. He was the first council member from here [Iqaluit]. He told the commissioner, why do I always get my mail to E7–551? My name is Simonie Michael. And they passed a motion. (Okpik 1985–95)

What they passed was probably Motion 29 (see below) on spelling of Inuit names. The research suggests that no motion dealing with Project Surname itself was ever passed. It did not originate with Stuart Hodgson. In 1966, Ben Sivertz had asked Alex Stevenson, Administrator of the Arctic, for his advice

> regarding Eskimo identification discs. It seems to me that there is only one justification for assigning a number to people and actually putting it on a disc. That is, if an absolute requirement exists for identifying people and the alternatives would be an unacceptable level of confusion. It strikes me that we should discontinue the number system and the disc system as soon as possible. (Roberts: 26)

Stevenson was reluctant to abandon the numbering system. Although couched in ethnocentric terms, he rightly said that surnames would not solve the administrative problem of how to list and locate Inuit. In Pangnirtung the Kilabuk, Kooneilusee and Akpaliapik families had already taken surnames and this had not made things easier for the record keepers. With three women named Annie Kilabuk in Pangnirtung, identification by Outsiders was as difficult as ever. Stevenson did not think to ask the people who shared those names to find their own solutions to the 'problem' or to administer the social insurance numbers other Canadians received.

> The discontinuation of identification numbers may be the ultimate aim of our administration but as Mr. Sivertz has intimated in his memorandum, there is still an absolute requirement for identifying Eskimos in the Eastern Arctic. The alternative would be an unacceptable level of confusion ... I could not responsibly recommend the discontinuation of the number system yet. I cannot emphasize strongly enough the need for continued use of identification numbers. (Roberts 1975: 27, 34)

In 1968, Administrator of Ordinances F.H. Murphy advised the Deputy Commissioner that, in his estimation, standardised spelling alone would not resolve 'the problem of identification' but 'would be another step in the right direction' (Roberts 1975: 28, 34).

Several years before Project Surname, Guemple observed: 'Surnames have been introduced into the [Belcher] Islands by the government in the last three or four years but are not widely used by the Eskimos' (Guemple 1965: 334). The issue was debated in the Territorial Council. On 19 June, 1969 Robert Williamson tabled the following motion:

Motion No. 18: List of Eskimo Names
MR. WILLIAMSON:
...

WHEREAS there has been for many years considerable confusion, loss of dignity, and loss of identity by Eskimo people because of the very inaccurate and badly misunderstood means of rendering Eskimo names in all official documents;
AND WHEREAS the naming system of the Eskimo people is extremely important to them and worthy of proper respect and accurate rendering;
NOW THEREFORE, I move that the Commissioner seek means to have sent out, on a regional basis, to each settlement a series of persons familiar with the local regional dialects and the standard orthography for Canadian Eskimo language, and in consultation with the individual adults, draw up a completely revised list of Eskimo names, using the modern means of spelling, this list from thenceforth to be the official way of rendering the names of the people at all times.
THE COMMISSIONER: Moved by Mr. Williamson, seconded by Mr. Simonie Michael.

There was no proposal for surnaming or renaming, only for respelling. In the discussion that followed, Williamson made a fatal error: 'It would not be an enormous task by any means for one person, perhaps somebody already in the employ of the Administration concerned, to consult with the people themselves about how their names should be written ...' He was right in assuming the need for consultation but wrong in assuming the task was not 'enormous'. Deputy Commissioner John Parker noted that 'Mr. Williamson has raised this subject before', saying Commissioner Hodgson had already given him 'the job of seeing that this was carried out ... However, we simply haven't had the time or the forces to do this job. It has not gotten that high up on the priority list ...' Action was further complicated because 'We gather that there simply hasn't been complete acceptance of the new orthography'. Councillor Duncan Pryde voiced strong support for Williamson's motion and added, 'we can't merely go to the settlements and write out the Eskimo orthography and tell the Eskimo people, 'This is your name.'. We must teach the Eskimos how to use the new orthography ...' Commissioner Hodgson told the Council,

We have decided after talking to a great number of people within the North, that the disc lists should be done away with and we are planning on converting the disc list over to Social Security Numbers. We believe [Inuit] should be the same as everybody else in Canada ... it would be just as easy to identify people and there would not be ... different types of numbers ... we have undertaken to try and do this in time for the Centennial. It will be quite an undertaking, but we are going to send a Tribunal into each settlement and at the same time we are going to try and establish family names and ... try and ascertain the correct Christian [!] names. I think Mr. Pryde probably expressed it better than any of us when he points out that it is not a very clear cut question. There are strong, strong oppositions amongst people within the North with regard to the new orthography ...

...

MR. SIMONIE: Mr. Commissioner, I support this Motion No. 18 because as I learn about this it could be good. I think most Eskimos in the Arctic don't like to be called by number and therefore I support this Motion. Also I have a number and I don't like being called by a number ...

...

AIR MARSHAL CAMPBELL: Mr. Commissioner, I wonder having heard that the Administration is conscious of this problem and they plan to improve the existing situation, if the mover of the Motion would consider dropping it ...

MR. WILLIAMSON: ... My Motion was introduced without any knowledge of what action had been taken by the Administration ... Ever since the very first Session that I attended in Resolute Bay I have been asking for some action on the development of the orthography which has for some time been in the hands of the Education Division of the Department of Northern Affairs ... By my calculations, something in the region of $300,000 to half a million dollars has been spent in salaries, staff conferences and transporting people around to bring about a proper spelling system for the Eskimo language. It is now in the region of 11 to 12 years since this work started, and nothing very effective has been done yet.

THE COMMISSIONER: Excuse me, Mr. Williamson, I don't like to bring you to the point, but are you going to withdraw the Motion or are you going to push on. I have to know because I think the idea, there was a suggestion that the Council spend no more time on it. I would hate to find yourself [*sic*] discussing a Motion that didn't exist.

...

MR. WILLIAMSON: ... Perhaps what I should have done, Mr. Commissioner, as I have done at previous Sessions, is to introduce a Motion asking for more action on the development of this orthography. What I was really trying to get at here is the feelings of the Eskimo people themselves about the way in which their names are mis-spelled or misrendered in so many parts of the North, and to seek some way of properly and respectfully rendering their names, whether by the use of this orthography or by some improved method ... This has to be in consultation with the people ...

THE COMMISSIONER: Just a moment now. Apparently you mistook my intention. Are you going to withdraw the Motion or are you going to continue the Motion. You must make this decision.

MR. WILLIAMSON: I think I answered most of the questions raised, Mr. Commissioner.

THE COMMISSIONER: That is not answering my question. What are you going to do with the Motion?

MR. WILLIAMSON: I think the suggestion since work is going ahead already; there is no further point in going ahead. It will be withdrawn.

THE COMMISSIONER: Thank you. (Government of the Northwest Territories June 1969)

I have left much of the text intact because so few people have read it, and because the tone of the debates can help us understand the nature of the Project Surname process. Apparently Williamson withdrew his Motion in deference to the Commissioner. Things were indeed under way, and Williamson's concern for cross-cultural respect and mutual consultation was lost in the bureaucratic shuffle, but not before his Motion No. 29, a restatement of Motion No. 18 focusing on orthography, had been passed.

> MR. WILLIAMSON:
> WHEREAS there is much confusion, annoyance, embarrassment for all people in the North, loss of proper family and cultural identity by the Eskimo and difficulty for administrators because of the very widespread and enormous inaccuracy of the spelling of Eskimo names,
> THEREFORE I move that the Commissioner seeks [*sic*] means of improving this situation by something like the following procedure:
> (a) appointment in each region of a bilingual person, trained in the standard orthography, preferably Eskimo, who will also be competent in understanding Eskimo family relationships;
> (b) this person to go to each Eskimo settlement in the region, and in consultation with the individual Eskimo people concerned, or their parents, to prepare a final and definitive name list, having reference to proper and accurate language usage and family records and preference;
> (c) all Eskimo name lists thereafter to be revised according to the improved spellings and accepted as official.

It is important that Williamson stressed intercultural awareness and respect. It is also important that he mentioned consultation with *parents* – female and male elders. His proposal avoided imposing a European family structure on the Inuit. Although the whole assumption that Inuit should be more consistently identified than other citizens is itself ethnocentric, the proposal considered the importance of a two-way process. Later in the Council debate, he further explained:

> The importance of the Eskimo name is something I have spoken of before. It is very important for each individual to be properly identified. In the Eskimo tradition it had an even greater significance, and there is a persistence of … traditional beliefs, whereby the name is the soul and the soul is the name. So if you misuse someone's name, you not only damage his own personal identity in the existing society, but you also damage his immortal soul.

Others saw the numbers as merely part of the process by which a state keeps track of its citizens.

> MR. SEARLE: Mr. Commissioner, I listened to my friend Mr. Williamson speak about the disc numbers and how there is need for one to keep one's identity. I agree that this is a need, but, you know, in this world of ours it seems to me that government agencies … are requiring all of us to have numbers … I just

took out my wallet and took out my social insurance card ... that we must all carry ... to everybody ... particularly the income tax people and the IBM machine that record [sic] all my data, I am [speaks his social insurance number], whether I like it or not.
DR. BARBER: What an unfortunate name! (Government of the Northwest Territories October 1969: 510)

Well, yes – and no. Mr Searle neglected to mention that Inuit numbers were *separate and different*, and given to one selected group of Aboriginal people as if they belonged in a distinct category. No one talked about why Inuit were not simply given social insurance cards. The members of the Territorial Council were Stuart M. Hodgson, Commissioner; John Parker, Deputy Commissioner; Dr Lloyd I. Barber (Saskatoon); Air Marshal Hugh Campbell; J. Gordon Gibson; Chief John Tetlichi; Mark Duane Fairbrother; Duncan M. Pryde; David H. Searle; 'Mr. Simonie' (Simonie Michael), Frobisher Bay (Iqaluit); Donald M. Stewart; Lyle R. Trimble; Robert G. Williamson (Government of the Northwest Territories 1968). Roberts writes that Project Surname was launched in 1970. Actually, it began a year earlier. Abe Okpik recalled:

The Commissioner – Stu Hodgson – was looking around for someone to work on it [Project Surname]. I was on holidays in 1969 out of Spence Bay – I was up there as administrator. I ended up in Edmonton – went down to the airport just to see who was coming off the plane. Well, lo and behold, Stu Hodgson and his wife came off. He said 'Abe, I got a job for you.' He shook my hand. I said 'What do you mean?' So I reported back from my holidays and Stu Hodgson sent me a telegram. My regional superintendent called me and said, 'they want you to go out and try and get rid of these disc numbers'. It became a Centennial project. (Okpik 1985–95)

Not surprisingly, resistance to the program did not take long to manifest itself. Departments of the Territorial and Federal Governments were particularly vocal in criticizing [sic] the ... program, and the concept of Project Surname. No one, of course, was prepared to put these objections and criticisms in writing, but objections were loud and persistent. "What about people using the same name?" "How will we keep track of the people who move around?" "How do we identify individuals?'" "How do we know we are paying the right person?" And so on ... In the interest of getting the job done, all of the objections were ignored, and though there will be problems, these are no less or greater than the same problems in other sections of our society ... The program was ready, and Abe, who had been totally involved in its development, was prepared to start his long trek. (Government of the Northwest Territories 1971a: 12)

To publicise and explain the Project the Government of the Northwest Territories published a booklet, *Project Surname*, authored by Abe Okpik, Project Director, with the 1970 Centennial logo and a cover illustration

Figure 3.2 Project Surname booklet.
Source: National Library and Archives of Canada.

featuring Inuit tossing disc numbers aside (figure 3.2). The Commissioner's introductory letter is filled with the importance of the occasion:

> It appears to me very fitting that this project should be started as we approach our Centennial Year 1970 and for this reason I have designated it as an important Centennial project. I hope that all Community Centennial Committees will assist Abe Okpik in making this project a success. (Okpik 1970)

There is no indication that 'Community Centennial Committees' had any bearing on Project Surname (or even existed). The booklet gave a Eurocentric explanation for the enterprise:

> A surname is what is commonly known as the last name. Commissioner Stuart M. Hodgson, for example, is known by his last name – Hodgson, which is his surname. Most people are called by their first names by their friends but it is the last name, the surname that they are identified by. You may call the Commissioner any name you like but you have to say his surname before anyone knows who you are talking about.

> WHY ARE SURNAMES CHANGED?
> Many people of Canada have changed their names ... Names that are hard to pronounce ... are too long [or] too similar ...

Well, yes. But this ignores the underpinnings. When names are changed for these reasons they are almost always the names of minority people who are accommodating those with more power. Many voluntary name changes imply upward mobility – for example, immigrants who 'Canadianise' their names to get better jobs. Some names are changed under duress – by immigration authorities who mis-hear, or do not ask, the name; by teachers or classmates who want to 'help' minority people seem more 'normal'. People in power seldom change their names. The booklet outlines legal and administrative arguments – easier inheritance and recordkeeping. Among the 'advantages': people will have 'the proper Native given name truly from your cultural background'. There is no indication of how Project Surname would help with this. Abe grew up in a fairly acculturated Western Arctic region and spent much time among First Nations people and Qallunaat. Either he was aware of Inuit naming traditions and was ignoring them, or had not learned them and was unaware of the contradictions inherent in his position.

He further argued that the surnames would 'lead, at age fourteen, to a Social Insurance number ...' but did not say why such a number could not be given without a surname – or why it was not simply given in place of the whole surname project (a far less costly enterprise, since it was already under way). It was inaccurate to say that 'Once you have chosen your surname it is yours, and yours only, for all time'. First of all, the conventional Euro-Canadian surname system is 'yours ... for all time' only for *men*. Although things are gradually changing, it was generally expected that a woman would abandon her fathers' name for her husband's at marriage. Second, hundreds of Euro-Canadians share surnames and often first names as well. In short, the arguments did not hold water.

People were given the option of keeping their disc numbers, either with, or in place of, surnames. 'It will not be up to me, or anyone else to influence you in your decision', they were assured. The contradiction was that Abe had been sent to collect a name for each Inuk, and, as in so many other 'voluntary' programmes, there was a good deal of social pressure to conform and comply. There was freedom to choose the name of any relative, but no acknowledgement of how this would undercut the existing culture. 'Think of your identity, the loss of your true name, when you think back on the use of disc numbers', Abe wrote, without mentioning the loss of 'true name' that accompanied the supposedly more enlightened new system. The argument for a new naming system imposed uniquely on Inuit ended with a wish that '1970 will be a year of unity among our peoples of the North, namely those of Innuit, Indian, White and all other backgrounds …' (Okpik 1970). On that note, the Project began.

How it Worked

The settlements of Holman Island (Western Arctic) and Pond Inlet (Eastern Arctic) were selected for a pilot project in late 1969. 'In addition to testing the program and procedures, the pilot project also tested the Eskimo people's reaction'. Abe's reports 'indicated a very encouraging and enthusiastic reaction'. There were 'minor adjustments' where procedures 'did not quite work'. At Pond Inlet the booklets arrived too far in advance; later, they were sent out to arrive about a week ahead of Abe's visit. In thirteen months he travelled more than 45,000 miles and interviewed about 15,000 people. Although he told me there were several complaints, the *Summary* author claims to know of 'only one case' in which an Inuk refused to choose a surname, 'Stating firmly that he would continue to use his disc number'. Because of impossible weather conditions, Abe missed the settlements of Whale Cove and Repulse Bay.

I started my trips in September – *this* time of year [our conversation took place in autumn 1985]. September 23 was the date, I remember it – 1969. I was called to the office. We had to draw up the pamphlet, map out the area where we should go. But there were no real airlines to go in and out with, eh? They gave us a budget – not very much … I said 'well we don't know what the *people* want'. I said 'I'll do it my way if I have to' … I went on a field trip. I took one place, Holman Island, which is the W District – my district.

They said 'What're you doing?' I said 'Well I got news for you'. So I had a little public meeting and went to church and announced my intentions. And I explained to them that all Canadians have a number to identify us. And I said 'You want to keep your number? Let's see how your names are spelled'. So we checked. I was doing quite a bit of studying before that on this one particular guy. He had eight children. Each one of his children were [*sic*] registered by different people passing through. There was an RCMP who had Ukrainian background. There was father La Pointe who was a Frenchman, Bishop Sperry, and the Hudson's Bay clerks were mostly from Scotland. Every child [in this family] had his name spelled differently. So I said, 'How would you like your name spelled?'

So I had that meeting and I was successful. I took it back to our office in Yellowknife. There was no [airline] schedule. You'd have to wait for a plane and just hope you'd get out. They said 'You ought to try the East'. Next was Pond Inlet. That time of year, it took three weeks. It was confusing … I had a public meeting. And there I found out how they wanted it done. They said … the name should live on. We had a meeting and they said 'Come and see us in the winter; it would be better with our family in the house'. (Okpik 1985–95)

Some people were reluctant to discuss names in a public meeting, preferring the privacy of their homes. Also, they wanted all family members to be present, and some were still out hunting, camping on the land.

At the meeting, someone said 'I'm named after my father'. Someone said 'I'm named after my auntie' … . 'I'm named after my mother's father' … So they were all brothers and sisters … They made their own structure. I said 'You can use the spelling, or if you don't like it or you don't like the name you can change it' … After nineteen years old you could go to the RCMP to the Justice of Peace – you have to go through a court to change your own name; there was an option then. (Okpik 1985–95)

Some kept their original names but adopted Christian first names and used their original Inuktitut names as surnames.

I'll give you an example. A man named … was adopted out to his grandparents. His brother has a different name … and a younger brother with still another name. One changed to their father's name; another said he would keep the name from his mother's grandfather; the third used his uncle's name. When I was a little boy I had three uncles. They still call me my uncle's name because I'm supposed to live like him. We're supposed to have spiritual guides. My uncle's name is Autaalik – great uncle. My Christian name is Abraham. My name was [originally] Abraham Autaalik. Younger people don't call me by my real name. But some young guys … still call me Uncle Abe.

I spent six weeks in Pang [Pangnirtung] because everybody was out on the land and I had an opportunity to travel. I would hire a canoe … I went into Eskimo Point [now Arviat] and it was really difficult because at that time I wasn't used to their dialect. Now I speak it. It was really a headache. I spent fifteen days in Igloolik. I brought a tape recorder. I've got lots of legends – gave it all to Glenbow [Museum]. The only place I missed was Whale Cove and Repulse Bay. There was only a hundred people in Repulse.

He sent a letter to the local priest in each of those communities, and they arranged for the work to be done by local people.

I kept right on going. I never took holidays. I wanted to get it done by the end of the Centennial year … .it was getting close to Christmas. I was living in Ft. Smith at that time … There was no flight from Yellowknife to here at that time … I had to fly south – had to keep going up and down from Montreal. I had to go back to Yellowknife every three months to compile everything and go to the Supreme Court of the Territories – Justice Department – to register a certain community and sign an affidavit saying 'Here's the people who've agreed to change …' Going to court meant I had to get a special order from the Council. Some communities were easier. Frobisher responded to me – they knew me. In Baffin they did know me … I couldn't get very far across Eskimo Point and Baker – I didn't speak their dialect and they were wary. The teachers were hardest to meet with. They thought the children were doing ok. They thought it was stupid … They thought that all the children should grow up and register their own names. All total I spent thirteen months out in the field. Then I spent two years, almost to the day – September. I had it about two-thirds done by the end of the Centennial (1970). Then I finally got it done in the office.

He hired a supervisor and four assistants to work with him in the Vital Statistics office.

I calculated one day before the last report – at that time there were 17,000 Inuit. I didn't interview all of them, but I interviewed the parents of all of them, except maybe three or four that weren't around. I spoke about almost each individual. Our population's doubled up since then. I spent about five months in this office. I was really pushing it … I'd do two hundred names in a day, starting ten a.m. and on through the night. After all this work I did, I forgot to write my own family's names! (Okpik 1984–2004)

Some communities took it upon themselves to correct the errors. In 1972 the Baker Lake Settlement Council appointed Councillor Armand Tagoona to correct and revise the community's name list (Sanavik Cooperative 1973: back page). 'Robert Williamson of Rankin Inlet Northwest Territories, elected member of the council for the Central Arctic region, said use of the numbers and related problems are contributing to Eskimos' loss of self-respect' (Leader Press 1969: 5). Yet the programme instituted in the disc numbers' place was even more offensive. Project Surname hopped onto the political bandwagon and produced a 'Bandaid'; it cleaned up the government's act in the interest of better public relations but left the old ethnocentrism in place and endangered Inuit culture. People speak of Project Surname as if it were a great storm. It 'came through'; it 'swept away'; it 'left in its wake'.

Qallunaaq, early 50s:
I was in Baker Lake … There were eight hundred people. It was just like a sausage factory … 'Do you have a surname? What's your father's name? OK. You're [new name]'. The late 1960s were an era of people who didn't

want to be put into pigeonholes. Project Surname ended up creating a situation which is just horrendous. Some people in the South see the North as a warehouse: you go in and you get out. (Alia 1984–2006)

The Politics of Surnaming

Accounts of the origins of surnaming are diverse and contradictory. One linguist says surnames were first adopted by those of noble birth and called 'sir' names (Ames 1941). Another attributes the derivation to 'surnoun – a name common to all members of a family' (Sykes 1982: 1074).

> The commoners followed the example of the nobility; but even as late as 1465 surnames were not universal, and Edward the Fifth passed a law to compel certain Irish outlaws … to take them [which specified,] They shall take unto them a Surname, either of some Towne, or some Colour … or some Art or Science, as Smyth or Carpenter, or some Office … . (Ames 1941: 9)

Therein lies the origin of many a familiar contemporary surname. While Project Surname was less precisely conceived, it followed the same principles and was linked to law: newly surnamed Inuit had their new names 'validated' by court procedure. Surnaming has always been tied to class distinctions and power inequities. A surname can be a mark of 'distinction' for those who inherit or pass it to future generations. Or it can be a mark of subjugation – a way of being followed or found if one is in an underclass (a Jew in Nazi Germany, an outlaw, a political 'criminal'). It can signify cultural absorption – a way of 'normalising' a marginalised culture. Motives for giving Inuit surnames ranged from affording them the *opportunity* to be 'like all other Canadians' to imposing a *requirement* to be 'like everyone else'. Surnaming is sometimes a way of controlling disempowered people.

> In 1916, all Thai were directed by royal decree to choose family names which children would take from their fathers, but even today these names are little used except on formal documents. (The Burmese still resist even this suggestion of paternal dominance and use no family names at all.) A Burmese woman does not take her husband's name … children's names bear no necessary resemblance to those of either of their parents. (Burling 1965: 100)

Although surnames were not quite decreed and the Inuit response not quite so extreme, the principle applies. In tampering with the country's naming patterns, the Thai government effectively altered the patterns of power. Resistance went far deeper than mere rejection of labels, to the very centre of a society that had enjoyed a more egalitarian system than the new regime could bear.

In Nunavut, the case of Project Surname demonstrates the close ties between renaming, colonial politics and policymaking and reveals the hazards of hastily assembled political 'projects' – for both those in power and those affected by it. The Northwest Territories Centennial was accompanied by much fanfare and a profusion of Royalty. A UPI Telephoto from Frobisher Bay (Iqaluit) 5 July, 1970 shows Commissioner Hodgson helping Queen Elizabeth don a parka. She is seated beside the equally parkaed Prince Philip, Princess Anne and Prince Charles.

> The monarch's itinerary among the Eskimos has been arranged to emphasize her role as Queen of all Canada, and to stress at the same time the role of these northerners as Canadians ... Queen Elizabeth of Canada travelled 5,000 miles across the Arctic this week impressing on Canadians that their big, rich northland is their inheritance to develop and protect. The trip, while following the familiar routine of a royal tour, was in fact a demonstration of Canadian sovereignty in the Arctic. (Walz 1970: 8)

In a radio message broadcast from Yellowknife, the Queen said: 'It is most important to bear in mind that thoughtless meddling and ill-considered exploitation is just as bad as wanton destruction' (Walz 1970: 8). The week-long royal tour cost the Canadian Government $750,000. The next year, 1971, Stuart Hodgson was awarded the Medal of Service of the Order of Canada, for 'the part he played in moving the Territorial Government from Ottawa to the new capital of Yellowknife in 1967, and since then establishing an effective public service in the North to serve the people' (Ernerk 1971: 4). The same issue of *Tukisiviksat*, published by the Department of Information of the Government of the Northwest Territories, noted that Project Surname was nearing completion, explaining:

> discs were first introduced as a method of properly identifying Eskimo people for social welfare purposes. The Territorial Government decided that they had outlived their usefullness [sic] and that a complete list of proper Eskimo names should now be compiled ... Official change of names is now under way for those persons who requested them. (Tukisiviksat February 1971)

The language is deceptive. Although people were apparently not 'required' or coerced into adopting surnames, it is not accurate to say that the surnames produced through a programme organised by government were 'requested'. Abe Okpik got his own Order of Canada medal for his work on Project Surname. In the 1970 Annual Report of the Commissioner of the Northwest Territories, Hodgson wrote:

> On New Year's Eve, at the stroke of midnight, the Honourable Jean Chrétien, Minister of Indian Affairs and Northern Development (later to become Canada's Prime Minister), flicked a light switch, and a ten-foot tall sign flashed

in bold red letters atop Yellowknife's high-rise apartment building – 1970 – Centennial. The celebration started and the North's most exciting year was under way. It was a year of unity and a year of progress. It was most appropriate that in this Centennial Year when 'Territorial Unity' was the theme, that the Federal Government recognized the need for unity in political development and completed its transfer of administrative responsibility to the Government of the Northwest Territories ...

On 1 April, 1970 the Commissioner raised the flag of the Northwest Territories at the Keewatin Regional Headquarters in Churchill and later in the day at the area office in Baker Lake, the heart of the Central Arctic. On that day the whole of the Northwest Territories became the responsibility of the Territorial Government, which has most of the powers of a Provincial Government, with the exception that non-renewable resources remain the responsibility of the Federal Government. The year of 1970 will long be remembered by people all across the 1,300,000 square miles of the Northwest Territories. It was an historic year in which unprecedented attention was focused on Canada's North [and] a year in which political developments steadily advanced, keeping apace of social and economic progress ... (Hodgson 1970: 7)

Progress included amendments to the Northwest Territories Act increasing the number of elected members of Council, 'thus increasing the representative nature of the legislative body' (Hodgson 1970: 3).

The Eastern Arctic (Nunavut) is the region least assimilated into southern Canada. Many Inuit in the Western Arctic already spoke English when Project Surname began. Many already had Qallunaat surnames. The people of the Baffin were far less acculturated, and few had taken surnames. Robert Williamson played a problematic role. As anthropologist, he wrote eloquently of naming in Inuit culture; as Territorial Councillor, he supported Project Surname (Hodgson 1969). His position harks back to a long tradition of intimacy between governments and anthropologists, prevalent in Europe and the United States as well as in Canada. His doctoral dissertation, filled with respect for Inuit culture – particularly naming – was published in 1974, long after he had gotten a position on the Territorial Council. His proposal to Council was far better thought out than the programme that was apparently already under way. Although the Territorial Council was only now discussing the subject, Territorial Secretary H.E. Cross reported that 'Council was told some five hundred thousand dollars had been spent in the last eleven or twelve years on the project' (Government of the Northwest Territories 1971). As one Qallunaaq put it:

Stu was known for acting on his own. He didn't go in much for consulting people. Abe got the flak. Everybody disappeared when it was over. Abe still lived here and had to deal with people. Some communities were worse than others; some people were very upset and others weren't upset at all. Stu

> Hodgson was so full of himself. Pompous. Not a bad guy. Did some good things, and cared about the people. But he didn't take to criticism. Mostly, people let him have his way. (Alia 1985–2006)

The Commissioner had a strong personality and a reputation for action. I have gone over and over the documents looking for an official start of the Project. One person who was around at the time said there was no official authorisation. According to another, 'He just *did it*'. Perhaps the idea originated with Simonie Michael's comments; perhaps the comments of a number of Inuit and Qallunaat had a cumulative effect. Certainly there was much talk and grumbling, and a climate of imperatives for change. What seems true today is that it is unfair to blame all of the mistakes on any one of the many players. Each is responsible; none is *totally* responsible. It is unfair to blame Abe Okpik, as some Inuit have done, merely because he remained a visible resident of the North.

Stuart Hodgson returned to British Columbia, out of the line of fire, out of the creation of Nunavut, and out of the continuing dialogue about the effects (good, bad and indifferent) of the project he spearheaded. It is inaccurate to pin the whole thing on Hodgson; the roots of Project Surname were firmly planted by Sivertz and others before him. Robert Williamson, too, was a cog in the wheel of intricate northern history. He has remained a respected member of the anthropological and northern communities. The one thing that is clear from the transcript of the Territorial Council Debates is that as soon as Williamson learned that the renaming programme was already in progress he withdrew his motion, backed off and refocused on consistency in spelling.

The various demands and actions of the past decade, to restore or protect Inuit names, suggest a need to reexamine policies. There was a precedent for the request made by Elise Attagutaluk and others that the government facilitate and pay for name changes. When it suited the government's purpose, legal and financial supports were put into place, as when Abe had the new names changed in the legal system at no cost to the individuals. Yet for many years, Inuit had to pay to *restore* names they had lost during Project Surname. In the early years of Nunavut Territory there have been changes. Alexina Kublu, Jose Kusugak and Peter Irniq are among those who have pressured government and organised projects for restoring people's names. A project is under way in which Inuit are helping to name the people in hundreds of thousands of photographs stored in Canada's National Library and Archives (figure 3.3). It began in 2001 with the collection of photographs by Richard Harrington. Before digitisation, the images were taken to Nunavut, where elders helped to identify them. In 2003, photographs were projected onto a screen in the Arviat community centre.

I✦I Library and Archives   Bibliothèque et Archives
    Canada   Canada   Inuktitut | Français | Help   **Canadä**
        Home > Browse Selected Topics > Project Naming   Important Notices

P   R   O   J   E   C   T

NAMING

SEARCH FOR PHOTOS   WEB LINKS   CONTACT US

introduction

introduction

THE STORY BEHIND PROJECT NAMING

voices from Nunavut

the Inuktitut language

photo collections

the naming continues

credits

The goal of *Project Naming* is the identification of Inuit portrayed in some of the photographic collections of Library and Archives Canada in Ottawa. It is an ongoing initiative, which enables Nunavut youth to connect with Elders and to better understand their past. It also helps to bridge the cultural differences and geographical distances between Nunavut and the more southern parts of Canada.

The collections depicting the people of Canada's North consist of thousands of photographs dating from the late 1800s to the mid-20th century. However, very few Inuit in these images were identified at the time these photographs were taken. Nunavummiut have never had a chance to assist in identifying these individuals because the collections were located far from their communities. Prior to digitization, there was no means of easily transporting the photographs to Nunavut. The naming of these still anonymous people has become very time sensitive. Today's Elders may be the last people able to identify these individuals from the past, whose names might otherwise remain lost forever.

During the first phase of *Project Naming*, photographs from the Igloolik (Iglulik) area, taken in the early 1950s by renowned photographer Richard Harrington were scanned and transferred to CD-ROM. Equipped with laptop computers, youth visited Elders living in that community, in order to identify the individuals in these photographs. The first phase was a great success, since more than three-quarters of the people were identified. Many Elders were able to identify their parents, other family and community members, and in some cases even themselves. Since then, the Project expanded to include other photographic collections at Library and Archives Canada, and covered additional Nunavut communities, including Kugluktuk (formerly Coppermine), Taloyoak (formerly Spence Bay), Pond Inlet (Mittimatalik/Tununiq), Pangnirtung (Pangnirtuuq), Cape Dorset (Kinngait), and Iqaluit (formerly Frobisher Bay).

When the locations of photographs are described in *Project Naming*, communities are listed by their Inuit name or by the English or non-Aboriginal name, followed by the other in parentheses. Most of the photographs were taken at a time when the non-Aboriginal names were considered the official community names. Today, with the creation of Nunavut and Native name recognition initiatives throughout the Arctic, some communities such as Iqaluit and Arviat have officially changed back to their original Inuit names. Although some are in the process of changing back, many still use both names interchangeably. Searches for photographs related to *Project Naming* can be done using both the Inuit and non-Aboriginal community names. The spelling of all Inuit community names is based on the *Map of Inuit Communities in Canada*, on the Inuit Tapiriit Kanatami Web site, and on the Northern Community Names Changes section of the Canadian Geographical Names Web site of Natural Resources Canada.

Project Naming is a collaborative effort between Nunavut Sivuniksavut, a special college program based in Ottawa, which serves Inuit youth from Nunavut; the Department of Culture, Languages, Elders and Youth

Figure 3.3 Project Naming home page.

Text: Project Naming Introduction © Library and Archives of Canada. Reproduced with the permission of the Minister of Public Works and Government Services Canada (2005).
Photo: 'Atootoo', Cape Dorset, Baffin Island, N.W.T., Feb. 20, 1929.
Photo source: Library and Archives Canada (Credit: J.D. Soper/Indian and Northern Affairs Collection/PA-101314.
Website source: Library and Archives of Canada (www.collectionscanada.ca/inuit/054301-e.html).

When the faces of the people in the photographs were recognized, members of the community called out the individuals' names. In other cases, youth went door-to-door visiting Elders ... Students studying at the Nunavut Sivuniksavut Training Program in Ottawa also participated in the identification of photographs for *Project Naming* ... For Mathewsie Ashevak, the most memorable aspect of meeting with the Elders was learning about their past way of life and listening to the memories and stories rekindled by the photographs. (Library and Archives Canada 2005)

During Project Surname, many people of Elise's generation were away in school – usually at the government-run residential school at Churchill, Manitoba. 'Kids came home and were told "You're somebody else" (1984–2006). Project Surname was part of a long and complicated history of benevolence, paternalism and racism expressed in public and private documents and in daily treatment of Inuit by Qallunaat. In January 1946 a series of photographs by Bud Glunz, distributed by government to the media, were given captions, each preceded by the following text:

The Eskimo is a happy, childlike nomad. He lives mainly by fishing and hunting ... (National Library and Archives of Canada 1946)

An article written nearly thirty years later was almost as patronising, not to mention mistaken, even in its praise of Inuit's 'natural' attributes: 'Dishonesty is almost foreign to the Eskimo's nature ... Since the Canadian Government made the Eskimo a ward of the state much of the primitive way of life has vanished. The overnight hunt is a thing of the past and the tent has been replaced by box-like structures with oil stove heat' (Cahill 1970: 24). This would be news to Inuit who still use their summer camps and hunt and fish in winter. The journalist did not forget to mention naming: 'The older men have such exotic names as Munga, Agvil, Omingmak and Tootalik. Their children who attend school and buy rock records at the Hudson's Bay Company store have such Christian names as Peter, Mary, Richard, Philip, Jean and Allen' (ibid.).

Women are absent from the story. One wonders where the reporter got the names 'Mary' and 'Richard', which would not be pronounced anything like this in Inuktitut, or even spelled this way. Nevertheless, his point is clear: at a time when social scientists had long since abandoned at least the obvious forms of ethnocentric writing, for this writer 'Tootalik' is 'exotic' and 'Richard' is 'normal', the very attitude that led to so many efforts to make Inuit 'fit into' Qallunaaq society. Some comments were even more disrespectful. After ten years in the Canadian Arctic, Dr Gordon C. Butler told a *New York Times* reporter: 'the Eskimos never had a way of life ... only a way of survival' (Walz 1970: 9).

There was growing protest against such attitudes both inside and outside government. As Keith Crowe (1984–96) put it, the post-1950s world was 'touched by the world revolution of expectations'. The wearing of numbered discs continued to conjure up images of dog-tagged armies and many people felt that names, whatever their cultural origins, conveyed more humanity and individuality. The next chapter looks at Inuit responses to the evolution and aftermath of Project Surname.

Chapter 4

'THE PEOPLE WHO LOVE YOU': CONTEMPORARY PERSPECTIVES ON NAMING IN NUNAVUT

Inuit society, in many respects, is as modern as its Euro-American counterpart. Inuit, however, continue to consider themselves to be Inuit. In spite of cultural and social change, they feel strong continuity between their past and present … . [and] do not perceive any major break in their personal identity. (Dorais 1997: 3)

Inuit feel continuity between their forebears and themselves, even when they are living in permanent communities, engaged in wage labour, attending school or local government meetings, or keeping records in Qallunaat languages. Genuine Inuit identity may thus find itself concomitantly in a 'traditional' as well as a 'modern' setting. (Dorais 1997: 106)

[I]dentity shows a lot in your Inuktitut name, because those are the names that are given to you when you're born by the people who love you. (Pitseolak in Alia 1995)

A Short History of Nunavut

In May 2005, a historic Partnership Accord was signed between Inuit and the government of Canada. The signatories were Jose Kusugak, President of Inuit Tapiriit Kanatami, and the presidents of Inuvialuit Regional Corporation (Western Arctic), Nunavut Tunngavik Incorporated, Makivik Corporation (Nunavik), Labrador Inuit Association, Pauktuutit (Inuit Women's Association), Inuit Circumpolar Conference Canada, the National Inuit Youth Council, and Andy Scott, Minister of Indian Affairs and Northern Development. The accord acknowledges constitutional recognition of Inuit as an Aboriginal people of Canada, living in Nunatsiavut (Labrador), Nunavik (northern Québec), the Inuvialuit Settlement Region, and many centres in southern Canada.

It recognizes the comprehensive land claim agreements signed by Makivik Corporation, the Inuvialuit Regional Corporation, and Nunavut Tunngavik Incorporated ... [and] the impending Labrador Final Agreement ...

It acknowledges the creation of the Inuit Relations Secretariat as a focal point for the renewed relationship between Inuit and the Government of Canada. (Inuit Tapiriit Kanatami 2005)

A few months later, in November 2005, Canadian Prime Minister Paul Martin invited Aboriginal leaders to Kelowna, British Columbia, to attend the first ministers' meeting with leaders of federal, provincial and territorial governments. 'It's the first time Aboriginal leaders have been invited to sit in on the top-level meeting, a spokesperson for the Department of Indian Affairs and Northern Development said' (CBC News 2005: 1). Nunavut Premier, Paul Okalik, was already included in the first ministers process. The new participants represented the Assembly of First Nations, Métis National Council, Native Women's Association of Canada, the Congress of Aboriginal Peoples, and Inuit Tapiriit Kanatami (ITK). A month later, in December 2005, the Labrador Final Agreement alluded to above was signed, bringing the 5,300 Inuit of Nunatsiavut ('our beautiful land') into a self-government agreement with the Government of Canada.

ITK – originally called Inuit Tapirisat of Canada (ITC) – has long been prominent in Canadian Aboriginal politics, and figures importantly in the Nunavut story. In 1973, ITC inaugurated a study of Inuit land use and occupancy that led to its 1976 proposal of a comprehensive land claim settlement that included creation of Nunavut Territory. The process gained momentum in 1979, when the federal government divided the Northwest Territories into two electoral districts. In 1980, ITC passed a resolution calling for the creation of Nunavut, but it was not until 1990 that Inuit managed to obtain an Agreement-in-principle between their land claim organisation, Tungavik Federation of Nunavut, and representatives of the federal and Territorial Governments. The Agreement covered both the land claim and division of the Northwest Territories into two political entities. Voters throughout both districts approved the proposed boundary for division in 1992, resulting in the signing of the Nunavut Political Accord, which set a Nunavut launch date of 1 April 1999.

Nunavut means 'our land' in Inuktitut. The territory comprises about two million square kilometres (800,000 square miles), about 30,000 people and twenty-eight communities. In keeping with traditional practices, there are no Territorial political parties (though candidates for federal election do have party links), and decisions are made by consensus.

The proposal advanced by John Amagoalik, to set an equal number of female and male members of the Legislative Assembly, was defeated in a 1997 plebiscite. The founding of Nunavut involved two separate Agreements – the Nunavut Land Claims Agreement Act establishing the rights of Inuit, who comprise 85 percent of the population, and the Nunavut Act providing for a public government with equal rights and representation for all Nunavut residents. These Agreements were adopted by Parliament and granted Royal Assent in 1993. While it was recognised that Iqaluit, with its well-developed communication and transport infrastructure, was the best choice for the central government, a pair of documents, *Footprints in New Snow* and *Footprints II*, produced in 1995 and 1996 by the Nunavut Implementation Commission (NIC), recommended decentralising some of the government departments and facilities. This was in keeping with the principles that had earlier guided establishment of several regional Inuit associations, served by coordinating offices of ITC/ITK in Ottawa and Iqaluit. *Footprints II* set out the structures and principles that became the foundation of the Government of Nunavut. On 1 April 1999, Nunavut Territory and the Government of Nunavut were officially launched (Government of Nunavut 2005).

Peter Jull calls this the most ambitious Canadian Aboriginal self-government plan and 'also one of the most practical, combining 'Canadian traditions of social and political philosophy with the needs of Inuit culture' and embracing environmental, economic and social values and development (Jull 1988: 12). While he agrees with Nunavut's importance in Canadian history, Premier Paul Okalik sees it somewhat differently. While the 'official creation of Nunavut on April 1, 1999 has been acknowledged as a landmark in Canadian history [and] ... represented the culmination of more than two decades of work by the Inuit of Nunavut to regain some control of their lives',

> What Inuit achieved on April 1, 1999 was not self-government, but a legislated guarantee that Inuit would participate in a meaningful way in the decision making process in the territory ... While the Inuit of Nunavut chose to express their rights through a public government structure, they retained their right under the Agreement to pursue self-government in the future if they so desire. (Okalik 2001)

He places this achievement in broader sociopolitical context.

> Inuit control began to erode in the 1950s when the Canadian Government moved nomadic Inuit families into permanent settlements, irreparably disrupting their way of life. This policy began a process of dependency ... In the years since moving into communities, Inuit became largely dependent on meagre employment opportunities and welfare ... poverty was endemic ... The resulting stresses on Inuit have been both dramatic and cumulative. Our

society was facing the spectre of a continuous slide towards social and cultural decay. (ibid.)

One of the leaders in the process was John Amagoalik. He headed the Nunavut Land Claims Project and was chief commissioner of the Nunavut Implementation Commission, 'which oversaw the establishment of Nunavut territory in 1999' (Etzel 2005: 75). While serving as ITC president in the 1980s, he also played a key role in the Inukshuk Project, forerunner of the Inuit Broadcasting Corporation and a key player in Television Northern Canada and its successor, the Canada-wide Aboriginal People's Television Network (Alia 1999, 2005).

Names and the 'Inuit Renaissance'

Inspired by the naming of the Maori cultural revival in Aotearoa (New Zealand) as the 'Maori Renaissance' (Alia and Bull 2005: 110), I have adopted the parallel term of 'Inuit Renaissance' to refer to the cultural revival in contemporary Nunavut.

Except where otherwise noted, the accounts in this chapter are from my conversations and interviews with Inuit and Qallunaat in, or concerning, Nunavut and the experiences with naming and identification (1984–2006). The stories told here were gathered during interviews, conversations, group discussions and debate at the 1989 Inuit Circumpolar Conference assembly at Sisimiut, Greenland; at the Inuit Tapirisat of Canada (ITC – now ITK), Pauktuutit (Inuit Women's Association), Tungavik Federation of Nunavut (TFN) and Inuit Broadcasting Corporation (IBC) offices in Ottawa; the offices of IBC and CBC Northern Service in Iqaluit and CBC in Yellowknife; the Prince of Wales Northern Heritage Centre in Yellowknife; Northwest Territories and Nunavut government offices; the offices of *NewsNorth*, *Native Press* (no longer publishing) and *Nunatsiaq News* in Yellowknife and Iqaluit, respectively; several Arctic policy conferences; at the annual Inuit Studies conferences, the International Association of Arctic Social Sciences and other conferences and meetings, between the years of 1984 and 2006.

In the earlier years most of the interviews focused on the experiences and effects of the disc number programme and Project Surname. As I spent more time in the North and got to know people better, there were fewer formal interviews and more conversations. A cluster of interviews were conducted for the radio documentary, *Nunavut: Where Names Never Die* (Alia 1995). More recent interviews and discussions took place in the years immediately preceding and following the signing and implementation of the Nunavut Agreement, from the mid-1990s to early

2006. A pattern emerged in the responses to the earlier interviews, which has appeared in other research experiences as well. I have called it 'the turn-around phenomenon'.

The Turn-around Phenomenon: 'No Problem' Responses

When I first asked whether an individual had experienced negative consequences as a result of government identification programmes I got a quiet, unequivocal 'no'. While this can be attributed in part to the cultural differences and my Outsider/visitor status particular to the study, there are certain generalities observable in other research projects and diverse cultural contexts. I first identified the pattern during the early stages of the Project Surname research. After several interviews, I learned to listen for nuances in the 'no problem' statements. In each instance, alternative attitudes and information would start to filter into the conversation. Sometimes there was an abrupt and unheralded shift. Here is an excerpt from an interview conducted in a small and close-knit Nunavut community in 1985:

> *Question*: 'Did the birth certificates and new names cause you any difficulty?'
> *Response*: 'No'.
> *Question*: 'What was it like when Project Surname came through?'
> *Response*: 'My sister's name was put down all wrong. My birth certificate has the wrong date on it and my old age pension cheques did not arrive until many years after I was old enough to receive them.

The sudden burst of negatives followed an entirely positive 'no problem' response to the initial questioning. After a time, I learned to show no surprise and continue as if the discussion had a natural progression. Once the experience had recurred several times and I began to see a pattern, it was difficult to avoid expecting it. I tried not to anticipate the shift, though it occurred in most of the interviews. I did notice a correlation between the informant's age and the degree of initial candour. People over thirty tended to be more positive and polite at the start, either because their generations were more closely tied to traditional ways of conversing or because age and experience made them more cautious (perhaps a combination of both). Individual personality was also a relevant factor. Those who described negatives at the start usually shared humour, informal talk and friendliness that seemed to indicate greater trust. Language figured less importantly. Of those who began in a more – or less – candid way, some were English speakers but others spoke only Inuktitut and volunteered the information through an interpreter.

There is one other factor particular to the research at hand. Especially where the Project Surname process was concerned, I received the public relations version of Abe Okpik's visits and only later did I hear another version that included problems and concerns. There are important reasons for this. An Inuk who was originally from the Western Arctic, Abe spent much of his life in the eastern regions of Nunavut. He married a woman from Pangnirtung and lived for many years in South Baffin, in Pangnirtung and Iqaluit. He was a public figure, a respected elder who throughout his life remained active in the community. In discussing Project Surname, most people treated him with respect, even when they criticised the project, or his role in it.

Many people predicted that the waves of outside interference with Inuit identity would mean the death of Inuit culture (see, for example, Davis and Zannis 1973). They were mistaken. Throughout all of the changes, Inuit kept their traditions alive. When Nunavut became official, making Inuit the 85 percent majority in their homeland, the cultural revival already under way became stronger. Today, as Jose Kusugak puts it, cultural revival – or recognition – is a dominant theme in Nunavut. Inuit are naming babies in the old ways, playing with or discarding the old disc numbers, reclaiming names that were lost or changed through Project Surname, and continuing naming practices that for a time became less public but were never lost.

> It's amazing. When the land claims got ratified … you remember when it happened, where you were … I know where I was; I know what time it was … Once that day happened, you kind of cleaned the slate and said, "Oh, good; we made it to this point … Now we can develop our own, with the good [parts of Qallunaaq society] – take some of their good parts, some of our good values, and mix the two to develop a synergy …'
>
> … Thirty years ago, they were telling us that the Inuit language is going to disappear, so why not just speak in English? Which Inuit heard, but totally ignored and just continued with their language. The naming system is another one of those society laws that was hard to continue, because of Christianity coming in, the surname project coming in … But again, it was continued because the Inuit ignored all of that.
>
> I think the land claims make it all easier to enhance the naming process. I don't think it's a matter of bringing it back; I don't think there was ever a time that it got lost. But now it's being brought back in the schools, where, if you bring your kids in … they actually register them into the classroom with their given names in Inuktitut. My little girl, for example … her classmates don't address each other by their Christian names, they address each other by their [Inuktitut] given names. It's really very nice. (Jose Kusugak in Alia 1995: 17)

> I have an eight-year-old daughter. Her name is Silaqanie. She's named after my grandmother. She has *no* Qallunaatitut name, because she's already got quite a few Inuktitut names. Those are the names that were given to her by my mother … Today, sometimes she gets scrutinised – as well as me – because we don't have a name like "Catherine" or "Margaret" or "Martha" or "Esmeralda"

or whatever. We get scrutinised because we do not have an English name; we do not have Qallunaatitut names … I do not *wish* to have a Qallunaatitut name. My identity is in that I am Peesee, named after my grandmother. (Pitseolak in Alia 1995: 18)

Underground Naming: Public and Private Behaviour

The removal of names and naming practices from the public eye is not necessarily a concession to cultural genocide. It often has precisely the opposite effect of preserving cultural practices in the light of pressures to assimilate. Sometimes those pressures have life-or-death consequences. The Shoah (Holocaust) survivors known as 'hidden children' were renamed to save their lives; the younger ones sometimes were so well concealed that they learned they were Jewish many years after the end of the Second World War (Jarvie 1984–94; Stein 1993). An Armenian-Canadian recalled stories in her family about relatives who were threatened with execution if they persisted in refusing to take Turkish names (Toukmanian 1984). Margaret Kahn (1980) reports an elaborately developed double-naming system in which Kurdish names of individuals and communities are kept intact but secret and publicly replaced by names of the dominant countries (e.g., Iraq). As a child growing up in Oklahoma, I learned early on that my Hebrew names were to be used only at home or in synagogue, were not on my birth certificate, and would sometimes become objects of derision if shared openly with people from the dominant culture.

In his monograph, *Eskimo Underground* (1974), Robert Williamson uses the term 'underground naming' – a term also used by Keith Crowe (1984–96; 1991) – to refer to the practice of maintaining traditional names in private while following dominant-society conventions in public. When one culture dominates another, visitors are nicknamed and talked about in ways not revealed to them, while the nicknamers preserve their own identities in private. Erving Goffman (1959) calls this 'back stage' behaviour. In the decades preceding the Nunavut Agreement, Inuit often adopted a system of 'underground naming', recording official Qallunaat names on documents such as birth certificates and keeping traditional names for private use. People were baptised and attended church, but retained far more of the old practices and beliefs than some missionaries would like to believe. A similar practice was reported at the Acoma Pueblo in New Mexico. Long ago, Spanish conquerors gave Acoma people surnames. Today, a system of underground naming is in place. People are given traditional Acoma names but use Spanish and English names in different contexts. The naming patterns fit into a more generalised cultural hierarchy in which Spanish-derived Christian celebrations are open to the public and traditional ceremonies are not (Acoma 1993).

According to Williamson's principle of 'underground culture', the process of acculturation 'develops ambivalences and social and mental strains on all sides (among both the non-dominant and the dominant societies) involved in the confrontation of cultures, though most notably among the members of the non-dominant group'. All societies reinterpret and reorganise values and structures, but the non-dominant culture 'seeks, because not only of ethnocentricity, but ... a basic need to retain reassuring and familiar patterns in a strange and perturbing situation – to defend itself from too-penetrating incursions of the alien value-system, by apparent acceptance of the dominant system ... passivity and withdrawal' (Williamson 1974: 7).

Reflections on the History of Inuit-Qallunaat Encounters and Inuit Identity

The Legacies of Disc Numbers and Project Surname

Project Surname met with a range of responses, from anger and resistance to (at least publicly) polite compliance. Abe Okpik said: 'We had a few retaliations from the young children – people going to school in Churchill, Manitoba – saying, "Why'd you change my name to this name?' But I said, 'You shouldn't protest to me, talk to your parents. At nineteen years you can take it over.' I just told them that there was a time of changing people's names. Eskimo Point [Arviat] and Baker Lake were more trouble.' At Eskimo Point, a man old enough to be getting his old age pension told Abe: '"I have one name and I live with it all my life. I would like to keep my name because when I go for a cheque, if you change it, it might not come my way. I'm not going to live forever." He said, "I use my name and I'll keep my number." Some of the people still go to court with numbers, you know' (Okpik 1985–95).

Alexina Kublu (see figure 4.1) was an adolescent during Project Surname. She recalls her own experience and feelings about the process and its results:

> As a child I knew I was Kublu; I knew I was Apuk; I knew I had E51287. That was all right ... Then I went out to school in Churchill and I came back and my mother gave me this little blue card. 'What is this?' I ask. She tells me it's to let me know who I am. It's a birth certificate. And the birth certificate said 'Alexina' – who I now knew I was – there was a 'K' – I assumed that was for 'Kublu' – and then there was a 'Piroatuk'. I said, 'This is to let me know who I

Figure 4.1 Alexina Kublu, 1998.
Photograph by Valeria Alia.

am?' So she explained to me that while I was out in Churchill, a team of people had come around with Project Surname.

I was pretty upset. Piroatuk was my grandfather's name ... I said, 'I am not Piroatuk ... I don't want to *be* Piroatuk'. My grandfather had died the January while I was Out, so there were these babies who were named after my grandfather. *They* were Piroatuk. And yet on their birth certificates they weren't even listed as 'Piroatuk' ... (Alia 1995: 9–10)

Kublu complained to Abe Okpik and was told that children under the age of nineteen had to take their parents' name, but when she turned nineteen she could seek a legal name change. She did, but had to pay a fee to 'get my name back'.

Elise told me she was stunned when, as a young adult, she received a birth certificate with her *husband's* surname on it. 'I sent it back and asked for correction and they just sent it back to me unchanged.' She had other Inuktitut names; Elise was her own name from birth, when she was baptised by a Catholic priest in Igloolik. Even after Project Surname, Attagutaluk was not her last name. 'When they did Project Surname, kids came back from school with new names. You go away and you come home, and suddenly, you're somebody else.' She talked about Abe Okpik's visit to Igloolik, recalling (as did women in other communities) a more pressured, less gentle approach than some have described. 'One woman didn't want her name changed. Abe said he couldn't leave town without a name for everyone.'

An Inuk from South Baffin said she would prefer to have the disc numbers back. Another Inuk from a different community said she wanted her own name and no numbers. I asked a Qallunaaq who was in the North during Project Surname whether there were public debates, and whether Project Surname was legislated. 'That's a good question', he replied. 'Apparently not.' He said it was both a national and a Territorial programme. 'In those days, people wore different hats – they were both NWT and federal.' A Qallunaaq who was in a different community during the surnaming project recalled a friendlier climate, with public meetings about the surnames. 'People came in groups. We had fun with it.' He did not think the renaming programmes meant the end of Inuit culture.

> The existence of a surname needn't stop the existence of a soul-name. In the 1970s a child of a friend died of leukemia. I was the last to see him alive, in hospital. When I went back a couple of years later his grandmother said '[he] is back again.' A baby had been born to a member of the family and given that name. There was no difference made between life and death: the name's new person meant the soul was alive and the person lived. The body is only a temporary place for the soul to be. But a problem does arise when the soul name is used for a surname.

I ask if this was taken into account in planning Project Surname. 'I suspect not. It was done so fast.' He questions my premise: 'Is renaming really a political question? It's administrative, sociological ... I guess it does become part of the political arsenal.' He mentions the cultural underpinnings that make Inuit particularly vulnerable to administrative control. 'Inuit never push ideas on people; so they're sitting ducks for someone who does.' In the mid-1980s, a Qallunaaq employee of the Territorial Government tells me that disc numbers were essential because, 'All Inuit had the same name or so close you couldn't tell the difference. You needed something logical. You had to have an order. There weren't any names.' I reply that there *were* names and they were not 'the same'. He insists this is not the case, and Inuit were 'impossible to identify'. Clearly the old attitudes of colonial administration persist in more recent times.

Project Surname created new identities and destroyed old ones, sometimes overnight. Not everyone had a say in the renaming, and the result was a tangle of inaccuracies and affronts to tradition. Not everyone thought of the name-changing as a voluntary process. Wives received husbands' surnames – created on the spot – overnight. Children were renamed while they were asleep or away at school. The stories of how people experienced Project Surname are many and varied.

> *Inuk elder:* I used to have only my original name. Some years ago we had to get a second name ... it was before Abe came up here. The RCMP told me I had

to get a second name. I picked my father's name. My wife uses the same name. I was brought up by a family by the name of … and their son's name was [my name]. Their son died and soon afterwards I was born. I was named after their son. All my children are named after ancestors. My wife and I decided the names together. I never wore the disc, just kept it. I didn't get a birth certificate until I was quite old – maybe fifty. Most Inuit people, the older people, they don't really talk good with the white man. So when we were asked what year we were born and we said we didn't know and the white man would just suggest 'perhaps you were born on this year'.

He mimes typing. 'It's all bureaucratic.' In a Nunavut community, I meet with several women and, with permission, tape our discussions. When I return to the tape, I realise that they spoke in order of age, with the oldest speaking first. I do not know if this was intentional or if the oldest person was also the most outspoken. I have changed the names (except for my own).

Elisapee: There has never been any complaint about the discs. I didn't like the second name I was given. But I had no choice but to get this name. That's the way it was. We had no choice. That's a complaint we have. Most people had a choice of *which* last name they were given. The way I got my name was my husband's parents were by that name, so my husband was given that last name. So that was it.

Valerie: Did all the women get the men's names?

Elisapee: As long as they were married they got the husbands' names.

Valerie: Is that a good reason not to get married? [joking].

Geela: Still the same today. A lot of unmarried people keep their same family names. It hasn't changed since then.

Valerie: There's more freedom than in marriage …

They laugh, followed by a chorus of 'ehhhh' (Inuktitut for 'yes'). I have understood something. There are many smiles.

Malaya: Especially here. There's hardly any marriages at all.

Valerie: There are fewer marriages in the south now, too.

We talk about these changes. They tell me that missionaries in the early days insisted on marriage. I ask if all of the visitors have made a difference in how people give names, and if they still follow the traditions.

Elisapee: This hasn't changed since we can remember. We still follow the traditional names.

Alice: A lot of times young children are called by the name of the grandfather or something. But on their birth certificates it'll name another name. Like for example myself. I'm not named after anybody in particular [referring to her Qallunaaq name] but a lot of people call me by another name which is of a dead person [her real Inuit *sauniq* name].

Valerie: Was that the name given to you when you were born?

Alice: Yes.

Valerie: So that's the real one.

Alice: Ehhh. The way it is, is – a child will be baptised with the names – Billy or something – but his name Billy would be on the birth certificate, but around town he would be known as somebody else, as the name of a dead person.

Valerie: But it won't go on the birth certificate.

Alice: It won't go on any record at all. But he *will* be known as another name. It's still followed today. Like right now my own baby is named by three different names which aren't going to be on his birth certificate.

Valerie: When you have a baby, who makes the decision about how it's named, about who it's going to be named for?

Elisapee: It used to be the mother's responsibility. Any name the mother wanted would go. These days it's between the husband and the wife. They agree on a name. My oldest daughter was named by my grandfather. But all my other children I named myself. All except one, which I told my husband, 'This baby, you're gonna' name him.' But the name my husband thought of I didn't like, so I had to find another name for him 'cause my husband didn't want to name him anymore because I didn't like the only name he could think of.

Valerie: What happens when you have the same name – real name – as another person?

Alice: There's a special name for it. It's *atiquruq*. It means that you have the same name. *Quruq* is something good. You share a good name.

Valerie: It's nice if you're friends. What happens if it's someone you don't like so much. (They laugh.)

Elisapee: It's just the same as not being friends. When Sallie meets with another Sallie on the road – when they meet on the road they're more than friendly. They seem more close because their names are the same.

Valerie: I have a friend Valerie; it's like that too, except we don't have a name for it.

They ask how to say my name, find 'Valerie' tricky and settle for 'Alia', which is closer to Inuktitut. When they ask about my 'real name' it gets complicated. I explain that a few years ago, I took my own last name. They immediately find a connection.

> *Alice*: It's like Meeka's last name ... she's not named after her husband's grandfather but her husband's grandmother instead, because they didn't like her husband's last name.

I first met Etoangat at his home in Pangnirtung. Qallunaat sometimes call him Etoangat Aksaiyuk – spelled 'Aksayook' by the organisers of the exhibit at Angmarlik Centre, cited in the Bibliography. He was then in his mid-eighties, and would live for another decade. He had a special and wonderful mix of dignity and humour, both in conversation and in his ways of dealing with Qallunaat authorities and programmes.

> My real name is Etoangat but my other name is after my step father. So I'm known on paper as Aksaiyuk. But I don't use it. Everybody calls me Etoangat. Some other people in my family were given another name.

He takes out a very old Bible and a certificate of baptism. There is a mistake on the certificate. 'I was born in 1901 but it says 1906. I think the government knows about the mistake.' In the Bible, it says he was baptised at Blacklead Island, 'way on the other side of Cumberland Sound. When the birth certificates were being put together it seemed like they were doing the right thing. Not making mistakes'. His corrected Certificate of Baptism is labelled 'Diocese of the Arctic, Church of England in Canada, 1901'. The Bible, dated 1927, carries the inscription, 'translated into Baffinland Eskimo'. The certificate also contains the note: 'parents not recorded'. 'The church didn't know who my original parents were. When they died I was adopted.' Neither his birth parents nor his adoptive family is recorded. According to Inuit custom, adoptive parents are as authentic as birth parents.

> Whoever wrote those up did it sitting by himself! (much laughter). Originally all names on birth certificates were done by the RCMP but then they decided that some of them might be wrong so they changed them. They interviewed all the old people ... starting asking us to remember as far as we could remember back. So I told stories of when I was a child as far back as I could remember. From that they came up with a date. Five years wrong. I was born before Christianity was brought here – when there were shamans. Before anybody knew anything about preachers or anything like that. When I was very young, Christianity was slowly coming up here. There were a lot of people opposing Christianity and wanting to stay with shamanism. But I was brought up as a Christian so I don't mind it at all. I'm not really a devout Christian ... not orthodox ... My wife had a powerful grandfather who was

the boss. He did the naming. He was a real hunter, a real good hunter and that put him way up in society. I grew up with meat always there. I was never hungry.

I've never been given a white man's name. Aksaiyuk was still not a white man's name. It's my name. It's nobody else's name.

He did not mind disc numbers because he found them helpful if there was a misunderstanding between Inuit and Qallunaat, such as a problem with two people having the same name.

The way it used to be was most people were named after people who had passed away. A person that passed away, even though he wasn't a relative of yours, your child could take that person's name. And when the birth registration got started we kept going with the naming from deceased people but we would put a different name on the birth certificate. I think second names are really necessary ... as long as they are traditional names. Like names of people who have passed on. There would be confusion now with so many people, and there's only so many people that died. I like having traditional last names because it identifies the families and households and helps identify what the family represents.

He asks if I have a husband. (No, but I have two children.) He will call me if he finds a good husband. 'But only if you can live on seal meat' (more laughter). Etoangat (figure 4.2) is an artist and a hunter. Following his own playful style, I ask if it costs more for a husband than a carving. 'Carvings are more expensive. Stone lasts longer than people.'

Alison Smythe (Qallunaaq), health care worker in her late twenties (name changed to protect her anonymity): There's a child who was adopted out who got two health care numbers, one for each name. (She laughs.)

Ms Smythe's dismissive laughter was typical of some of the younger professionals, among Qallunaat I encountered. Like some of the others, she had no interest in trying to correct the errors or help the recipients of those errors to get them corrected. One of the early surprises was the discovery of more RCMP officers than other professionals who were dedicated to collaborating more than colonising, and had taken greater care to educate themselves. I had mistakenly assumed that teachers, doctors, nurses, social workers and others in the helping professions would automatically be more involved in the communities and more collaboratively inclined. All of us are on a steep learning curve.

The academics are a mix. On one flight North I met an American scientist who expressed surprised delight at the improvement in his research in recent years. For years he had studied northern conditions only in summer. Although he still came North only in warmer months, his research team had grown and changed. In the old days he came with

Figure 4.2 Etoangat, Pangnirtung, 1985.
Photograph by Valerie Alia.

Qallunaat students and colleagues, who also travelled only in summer. Now, he was required to include Inuit in Nunavut-based research projects. I was shocked that *he* was shocked to discover that 'scientific knowledge' was furthered by having a multicultural, multidisciplinary team, some of whose members lived in Nunavut year-round, were able to consult other Inuit in Inuktitut and to understand oral and written information inaccessible to Qallunaat scientists. Not only that, their year-round presence meant they were able to study conditions unavailable to their Qallunaat drop-in colleagues. I found it hard to believe he hadn't thought of this before. I have found that attitudes (and possibly, hiring practices) seem to have improved in the past decade or so, though old attitudes die hard. One major difference is that more Inuit are in leadership positions in the schools, health centres, social service centres and other offices.

Jonathan Karpik (not his real name), a well-educated Inuk professional in his early thirties: I remember when we didn't have last names. I went to sleep [Jonathan Maniapik] and woke up [Jonathan Karpik]. Abe Okpik came through and everything changed. Abe went around changing names. Traditionally there was no limit on how many people could have the same name. Reincarnation is very important. The person named has the same characteristics as the dead person. Sometimes there's even a scar. My son has a birthmark in the same place as the person he's named after. Abe's defensive now and says he'd support people who want to re-change their names.

Jose Kusugak, Inuk political leader: A child was named somebody-or-other, and the child gets really sickly and is about to die. Then they change the name of the child to another person, and the child will miraculously be cured. We're not talking about yesteryear; we're talking about today.

My original name was Amauyuk. As a matter of fact, it was Amauyuk E3917 ...

Mick Mallon, Qallunaaq educator who, with his wife and colleague, Alexina Kublu, specialises in teaching Inuktitut: ... I first started out in Povungnituk ... I was a teacher, but I also had to do administration. When a baby was born, I had this little pile of disc numbers, and the father and mother would come along; the birth certificate would be issued; and ... people would give me one English name and one Inuktitut name. I had the brilliant idea of saying to the father, 'Why don't we give him a *third* name ... which would be your name? Then, everybody will be able to keep track of who's whose father.'

I must admit that I didn't know anything about all of this that [Kublu has] taught me. People were very nice to me ... [they] would come into my office – into my living room – with two names for the child, and they'd go out from my office (usually; one or two people said no) with three names for the child, plus the next disc in order as I put my hand in the drawer. I did try to keep them in order, so in a way you could find out the order of people's birth.

So every Inuk – sorry, we're going back in time; every *Eskimo* – in those days had his own disc number, which was kind of like a little stamp on the forehead, which was indelible. (Alia 1995: 6)

Alexina Kublu, Inuk educator and linguist: When disc numbers were first handed out they were given by family grouping. My oldest brother was already born at the time they dished those numbers out, so my father being E5456 and my mother E5457, my brother was E5458. But then they were given ... as they [children] were being born. So, being E51287, I knew that the person with E51286 was the person born just before me ... We used to have fun, as kids, trying to remember people by their disc numbers. It was just a game. (Alia 1995: 6)

George Quviq Qulaut, Igloolik and Nunavut leader ('E5' refers to the prefix E, for Eastern Arctic and 5, for Igloolik) *and Valerie Alia:*

GQQ: When Project Surname came in, we had disc numbers. Mine was E51285 ... my disc number or my dog number. But, seriously, for some strange reason I had carried it with pride ... At that time I didn't know what was going on. But later on, when I started thinking about it, I thought, 'I feel like a dog or something'. But then I accepted it and adapted it. And to make it easier and just not to forget what they had done to us, I built a house [for] my mother and with her permission I put a number of the house, E5777. That was her disc number. Because we had to put house numbers. Whether I was proud of it or not, I wasn't sure. But it became something more personal; the number itself became more personal.

VA: By putting it on the house you took it over?

GQQ: Yes.

VA: How did other people in Igloolik see the numbers?

GQQ: Some are very happy to get rid of it. Some would make a mockery of it. They would do something, like, if they want to put a number on their boat or their skidoo, they use the E5 number. It's also used on combination locks.

Keith Crowe, Qallunaaq northern historian and former northern administrator who is a fluent Inuktitut speaker: I just got a letter one day from ... Ottawa, asking me if I would approach the Inuit of Cumberland Sound and ask them if they would adopt surnames, for general administrative convenience ... I talked it over ... we had a kind of impromptu council ... with Etoangat and Kilabuk, of course (who was in on just about everything) and maybe some of the older camp leaders. They said, 'Okay, we'll pass the word around'.
All I really did was sit back and – they arrived on my desk ... one way or another. As far as I know, it was all really done on a family basis. At that time people were living in camps that had anything from three to ... twelve families – all pretty well closely related ... We formed a little committee to decide on the spelling and so on; we sat up a long time and thrashed out these spellings – which were never adhered to ... I came up with this whole list of finished spellings, which everyone agreed to. A few years later I went back to find ... they were all being spelled the way people heard them again. (Alia 1995: 8)

The term 'disc list' persists despite the obsolescence of disc numbers. An RCMP officer, an Inuk woman from Baffin and a Qallunaaq art historian from Ontario all told me the disc system worked better than the surnames, despite its negative connotations. Neither system was able to prevent the loss of large numbers of Inuit during medical evacuations of the 1940s and 1950s. Until the mid-1950s there was no formal programme established to maintain contact among family members involved in the evacuations. Children and adults were sent south, most often to hospital to be treated for tuberculosis, and many people never found their homes or families again. It happened in Martha Flaherty's family:

My number was E91900. But when you're in a family, it doesn't go by E91900, E91001, E91902 – it doesn't go by that. The next child in that region ... will have E91901, but it's not your family. Disc numbers had a lot of negative impact on Inuit – for me anyway. We lost my sister for close to five years; we didn't know where she was. We were relocated to Grise Fiord from Northern Quebec. When we were relocated to Grise Fiord, we had to drop her off somewhere south because she had TB [tuberculosis].
After, I think, three years, because the government didn't know where we were – they thought we were somewhere up North; they weren't even sure – they sent my sister to Inukjuaq, which is northern Quebec. She stayed there for a year while the government was trying to find out where we went. A year later, they sent her to Resolute Bay, thinking we were there – because they

couldn't find us – so she spent another year there. Later, she finally came home. My parents were very frustrated. I remember them being very worried about where my sister was; they didn't know whether she was alive or dead. They didn't even have proper records of us. (Alia 1995: 7)

Members of the younger generation are turning the sadness and frustration experienced in Martha Flaherty's family to irony, anger and determination to create their own future. In recent years, two albums by Inuk singer-songwriters use disc numbers as a motif. In 1999 Susan Aglukark released *Unsung Heroes*. A beautifully photographed booklet accompanies the CD. Its pages are ringed with countless disc numbers in soft grey print: 'E-0224 E-0225 E-0226', and so forth. Two pages contain photographs of discs, showing the side that features the text: 'Eskimo Identification Canada' circling the British crown. One of the songs is titled 'E186'

Naasautaa …
Stole your name E186

Generations come and go
You can't wipe away what's written in the soul
And history comes and goes
You can change what's written
But you can't change the course

Naasautaa …
Worn that chain E186.
Naasautaa …
Stole your name E186
… changes can be the fall
If you define people with a number on a chain
…
So go on as unsung heroes
Don't let chains hold you
…
History's shame E186 …
Stole your name E186 …
Naasautaa
It's not your shame E186. (Aglukark and Irschick 1999)

In 2002 Lucie Idlout released an album titled *E5–770, My Mother's Name*. The CD itself is designed as an expanded photocopy of that disc, coloured in the reddish-brown of the original discs – a colour that is repeated on the pages of the accompanying booklet. On one page, a striking black-and-white photograph of the artist is heavily washed in the red-brown of the identity discs, linking Lucie Idlout with her mother's government-imposed identity. The title song, 'E5–770' is delivered in a rush of fury, relentlessly paced and presented in a deep, rough-edged voice that – for all its kindred content – is worlds away from Aglukark's gentler, lyrical 'country' singing style (Idlout 2002).

The surnaming programme resolved neither the indignities nor the administrative difficulties created by the disc numbers. In 1985 in one Baffin community I visit, each record keeping office – school, nursing station, RCMP, government headquarters – has its own spelling for each Inuk's name and sometimes a different spelling for the surname of an individual's family. The more communities grow, the harder this becomes. It is impossible to compile an alphabetical list or an accurate telephone directory; the 'same' name was spelled Qappiq, Karpik and Karpiq on different lists. Some people tell me the authorities ignore or override their decisions about their own family names. A nurse in her mid-thirties reports: 'We have twins who are seven years apart on their birth certificates.' I ask why, since she knows about the discrepancy, she has not corrected the error. She gives me a vaguely amused look and replies: 'They're young, and they know they're twins.' Asked if she will fix the mistake, she replies breezily: 'It's up to the family.' I wonder what will happen to the twins at school, and later when it becomes time for them to receive old-age benefits. I no longer wonder why so many Inuit have told me people do not like to ask for medical help, especially at night. In several communities, I hear stories which reflect two extremes: doctors and nurses are spoken of with affection and respect, or with fear. They are seen either as warm and caring, or as cold and intimidating. None of the stories are about people in-between. I suspect that this means one of two things: either health care workers fall into two extremes, or the middle-of-the-road ones don't merit storytelling. A Qallunaaq RCMP officer in his fifties has a very different attitude:

> I've spent all my life in the communities. I see a need for more cross-cultural awareness among my colleagues. I grew up in the North. My father was a [occupation]. I spent a lot of time learning about Inuit attitudes and traditions. It's a matter of respect, and usefulness. If you're going to do your job you have to be, almost an anthropologist. You have to learn about how people feel, learn about the culture. I've been asked to mediate family disputes – like how to decide about an adoption – when the families are having trouble and want someone who knows enough, but is an Outsider.

He said ethnocentric and racist attitudes in Canada parallel those of South Africa under apartheid (a view later voiced by Inuit and other Aboriginal leaders and used strategically in national and international negotiation). A Qallunaaq in her mid-forties recalled:

> In Pond Inlet, when a son was adopted out, the order of his names was reversed; they just reversed the names. Maybe later they would drop the

second name and take a new one. Inuit seem to be evolving a semi-secret/secret naming [system] with respect to white society. You still see some marriages which are prearranged from birth.

One lively interview ends in an invitation: 'Stay with us next time.' Sharing birthing stories and other tales of women's lives, it is hard to remember that there was ever a language barrier, or that these are not women I have known for many years. At least one Qallunaaq reversed the cross-cultural dialogue and changed her European name in a way she felt would conform more closely to the Inuit way. Georgia, 'the qallunaaq with one name', is a writer, baker, missionary and community organiser who has lived in the North for decades. She was living in Repulse Bay in 1972 when the last stage of Project Surname was completed. She heard much talk in the community of the need to take additional names. 'I went to court and had my name changed to just Georgia because traditionally – and at that time – the people used just one name' (Edgar 1989). As a newcomer to the North, she told me she felt the change should be in the other direction – that she should express respect for Inuit traditions, rather than imposing Qallunaaq ways on them.

Criticisms of the politics, logistics and effects of Project Surname began soon after its completion. Father Rousselière, who would become one of Project Surname's most outspoken critics, began with a gentle warning:

> For several years, many have been advocating the suppression of [the number] system claiming that it recalled ... the army, the jail or the concentration camp, that it is a manifestation of racial discrimination. They insist on all Eskimos being obliged to have a surname. Several years ago ... a first step in that direction had been made in the schools by giving children their father's name ... sometimes changing last or first names when they were thought to be too complicated. Two years ago [in 1969] the government decided to assign to the Eskimos a surname, the choice of which was left to the heads of families, and a specially appointed official travelled through all the Eskimo villages ... That campaign met with some obstacles. (Rousselière 1971: 12)

The 'obstacles' included variations in spelling. Inuit in the Eastern Arctic 'and in Protestant surroundings' (most Inuit were Anglican) 'have only a Christian name, generally borrowed from the Moravian translation of the Bible'. He cautioned that 'embarrassing situations' might arise from the naming of children of Inuit mothers and Qallunaaq fathers after their fathers 'even if they have never been legitimatised'. This was a 'problem' only in Qallunaat Christian terms, not in terms of Inuit practice. He wisely cautioned government to pay attention to Inuit naming traditions, citing Knud Rasmussen and Svend Frederiksen, who 'have underlined the importance of the name, considered as the soul, in the traditional

Eskimo ideology. It would be regrettable if such a fact was not taken into consideration'. Indeed, it was not.

> If the Eskimo must absolutely adopt a surname *for the benefit of the bureaucrats,* why could he not keep as an intermediary name – *recognized by the Vital Statistics* – his own Eskimo name? … A fairly amusing coincidence! It is precisely at the time when a move is afoot to rid the Eskimos of their registration numbers that a social security number is bestowed on each one of the whites in the North West Territories. Let us wager that few objectors will be found! (Rousselière 1971: 12–13)

This crucial point, which Father Rousselière raised as a postscript, never saw the light of day. The question no one asked was why someone did not simply convert the disc numbers to Social Insurance numbers, and leave Inuit names alone. That process could have taken place in an office, at minimal cost to taxpayers and minimal cost to Inuit culture. Father Rousellière objected on many grounds. In 1972, after the renaming project was completed, he wrote:

> The results are known: lists have been submitted; everyone received a birth certificate. A word describes the situation almost everywhere: it is a real mess …
> 1. Why did not the Government instruct a local Eskimo to carry out an investigation in each place? There were certainly almost everywhere men who could have done it at a much lesser cost to the Government.
> 2. Why was not the standardised spelling adopted, at least in the East, since the Government spent tens, nay hundreds of thousands of dollars in its development? Such spelling may not be perfect; at least, it is a logical system …
> If it is objected that the Eskimos chose their surnames freely, we will reply that a choice implies an alternative. Well, where is the alternative when an Eskimo has always seen his name wrongly spelt? When anyone is given a new tool, he is properly instructed in its use. The Latin alphabet was imposed on the Eskimos and most of them have never heard an explanation as to how they should use it. The result is a complete fiasco. (Rousselière 1972, no page number)

Apparently he thought the process was already too far gone (or its conclusion too foregone) to allow a revision of approach.

> We do not question the good will nor the competence of the civil servant entrusted with the task of drawing up the lists of names. However, what could he do within a few days, in a village where the inhabitants were totally unknown to him? It had been agreed that he would return to each place and check all the names. However, the Government was in too great a hurry, wishing apparently to rid the Eskimos of their administrative numbers in 1970, the Centennial Year of the North-West Territories, through a sort of Slave Emancipation Act!! … As a matter of fact, the ensuing situation is worse now than it was formerly – G.M.R. (Rousellière 1972, no page number)

Cleaning up the Mess: the Aftermath

The errors resulting from Project Surname left Inuit with an obstacle course of red tape and expense. It was not until the Nunavut government was in place at the end of the twentieth and the start of the twenty-first century that people finally were able to begin seeking corrections. Back in the 1980s, getting the errors corrected involved both difficulty and expense, as shown by the following extract (the grammatical and syntactical errors are in the original):

> BIRTH REGISTRATION
> … In a lot of cases they put down as single women even if the woman is married. When that happens the records will show that the child doesn't have a legitimate father and they'll put down mother's maiden name as the child's last name. And if the parents want the surname of the father, if the child is over a year old then they would have to go through change of name and that can cost quite a bit. (Kilabuk-Bourassa 1985)

In our conversations in Greenland and Nunavut in the late 1980s and 1990s, Abe admitted there were problems. Instead of clarifying family relationships and community records, the renaming had confused them further. He told me he had approached the Justice of the Peace about the possibility of having people re-register their names. 'They feel that they're losing identity. We need to revitalise something that they did long ago and did wrong, to make it more simple to understand … Because after a certain time of life your identity becomes just another bureaucrat paper.'

A Baffin educator attributed the 'horrendous situation' less to the mood of the 1960s than to southerners who continued to see the North 'as a warehouse: you go in and you get out'. The attitude persists. In Ottawa in 1987, a young lawyer on his way North said, 'I'm planning to go North for a couple of years so I can make my mistakes before I practice down here.' In the mid-1980s, nearly twenty years after disc numbering had ended, an RCMP officer told me that the list of community members was still known as 'the disc list'. Old labels die hard. In his introduction to the first (1981) edition of the Inuit Artists Biography Project, Michael Neill protested the replacement of the disc number system with the new surnames.

> The naming of a child was very important … a person did not just decide to change his name arbitrarily … A child leaving the community to attend school could have a parent's name added. Consistently teachers would refuse to use a person's proper name, opting instead to use the baptised name. A female might have a husband's name added for identification by a local (usually not native) administrator. Nicknames were occasionally used in 'official' lists. (Neill 1984: 7–8)

In one of several conversations in Toronto, in the 1980s and early 1990s, Neill told me: 'you could identify someone at a distance and it didn't interfere with local usage. It was a clear identity and Inuit had a clear understanding of what it was for. Project Surname meant an ending to the cultural orientation of the name. The thing that concerns me is, it's another corner knocked off the culture; and how many corners can you knock off before it becomes another culture?'

Gender, Culture and Community

While continuing the Inuit naming traditions, Napatchie has adapted them to the cultural diversity of her family and community.

> My oldest is seventeen. His first name is Patrick ... that's the name I picked, 'cause he was born on St. Patrick's Day. But traditionally he's named after my dad's cousin, who died not too long before Patrick was born. A lot of Inuit people say that if a baby has been born ... if he started crying ... for no reason ... we know that that person who passed away, even after the baby was born, probably wants to be named through that baby. So a lot of babies are named after the person who has died, even after the baby was born. And they would stop crying and we would know that person wanted to be among the family ... named with that baby. My youngest daughter, we named her Kirsten, but she uses her middle name more often ... because that's the way she acts – she's got the personality of that person that we named her after – Ninyurapiq, and she prefers Ninyurapiq to her English name.

The Pangnirtung elder, Kudlu Pitseolak (see figure 2.5), in her mid-eighties when we spoke, provided a woman's perspective on the identification programmes and their relation to Inuit naming. Her account makes it clear that traditional ways of naming persisted throughout and despite the various efforts of Qallunaat to bring in their own beliefs and agendas. 'I was baptised by Reverend Peck as Malaiya at one time. But a person by the name of Kudlu who was my relative died before I was born. So I got Kudlu instead of Malaiya and kept Kudlu instead of Malaiya ever since.' There was no conflict of priorities: when her namesake became known, her family reverted to the traditional way of *sauniq* naming and left the missionary-given name behind.

> In the old days we concentrated on survival. We didn't care about things like birth certificates. Before when I was living in the camp we would look in the Bible for good names for our children. That's how we would get the names – from the Bible. My husband and I would agree on a name. When Project Surname came, my husband left town along with some of the other hunters, with some of the art that they had made to sell. And when he came back he

called 'hey, guess what? I just got a last name!' So my husband told me that we would be having a second name of his father. He was Pitseolak, the name of his father. So we were amazed at how we would have two names. How could I be named another name while my husband was still alive? I didn't like this. The women weren't involved at all, only the men ... Because Abe Okpik was a man, he worked with the men. (Alia 1994)

Kudlu was not the only person who was dissatisfied with the surname project. Elise Attagutaluk, who was stunned to receive a birth certificate with her *husband's* surname on it, was one of the first people to attempt to address the problems. In 1985 she presented a resolution to the Annual General Meeting of Pauktuutit (Inuit Women's Association):

RESOLUTION #85–15
Many Inuit in the Northwest Territories have been obliged under Project Surname to have erroneous last names. They now are forced to pay money to change their names as a result of government incompetence.
BE IT RESOLVED THAT: the federal and Territorial Governments set up a programme to support Inuit in the Northwest Territories to have their surnames changed back to the real names of their families.
AND THAT: the necessary costs in legally changing these surnames be fully assumed by the governments.
MOVED BY: Elise Attagutaluk
SECONDED BY: Leonie Qrunnut. (Alia 1994)

The requirement that Inuit pay the costs of legal name changes to correct Project Surname's errors was a less sinister echo of the requirement in Germany that Jews pay the government for the 'privilege' of receiving acceptable German names. Those who could not afford the higher fees paid less, and often received derogatory names (*Toronto Star* 1991).

Continuing, Reclaiming, and Reasserting Culture: Inuit Perspectives

The resolution passed. Its cause was taken up by others, among them Peter Irniq, who changed his name legally from *Ernerk* to reflect its proper pronunciation. A long-time advocate of cultural continuity and respect for naming traditions, he clarified his own position:

Inuit had several names from, since time immemorial. When the missionaries came, they gave us Christian names. Peter ... was not the chosen name for me by my parents; it was a chosen name for me by a priest who baptised me in 1947. (Alia 1984–2006)

When I was growing up in Repulse Bay, I was known by two names, Peter Ernerk and Peter Erneck. That was depending on who you talked to. If it was the Hudson's Bay Company, it was Ernerk; when I was about to go to school in Chesterfield Inlet, they knew me as Ernerk, that was by the Roman Catholic Church. The school records show that I was Erneck at the Residential School. Then, for a time, I was known as Peter E3–546. And only the baptismal name [Peter] and the number. Then, Project Surname came along. We had to have family surnames, like all the other Canadians. This is just so … 'Eskimos could be part of the main stream of the Canadian Society.' But, the Project Surname was ten years too early, when we Inuit were just beginning to have our say in our own life … I never felt right about the spelling of my own name. So … I decided to do something about it in Nunavut. You know what, Nunavut listened. (Irniq 2000)

In 2000 a new law review committee called Maligarnik Qimirruijiit was formed in Nunavut. Among their assigned tasks is a review of the effects of Project Surname and implementation of legal correction of some of the errors. Peter Irniq has campaigned for this for many years and is gratified to see it 'finally becoming a reality' (Irniq 2000; Spitzer 2000)). Another project spurred by Peter Irniq is the current effort to name the Inuit in the photographs mentioned earlier, which reside in Canada's National Archive. They were taken between 1920 and 1950, mainly by visitors to the North. The photographers were missionaries, travellers and explorers, traders, doctors, National Film Board camera people and others. They rarely recorded the names of the people whose images they brought home, and sometimes publicly distributed. Peter Irniq proposed that Inuit studying in Ottawa be engaged to bring copies of the images back home and work with elders to identify the anonymised individuals. 'The results were unexpected and moving. Many hundreds of individuals were identified. In one case a young student, Tommy Akulukjuk, was told that a middle-aged man, smiling at the camera, perhaps because he had just been fitted with spectacles, was his great-grandfather' (Conlogue 2004: R4).

George Quviq Qulaut is equally determined to help keep Inuit naming traditions – and the people who carry the names – alive.

> Two or three years after my father's death Project Surname came along and it was very hard for us … It was very hard for me to say my father's name, it was so recent ago that he had passed away; it was very emotional … not only for myself but for my mother and my sister.

His family agreed to take a surname but respected the customary taboos by avoiding actually using the name for several years. Peter Irniq also discussed this tension between the new surnames and traditional avoidance taboos.

> You are forced to say the names and it makes you feel very uncomfortable. Some people's names, you can never say them at all, even alone [because] if they could hear you through the spirits, they would be insulted if they knew that you had mentioned their name. We would never use those as surnames.

His oldest daughter carries the name of an elder who passed away a few months before she was born, and was also named after George's father. Like many Inuit, she carries the names of female and male relatives because 'all Inuktitut names are unisex ... there is no woman name or man's name. It works well'. His commitment to continuing the culture is strengthened by his knowledge that he himself almost lost it.

> At the age of ten I couldn't speak my language, Inuktitut. My culture was completely gone. In order to be with my parents I had to re-learn the whole thing ... I had no one to talk to. The only people that spoke Inuktitut were my parents and the only person who spoke English was my grandfather. I went back home and played with the children and relearned the pronunciation and the whole system. (Alia 1984–2006)

Kiviaq was born at his parents' camp, near Chesterfield Inlet. When his family was brought south to Alberta, he was renamed 'David Ward' and given a birth certificate with that name on it. Now a lawyer in Edmonton, he had to petition the province of Alberta for the right to restore his original Inuktitut name. He finally won back his birthright in 2001, having had to fight the province's name laws. Because Alberta law requires that each individual have a given name and a surname, his application was rejected. He appealed. Government Services Minister David Coutts granted the request, saying,

> Your current legal name [David Ward] marks your loss of contact with the community of your birth. You wish now to formally reassert this personal connection to your culture by taking the name you were given when you were born. This gives your application to take a single name a unique cast. (Weber 2001)

On celebrating the decision, Kiviaq said, 'I feel so different you can hardly believe it. I am me. I am not a figment of somebody's imagination who said, "We'll give him a white name. We'll make him a white person"' (Weber 2001). Although obviously well-intentioned, the reporter for the *Edmonton Journal* got the story only half right, apparently basing his information more on assumptions than research. He understood that 'naming carries a political charge for the Inuit'. He informs readers that each Inuk was given 'a metal disc with a number on it' and that 'surnames were restored in the early 1970s' ... (Weber 2001). In fact, the discs were not metal, but fibre, and there was no such restoration of surnames. He seems to have missed the point of his own story: no surnames were 'restored' because Inuit had no surnames. By moving south long before Project Surname, Kiviaq should have escaped being renamed. Having landed in a province that had legislated surnaming, he in effect fell victim to his own private surname project.

Some people question the traditional practices and choose not to follow all of them. An Inuk of about thirty said:

> I could never say this to my family or friends, but I'm against the traditional way of giving people names. It puts such a burden on the kids. Makes them think they're supposed to *be* the person they're named after. They need a chance to be *themselves* and like themselves for who they are. I know it's not a popular view, but it's what I think. I don't like the idea of telling children they *are* their namesake. I've been thinking it's a lot to put on a little kid – to be told they're someone else. It's a lot of responsibility. You have to find a way to get your grandfather or grandmother reborn – find a kid to give the name to. It's a lot of pressure on the family all around. (Alia 1984–2006)

It is not just Inuit who take Qallunaat names. Some Qallunaat are adopting Inuit names and ways of naming.

> I notice that Qallunaat are starting to name their children … after Inuit. It's like they're saying, 'We approve of your culture; I like your culture; I like your people; I like your language. That's why I'm naming my child after your people.' (Deborah Evaluardjuk in Alia 1995: 19)

The French anthropologists Bernadette and Pierre Robbe study naming traditions among Kalaallit (Greenlandic Inuit). After years of collaboration and friendship, their family and the families of Kalaallit have become closely and permanently intertwined. When their first child was born, they decided to give her the name of a hunter, Yanu, who had been a close friend of Pierre's and had recently died.

> I sent a telegram to Greenland to say, 'We have a girl and we have given her this name'; they answered, by telegram too, that they were very happy to know that Yanu was born in our family. Then we went back to Greenland, the summer after that. We were with our daughter … the sister of [Yanu] was very, very happy, because he was living in France [in the person of the Robbe's daughter]. It was a new kind of life, without ice – without dangers … She said, 'I am very happy because now he will not have the risk of going through the ice'.
>
> Some years after, we were once more in Greenland with her. At this time there were still kayaks in the village. Our daughter saw a kayak … and she made some [mimicking gestures]. And the sister of the man – she became the sister of our daughter through the name – said, 'Oh, she wants to kayak'. After that, she asked her husband to build a kayak. He did it. He spent more than one week making this kayak of wood, skin and with every artefact on it. It was very, very hard work … and only because the sister of the name thought that, because our daughter had made these gestures … It has very strong meaning.

People used to say, 'Names don't die'. The name is something which is always living. (Pierre Robbe in Alia 1995: 19)

Inuit are finding ways to balance old and new ways of naming and Inuit and Qallunaat conventions in their contemporary, sometimes multicultural lives. The main thing is that it is their choice, and not whatever government programme may be fashionable at the moment. In 1995, Martha Flaherty, then president of Pauktuutit (Inuit Women's Association) addressed the annual Inuit Studies Conference, which was being held in Nunavut for the first time:

> During a couple of annual meetings, we have discussed the topic of kinship in the North, of the Inuit people. I think this is only a tip of the problem in the North. I think it's very important that we deal with the whole situation ... not just ... surnaming of the Inuit people but also the kinship of the Inuit. And I think this should be dealt with by the real people of the communities. [One of the objectives of the Nunavut Final Agreement is] 'to encourage self-reliance and cultural and social well-being of Inuit.' I think this ... is perhaps much more important than the land ownership rights and billion dollars Inuit receive as compensation. If we cannot preserve our culture and our dignity as Inuit throughout this process, we will not survive as a people.
>
> Some of you might dismiss this remark of mine, and think ... that I don't know how valuable land ownership, our own government and our compensation package can be. I can only remind you that power and wealth are meaningless if they are misused and the spirit of our people is broken. (Alia 1995: 21)

Rachel Attituq Qitsualik is a Nunavut journalist who is skilled at translating between generations and cultures. Born into a traditional Igloolik family, she has focused on Inuit sociopolitical issues for the past twenty-five years. In a piece titled 'Playing Cowboys and Inuit', she explores the ramifications of multicultural identities and lives:

> ... my nephews are part Inuit, part Chippewa. Under the Canadian Constitution, they are termed 'Aboriginal' ... So which rights do they have? Their father's? Their mother's? ... to what degree do their descendants have to be one or the other? My grandfather was part Cree on my mother's side ... does the fact that my father was half white dilute our rights, even though culturally he was 100 percent Inuit? let's say I moved to Alaska ... [or] ... from Alaska to Canada. What rights do I lose, and what rights do I take on? Who determines that? The American government? The Canadian government? ... These are only a few questions, and already the thought of them makes me feel more like a specimen than a person ...
>
> 'No, we're not called "Eskimos" anymore.' ... How did it happen that Inuit came to need an instruction manual on how to be 'Inuit'? Despite the criticism sometimes leveled at it, I'm pleased at the progress toward Inuit self-definition. Labels can be a good thing – but only when one is

empowered to label oneself as desired. Perhaps one day it will be Inuit who state what 'Inuit' are, and all that such a label entails. One of my little nephews was once heard to say while playing Cowboys and Indians, "I'm not an Inuk or an Indian. I'm a cowboy." I guess that makes me the cowboy's aunt. Can I be a cowgirl? *Pijariiqpunga.* (That's all I have to say on the subject.) (Qitsualik 2003)

The comments which follow are from interviews and, in the case of John Amagoalik, a speech, recorded for the radio documentary, *Nunavut: Where Names Never Die* (Alia and Moss 1995).

> We started listening to our elders ... they don't want us to lose our culture, language, and our identity ... (Deborah Evaluardjuk)

> My identity is in that I am Peesee, named after my grandmother. I also have four other names that were given to me when I was born ... For a long time, I kept thinking, should I say Katherine is my name ... even though it's not – because everybody else has a *Qallunaatitut* name. But no, it's part of my identity that I am Peesee. (Peesee Pitseolak)

> I think many people in Nunavut, especially the Inuit, are going to reclaim their traditions in order to be stronger in life. I want to ... make sure that our names, our community names, are properly spelled ... so that they mean something fifty years from now. My ancestors left this land for us and we are borrowing it from our children and grandchildren, so we must do it right. We must leave those proper names the way they are, for them to remember. (Peter Irniq)

> In the schools [children are registered] with their given names in Inuktitut ... I don't think it's a matter of bringing it back: I don't think there was ever a time that it got lost. (Jose Kusugak)

> Inuit have experienced, over the years, a severe loss of pride and a crisis of identity ... We have a unique language, which is surviving incredible odds: wave upon wave of other languages have made it very difficult for our language to survive, because we're so small in numbers and others are so enormous ... people kept telling us, "You're going to be extinct. You're going to die in fifty years ... We decided to prove them wrong. (John Amagoalik, 'father of Nunavut')

Chapter 5

HOMELANDS AND DIASPORAS: CONCLUDING THOUGHTS ON THE POLITICS OF NAMING

Names and the Politics of Place

It is not just personal names that have deep meaning for Inuit. As George Kuvik Qulaut explained, 'Each one of our names means something, they all have meaning; geographical names are the same way.' Since 1972, Linna Weber and Ludger Müller-Wille have worked with Inuit elders and with Avataq Cultural Institute in Nunavik (northern Quebec) on mapping projects aimed at recording traditional place names. In the mid-1980s, Ludger Müller-Wille and this author were among the members of a team of Aboriginal and non-Aboriginal people who met in geographical names symposia with the Canadian Permanent Committee on Geographical Names to help correct, add and restore Aboriginal place names to Canada's official maps. Müller-Wille's view is that

> Place names are political symbols [they] are dynamic; they change, depending on who is in a place or region to name [the] spaces and places. So there are ... dimensions ... which we could call political identity. Inuit have put forward the claim that places that carry non-Inuit names should be changed back to the Inuit names that are being used by the local Inuit community ... I would say that place names are one element of personal identity. (Alia 1995)

The elders, most of whom were hunters, started from a place where they had camped and 'travelled' on the maps, following their travelling and hunting routes. They did not need maps to find these places. 'The maps were all in their heads. Through the oral tradition you have the names memorised ... and the sequence in which they appear ... and when you have this you can't possibly get lost.' There are traditional songs that record the places and their locations and special qualities. Some of the elders on the mapping project sang songs in which all of the place names of a given area were sung, in the sequence in which they were travelled. Place names contain important spiritual and environmental information.

> There are references to sacred sites [and] gravesites ... [and] references to spirits ... The names themselves contain warnings for hazards where there might be places on the lakes where there is always open water ... covered by snow ... They have warnings about bad water conditions, tidal conditions, wind conditions, information about places where you won't get good fish [or] a lake that might yield fish [that] are always skinny and no good to eat, so you better avoid it if you're hungry. Then there is all the good information: good places to fish, good places to hunt, what kind of animals are in those places, what kind of hunting methods are the best to use in that place. [It's] all in the names. (Weber in Alia 1995)

In traditional Inuit society land and person are almost inseparable; the world is divided not between persons and places but between named and unnamed things. The particular band or dialect group is often defined by a prefix followed by a common suffix, -*miut* ('the people of' or 'the inhabitants of'). 'Boundaries between the haunts of neighbouring groups are ... rather clearly formed – at least *in the minds* of the constituents – by the termination of place names relating to one group and the beginning of those of another' (Correll 1976: 173).

Keith Basso calls names 'a mnemonic peg on which to hang a social history '(Rassky 1988), a view extended by Mark Nuttall's observation that names show 'ownership by a person or group' but more importantly, 'establish power and Territorial claim'. (Nuttall 1992: 50). In the Unalakleet community Correll visited, he was told that each person had a personal name with a place-name counterpart 'somewhere in the surrounding country'. Place names were only spoken in the dialect of that group which was identified with the area. Speakers of one dialect who were visiting the territory of another dialect group used the host group's pronunciation of place names. One group taught the place names to children by chanting the names of topographic features in sequence as they occurred in nature.

> I've been intrigued for quite a long time ... I've remained of necessity an Outsider, and the North has remained for me a convenient place to dream about, spin tall tales about sometimes, and, in the end, avoid. (Gould 1971)

The pianist and broadcaster, Glenn Gould, was one of the Qallunaat who expressed a romantic and essentially fictional connection to the North. His famous radio documentary, *The Idea of North*, explored the strong identification of Canadians with the North – a 'North' more imagined than experienced by most Qallunaat. In 1995, when I finished my own radio documentary, *Nunavut: Where Names Never Die*, Lorne Tulk, the CBC genius who modestly and patiently brought his technical wizardry to the task of pulling it all together, gave me a set of tapes. Having moved to Canada a decade after its broadcast, I had neither heard nor heard *of* Glenn Gould's landmark series. Quietly, Lorne confessed to having performed his magic on Gould's series as well as mine. Gould brought to the public ear the centuries-long fascination of Canadians with 'their' North – a North less lived in than dreamed about, portrayed to this day by painters, dancers, explorers and musicians. Sherrill E. Grace analyses this motif of Canada's national identity in her book, *Canada and the Idea of North* (Grace 2001). The romantic visions serve sometimes to conceal the continuing invasions – seen most prominently today in the efforts of U.S., Canadian and European governments, corporations and individuals to exploit the potential of northern mining, oil and gas reserves, uranium, strategic positioning, and people. Inuit still struggle with the need to communicate the realities of the *inhabited* North to visitors and policy makers. Currently, they are publicising the effects of global warming and Arctic pollution.

Place names express and identify the Canadian landscape. Northern place names reflect the activities and travels of all of the residents and visitors. Over the centuries, visitors put their own names on places Inuit had known and named. Indigenous people have not always welcomed the renaming of their ancestral lands.

> Alexander Mackenzie came to our land. He described us in his Journal as a 'meagre, ill-made people ...' My people probably wondered at this strange, pale man in his ridiculous clothes, asking about some great waters he was searching for. He recorded his views on the people, but we'll never know exactly how my people saw him. I know they'd never understand why their river is named after such an insignificant fellow. (Kakfwi in Holmes 1989)

In the Western Arctic and sub-Arctic region comprising today's Northwest Territories, Dene peoples had called the river Dehcho long before it became known to others as the Mackenzie. In the Eastern Arctic the sixteenth-century explorer Martin Frobisher left his name on a body of water and a community that would later become the capital of Nunavut. When the official name of Frobisher Bay was changed to Iqaluit in 1987, the change reasserted Inuit sovereignty and removed the name of a visitor from the map and the mental landscape. It heralded bigger change to come: creation of the Canadian Territory named for the Inuit homeland, Nunavut ('our land'). The impression given by older maps, of a North more *visited* than *lived in*, has changed. Today's multilingual maps reveal the diversity of linguistic and cultural influences – and people. It is a more accurate picture, placing Inuktitut front and centre as befits a region whose population is 85 percent Inuit.

The Power of Place

> The colonial habit of place-naming reduces the landscape to an impersonal piece of territory ... awaiting 'discovery' ... empty ... Throughout northern Greenland there are places named after kings, queens, explorers ... Names ... indicate ownership by a person or group. More importantly, they establish power and territorial claim ... (Nuttall 1992: 50)

In *The Arctic Grail*, Pierre Berton makes two major errors: he assumes that Inuit never cared about seeing Inuktitut names on maps and he misses the political importance of mapping and naming. He laments the Inuit heroes whose names are hidden beneath those of Qallunaaq explorers, yet says 'Parry's name dominates, as no doubt it should' (1988: 637). He wants it both ways – dignity for Aboriginal peoples, supremacy for White explorers.

> What of Akaitcho ... without whose presence all would have perished? One searches the map in vain to find his name ... the haunts of the original people continued to bear the names of strangers – and still do today ... This didn't bother the originals ... Nor would it concern them for an instant that their names should be left off the maps of the Arctic. (Berton 1988: 630–31)

He could not be more wrong. There is no indication of which 'originals' he consulted, but the declaration that it 'is not their loss that the map ignores them; it is our own' implies that 'we' readers are non-Aboriginal. Did Berton really think that no Aboriginal people read books? Did he really think that maps are only for the inheritors of colonial treks across the land? As for Aboriginal people, it is indeed 'their' loss. The Aboriginal participants in the aforementioned geographical names symposia and the Inuit participants in elders' mapping projects said so many times. As Brody reminds us, 'A map is neither artefact nor romance. It is a political document, tied to past and present power relations, at the very centre of economic (land claims, etc.) and cultural progress' (Brody 1983). The geographical names symposia culminated in a set of resolutions that would forever change Canadian maps – and consciousness. In 1987 the government expressed its commitment to a new policy of inclusion.

> The geographical names of the aboriginal peoples of Canada are an important and integral part of Canada's cultural heritage. The aboriginal peoples have inalienable rights regarding the perpetuation and use of their geographical names, which are preserved mainly in the oral tradition of the elders, the wise bearers of cultural knowledge and customs of their respective communities.
>
> The collection of native geographical names should be accelerated throughout Canada and the systematic and spatial coverage of cultural and linguistic areas of the indigenous peoples should be ensured. Indeed, there is an expressed need to record native geographical names and associated

information efficiently and accurately as soon as possible. (Canadian Permanent Committee on Geographical names 1987: 1)

That was only the beginning. The document committed the government to facilitating and funding name collection projects, fostering 'ongoing formal relations ... between the provincial and Territorial names authorities ... and the native communities, groups and authorities ... on the subject of developing inventories of native geographical names, with the necessary procedures to be put in place as soon as possible' . It further called for inclusion of Aboriginal people on the boards and bodies responsible for official naming, and to annual, ongoing review (Canadian Permanent Committee on Geographical Names 1987: 5). In the years that followed, Aboriginal names increasingly appeared on Canada's maps.

Borders and boundaries

I know they don't want us here ... .They'll find out who we are. They'll tell us to go back to where we come from ... we are the speckled-Irish ... we're aliens and we'll never be Irish enough, even though we speak the Irish language ... (Hamilton 2003: 1–2)

It's the name that causes all the trouble. The Irish name: Ó hUrmoltaigh. People jump back with a strange expression and ask you to say it again ...

'What's that in English?' they ask. But you can't betray your family name. My father says we can't give the English version, Hamilton, no matter how often they ask for it. We can't even admit that an English version exists ...

Your name is important. It's like your face or your smile or your skin. (Hamilton 2003: 108)

Michael Hechter took the internal colonialism model developed by Lenin and refined by Gramsci a step further. Recalling Marx's view of England as divided into 'two hostile camps', English and Irish, he proposed a continuum of integration, with a (hypothetical) society that places no value on economic and cultural integration at one end, and the 'perfectly integrated' society with highly valued cultural and economic integration at the other. In this model, *external* colonialist power is imposed from outside the homeland, as part of conquest (thus, renaming of a country or a people in the language of the conqueror). In contrast, *internal* colonialist power is imposed from within the homeland on racially, ethnically, or gender-defined groups (thus, the giving of slave-names, husband's names at marriage, and government-sponsored surnames) (Hechter 1975; 1986). More recent perspectives on 'homeland' and 'diaspora' suggest that the internal-external dichotomy is insufficient.

As we saw earlier, the characters in *The Namesake* are forced to make choices that fit neither their original 'homeland' nor their new home in 'diaspora'. Having moved far more than geographically, from Calcutta to Cambridge, Massachusetts, Ashoke and Ashima are in a third 'country' of their own making. Their son has progressed from the appellation, 'Baby Boy Ganguli', to Gogol Ganguli. But Gogol is a 'pet name', meant only for private family use. The parents have given him the 'good name' of Nikhil, which is meant to be the name he uses in public. He has his own ideas and preferences, and in school there is much confusion. In the ensuing identity struggle, the parents choose Nikhil, the son chooses Gogol, and the teacher remains entirely outside the loop, wondering merely which name is the 'first' and which is the 'middle' name. Those categories are irrelevant to the family, and the intercultural impasse remains. The system makes no place for Bengali customs in Diaspora, or the creation of new customs at the intersections (Lahiri 2004).

To understand the politics of naming, it is necessary to separate voluntary from involuntary migration and to broaden our understanding of territory, communication, and culture. In the mid-1980s I discarded the internal-external model for what I called a 'multilevel view of colonialism', based on a Chinese box image that grouped people into units of increasing size and scale (Alia 1989: 128–29). Today I find even that expansion too restrictive – at once too linear and enclosed. I think what is needed is a much more fluid conception of intercultural and multicultural reality.

As Appadurai notes, 'Natives, people confined to and by the places to which they belong, groups unsullied by contact with a larger world, have probably never existed' (Appadurai 1988: 39). Clifford takes the next step, calling on researchers to 'focus on hybrid, cosmopolitan experiences as much as on rooted, native ones ... the goal is not to *replace* the cultural figure "native" with the intercultural figure "traveller" [but] ... to focus on concrete mediations of the two, in specific cases of historical tension and relationship' (Clifford 1997: 24). He further asks how one culture may be a site of travel for others, how spaces are traversed from outside, and to what extent one group's core is another group's periphery (ibid.: 25). He challenges ideas of 'homeland' and 'diaspora' and calls for a more fluid way of understanding cultural and geographical movement.

Consider the images of the tourist's Inuk in sealskin and fur, singing only old songs, living only in old ways. In Nunavut, country music is far more prevalent than the 'authentic' throat singing that is invariably imported to southern folk festivals (with singers suffering the physical discomfort of caribou parkas and sealskin mukluks in southern heat). The old 'whaler dances' derive from a marriage of British and Inuit cultures. The culture is complex and changing. I have had to struggle with the temptation to seek the preservation of what I perceived to be 'Inuit naming', until forced to admit that in a pure sense, there is no such thing. Inuit will continue the process of linking old and new, Qallunaat and Inuit. Gail Guthrie Valaskakis clarifies the intricate relationship between tradition and transformation, coloniser and colonised:

> In the writing of Outsiders, Native American traditional practice is often misunderstood as feathers and fantasy or, worse, as oppressive reification of the distant past. But Indian traditionalism is not these; nor is it lost in transformation or revived as a privileged expression of resistance. It is an instrumental code to action knitted into the fabric of everyday life ... (Valaskakis 1988: 268)

Past and present, 'inside' and 'outside' cultures are inseparable. Valaskakis's eloquent description of her Lac du Flambeau Chippewa childhood reflects the experiences of Inuit and other colonised peoples.

> We were very young when we began to live the ambivalence of our reality. My marble-playing, bicycle-riding, king-of-the-royal-mountain days were etched with the presence of unexplained identity and power. I knew as I sat in the cramped desks of the Indian school that wigwams could shake with the rhythm of a Midewiwin ceremonial drum, fireballs could spring from the whispers of a windless night, and Bert Skye could (without warning) transform himself into a dog. I knew that my great-grandmother moved past the Catholic altar in her house with her hair dish in her hand to place greying combings of her hair in the first fire of the day, securing them from evil spirits ... we were equally and irrevocably harnessed to each other ... I was both an Indian and an Outsider. (Valaskakis 1988: 268)

Mary Louise Pratt refers to 'the space of colonial encounters' as a 'contact zone'. Her aim is 'to foreground the interactive, improvisational dimensions of colonial encounters so easily ignored or suppressed by diffusionist accounts of conquest and domination' (Pratt 1992: 6–7). A 'contact' perspective emphasises 'how subjects are constituted in and by their relations to each other' and treats relations among colonisers and colonised, or 'travelers and "travelees"', not in terms of separateness or apartheid, but in terms of copresence, interaction, interlocking understandings and practices, often within radically asymmetrical relations of power' (ibid.: 7). In my research on indigenous media, I have found that, although culturally distinct, the world's indigenous communities have collectively experienced many of the elements of diaspora. Small numbers of people are scattered over great distances, some far from their homelands, as in Oklahoma – where survivors of forced relocation landed at the end of the 'Trail of Tears' – and the High Canadian Arctic, where Inuit were moved from Northern Quebec. Some reside in homelands newly 'legitimated' by dominant governments – as in the instances of Nunavut Territory and Greenland Home Rule.

Starting from what Pratt (1992: 7) calls 'autoethnographies', indigenous people are developing their own news outlets, using satellite, digital, cable and the Internet to strengthen their culturally and linguistically diverse voices and disseminate information to a rapidly expanding global audience, simultaneously maintaining or restoring particular languages and cultures while promoting common interests. Their progress is consistent with Ien Ang's idea of the 'progressive transnationalization of media audiencehood' (Ang 1996: 81). However, Ang's construction implies a unidirectional crossing of national boundaries and should be extended to account for instances of internal colonialism and boundaries between ethnicities and regions. The alternative is a fluid, constantly changing crossing from boundary to boundary and place to place – the *inter*nationalisation of indigenous media audiencehood and media production, which I have called the New Media Nation (Alia 2004b: 36).

We need to rethink the idea that missionaries and governments 'conquered' indigenous peoples. 'Underground' cultural retention is far more widespread and far stronger than has been thought. In the case of Nunavut, the religious and social customs of the colonisers did not necessarily subsume or subordinate those of Inuit. There is far more mutual accommodation, and mutual learning, than is conventionally acknowledged. As Nuttall observes, some 'aspects of the existing traditional cosmology, such as name beliefs ... still lie beneath the surface, having been glossed over with the veneer of European Christianity. During the time of the early missionaries the two belief systems probably existed side by side ...' (Nuttall 1992: 60).

We must reassess the nature and the extent of cross- and intercultural exchange, with minds open and political agendas set aside. Along with innumerable problems and challenges, Nunavut is ushering in an era of cultural renewal. It is worth asking if there is something inherently colonialist about surnaming itself. Surnames appear when populations increase or societies get more 'developed'. We need to discover whether increased complexity or substantial population growth ever occur *without* colonisation – whether, for instance, there can be a relatively pure form of confederation or association.

The reinstatement of indigenous place names in Canada preceded the restoration of personal names by more than a decade. Even today, Canada continues to make sure that its citizens are named, numbered and surnamed, while loosening its grip on the naming of places.

The evolution of name laws in Greenland provides a useful view of power balances and change, and a basis for speculation about the relative importance of personal and place names in determining power relations. In the 1980s and 1990s, new naming policies emerged from what some called Greenland's 'cultural crisis'. Until 1989, naming powers in post-home rule Greenland remained split between Denmark and Greenland.

Greenlandic people had earlier gained control over place names, while family names (surnames) continued to be supervised by the Danish ministry of justice, and given names by the ministry of religion (Olsen 1985, 1988; Schechter 1988). In Canada, Aboriginal place names were restored long before attention was turned to personal names. Government regulation of Inuit names followed a sequence which attaches more power to personal than place names, and is based on Ottawa standards (as it is on Copenhagen standards, in Greenland). Those policies are clearly based on Qallunaat views of naming. In the Inuit cultural context, there is apparently no power discrepancy between the two kinds of names, or even a distinction that we would call 'personal' or 'place'. There is much to be learned from exploring a politics of identity.

> This is ... a time of confused and chaotic passage. All the old pecking orders have been pulled down or ... pulled apart ... people hitherto deprived are reaching for some better distribution of the rights and privileges of belongingness and the satisfactions of self-esteem. (Isaacs 1989: 219)

The Circumpolar Context

Project Surname was a backward move at a rapidly forward-moving time. It was organised at the very turning point at which Inuit identity and participation were being reasserted and integrated across national boundaries. The Canadian legitimation of the land Inuit have long called Nunavut arrived at a time of increasing global activity among Inuit – what some call a pan-Indigenous movement. In November 1973 – barely a year after the last Project Surname changes had made their way through the Canadian legal system – Denmark hosted The Arctic Peoples' Conference at its parliament in Christiansborg. Participants included Sámi organisations from Norway, Sweden and Finland, organisations from Greenland, Inuit and Dene organisations from the Yukon and Northwest Territories in Canada. At the time, the Alaska Federation of Natives was embroiled in land claims negotiations and was unable to participate. As has often been the case with landmark activities in the Arctic, the 'mass media paid only moderate attention to the conference' (Petersen 1984: 725). The conference produced two resolutions demanding recognition of Arctic peoples, and their right to participate in northern development, and set up a working group to continue the politicisation process.

Alaskans, who missed the conference because of their claim-in-progress, took the next important step. Eben Hopson, the energetic visionary and Mayor of Barrow, sent out a call to participants at the Arctic Peoples' Conference and began the process of creating the Inuit Circumpolar Conference (ICC), formally launched 13–16 June, 1974 at

Barrow, Alaska. It was dedicated to providing a strong voice for circumpolar peoples, increasing Inuit control over their own destinies and influence over administration, and use, of the Arctic. Hopson was too ill to attend the second ICC assembly at Nuuk (then Godthab), Greenland, and died soon after hearing that his vision had become reality: the Nuuk assembly had unanimously passed the ICC charter (Petersen 1984: 726). From the start, ICC declared itself under four flags: United States, Canadian, Greenlandic and Russian. Until Siberian Inuit first attended ICC assemblies (unofficially in 1989, officially in 1992), a chair and Soviet flag were reserved at each meeting to symbolise their presence. Canadian Inuit are strong participants in ICC. There are cooperative projects between East Baffin and West Greenland. Canadian Inuit reflect on Greenland's experience with home rule, as they develop Nunavut.

As Nunavut unfolds, the legacy of Project Surname unravels. Inuit are reasserting cultural dominion and reminding visitors that Inuit culture was never lost. It is no easy task to make sense of centuries of cross-cultural contact, much of it dominated by a climate of unequal power. *Nunatsiaq News* editor Jim Bell cautions that the Nunavut Agreement endangers the concept of Aboriginal peoples' 'inherent right to self-government':

> The *Nunavut Act* is ... a delegated form of self-government. It's really a slightly modernized version of the *Northwest Territories Act*, the NWT's 'constitution," which northerners have for years denounced as an instrument of federal government colonialism. The *Nunavut Act* even says that any law passed by the Nunavut Legislative Assembly may be disallowed by the federal government within one year of its being passed. And there seems to be no iron-clad guarantee that would prevent Parliament from unilaterally changing the *Nunavut Act*. (Bell 1993: 2)

Such cautions bear watching. The poetry of Mary Carpenter Lyons and Looee Okalik shows the depth of feeling people have for the formal acknowledgement that Inuit hold 'Title to the land of many tales, many footsteps ...'

> Nunavut speaks to the soul of the Inuit. It's like a promised land ... (Mary Carpenter Lyons in Petrone 1988: 200)

> Poetry on Signing of the Nunavut Agreement
> ...
> Precious, precious we are,
> Precious they were yesterday
> and precious they will be tomorrow
>
> We have arrived to one of our many goals in life
>   Let us wake up
>   and make a difference ... (Okalik 1993: 10)

Changing Names:
Clues in the Search for a Political Onomastics

Plenty of people changed their names: actors, writers, revolutionaries, transvestites ... European immigrants had their names changed at Ellis Island ... slaves renamed themselves once they were emancipated ... (Lahiri 2004: 7)

Renaming and Political Upheaval: Colonisation and Resistance

Nations, cities, topographical features – and people – are renamed with each regime change, colonial incursion, liberation struggle or celebration. Brian Friel's play, *Translations*, 'centres on the specific moment when Anglicans were put upon the Irish landscape. In the 1830s, the British Army's Royal Engineers conducted the Ordnance Survey to produce a definitive six-inch map of Ireland. In the process, they re-named the country' (Quigley 1982: 14–15). Friel scripted the following conversation between Owen, an Irish assistant, and Yolland, a British engineer:

OWEN: What is happening?
YOLLAND: I'm not sure. But I'm concerned ... It's an eviction of sorts.
OWEN: We're making a ... map ... Is there something sinister in that? And we're taking place-names that are riddled with confusion and ...
YOLLAND: Who's confused? Are the people confused?
OWEN: ... and we're standardizing those names as accurately and as sensitively as we can.
YOLLAND: Something is being eroded. (Friel 1982: 43)

Michael Quigley sees that passage as presenting, not just the Irish situation, but 'The whole story of colonialism. "Eviction" is the cruel reality; "confusion" is the self-righteous claim of the colonist, to greater knowledge, to higher civilization, to a firmer grasp on progress' (Quigley 1982: 14–15), just as the perpetrators of Project Surname and the disc number system saw themselves as bringing Inuit into the current century and eliminating the 'confusion' of Inuktitut naming. Friel does not simplify as much as Quigley does; he has Owen and Yolland change and exchange roles and views. He is concerned that, as Owen says, 'We name a thing and – bang! – it leaps into existence!' (Friel 1982: 45).

Yolland's remark, 'Who's confused' echoed in debate on the floor of the Northwest Territories Council Chamber in July 1968, when Robert G. Williamson observed that 'there is much confusion, annoyance, embarrassment for all people in the North' and 'loss of proper family and cultural identity by the Eskimo' as well as 'difficulty for administrators ... (Roberts 1975: 28). As in the Ireland of *Translations*, the 'confusion' seen in Nunavut was that of the colonial administrators. In Nessa Rapoport's story, 'The Woman Who Lost Her Names', Sarah loses her identity in a series of experiences that effectively demonstrate her colonisation by her husband, family and community. As a child of recent immigrants to the United States, she was 'persuaded' to assimilate by a benevolent but misguided teacher.

> When she got to school the kindergarten teacher sent home a note. The family read it together, sitting around the kitchen table. 'Dear Mrs. Levi, we have decided to call the child Sally for the purpose of school as it will help integrate her and make the adjustment easier.'
> 'What's to adjust?' the brother next to her asked. (Rapoport 1980: 138)

Names: Avoidance, Change, and the Limitation of Power

In Maxine Hong Kingston's *The Woman Warrior*, 'No Name Woman' loses her name posthumously. She is deliberately removed from the family record, having shamed her family by out-of-wedlock childbirth and suicide. 'We say that your father has all brothers because it is as if she had never been born', Kingston's mother tells her (Kingston 1976: 3). A similar avoidance taboo is depicted in Jewish writer Sholom Aleichem's Tevye stories. The daughter who marries a non-Jew is erased from the family history. Again, the reason is that she has shamed her family and community. As in the Chinese family, the Jewish daughter's name is never spoken again. I have heard of more extreme cases in which families have actually conducted funeral services for still-living daughters. To lose or be denied one's name is to lose one's life. To be forbidden to speak a name or call attention to its owner is to experience a kind of linguistic imprisonment.

> When she calls out to Ashoke, she doesn't say his name. Ashima never thinks of her husband's name when she thinks of her husband, even though she knows perfectly well what it is. She has adopted his surname but refuses, for propriety's sake, to utter his first. It's not the type of thing Bengali wives do ... instead of saying Ashoke's name, she utters the interrogative that has come to replace it, which translates roughly as 'Are you listening to me?' (Lahiri 2004: 2)

A Mongolian wife spends her fertile years observing an elaborate complex of taboos that forbid her to speak her husband's name, the names of members of his family, or words that resemble or recall those names. In effect, she must speak a private language of her own creation, one that clarifies daily that she is subordinate to her husband and his kin. The purpose is to prevent her attracting her husband's attention (Humphrey 1978). Similarly, Pete Steffens tells a story of Orthodox Jews forbidding women to sing at Jerusalem's Wailing Wall. The authorities explain that it is not the act of women singing that is the 'problem', but the possibility that men may hear (and be attracted to) them.

Before the Second World War, Jews were cut off from the rest of German society by physical ghettos and by the ghettoisation of restrictive lists of 'official Jewish names' (Kaganoff 1977). Among the variables affecting the positive or negative consequences of name-changing is the degree of voluntariness involved. Sarah's teacher made it clear that taking an 'American' name was desirable, if not required, in the new country. Under Project Surname, Inuit were similarly 'persuaded' rather than 'required' to adopt new names. In both cases, the renaming threatened to undermine traditional names and naming practices. 'The Chinese I know hide their names. Sojourners take new names when their lives change and guard their real names with silence' (Kingston 1976). As in the experience of Inuit and Jewish 'underground naming', subjugated or marginalised people often adopt a public attitude of compliance with authority while privately defying it. Toni Morrison's novel *Song of Solomon* contains a prime example of this practice. There is no official recognition of Not Doctor Street, yet it has persisted through generations of reference.

> Town maps registered the street as Mains Avenue ... the only colored doctor in the city had lived and died on that street ... his patients took to calling it Doctor Street ... Envelopes began to arrive addressed to ... Doctor Street. The post office workers returned these envelopes ... Then in 1918, when colored men were being drafted, a few gave their address ... as Doctor Street. In that way, the name acquired a quasi-official status. But not for long. Some of the city legislators, whose concern for appropriate names and the maintenance of the city's landmarks was the principal part of their political life, saw to it that 'Doctor Street' was never used in any official capacity ... (Morrison 1977: 3–4)

Thus, the stage is set for a continuing tension between official and unofficial labels and the power relations they represent. The public officials eventually post a notice saying that 'the Avenue ... had always been and would always be known as Mains Avenue and not Doctor Street'. 'It was a genuinely clarifying public notice because it gave southside residents a way to keep their memories alive and please the city legislators as well. They called it *Not* Doctor Street ...' (Morrison 1977: 4). The history of colonialism is filled with similar accounts of overt compliance and covert defiance. In Kurdistan – a nation that continues to exist in the consciousness of its people – Kurdish names are used in secret and, as we saw earlier, official names dictated by the dominant countries are the public front (Kahn 1980).

Liberation Renaming

Often, people celebrate liberation by giving or taking new names to symbolise rebirth. I did this myself, replacing a former 'married' surname with Alia, to celebrate moving to a new life and a new country. In utopian communities or religious orders we can observe that newly liberated nations and individuals bestow or adopt new names, sometimes celebrating the occasion with elaborate rituals. The transition between old and new names is not always smooth; there are conflicts and contradictions. In the past decades, Scotland has seen a revival of Gaelic language and culture, especially in the Highlands. In 2003 a man called Austin Boyle was granted permission to give his newborn daughter the Gaelic given name of Aoife. At the same time he was *denied* permission to give her a Gaelic surname. 'According to the rules, if a surname is translatable into English then that name must be used.' The irony is that the government spends £13 million annually to promote Gaelic language and culture in Scotland, but 'Mr Boyle was told he could only register his child in English'. In protest, he refused to register the birth, flouting the law requiring him to do so. He said that in Wales a parent can register the child's name in Welsh and English, but Scotland permits only English. 'It is crazy, but Gaelic has no legal status in Scotland' (Seenan 2003: 10). Clearly, taking Gaelic names can be an act of liberation only if the laws are made consistent. This case points to the hypocrisy of policies that proclaim cultural restoration while preventing its implementation.

In South Africa, new names have been appearing, in celebration of the demise of apartheid in 1994. In an article titled 'New Start, New Names', the *Natal Mercury* of 23 December 1995 reported the renaming of a fleet of ships, which formerly had honoured pro-apartheid politicians such as P.W. Botha and Jim Fouche. 'P.W. Botha will be mortified to hear that *his* strike craft will soon be known as Shaka' (Koopman 2002: 5). Adrian Koopman documents the widespread name changes in South Africa since 1994 – changes to the names of people, institutions, objects and places (Koopman 2002: 6). Bertie Neethling has documented numerous changes to Xhosa nomenclature. In 2000 he reported an 'onomastic renaissance' in which African names were rapidly moving from underground to society's front lines (Neethling 2000).

The notion that keeping one's 'maiden' name in marriage expresses one's 'own' identity, at least in Western cultures, is miguided; it retains a male-dominated identity, simply replacing the husband's name with the father's. Carol Christ uses the term 'new naming' to reflect the difference between name changing and naming anew. 'Women's rituals simultaneously name, validate, and create new possibilities of being for women in a new world – new culture and new community. Participating in a ritual of the new naming brings women's experiences and visions out into the open and through sharing transforms them from private into public reality' (Christ 1980: 13). Here again, underground naming is emerging aboveground.

Shakespeare's Juliet tells Romeo to 'Deny thy father and refuse thy name ... 'Tis but thy name that is my enemy'. Romeo replies, 'Call me but love and I'll be new baptiz'd ...' The themes of rebirth, renewal and rebaptism are not just Romeo's (or the playwright's) invention; they reflect the attitudes and practices of many cultures. The distinction Juliet draws between 'self' and 'name' is not universally accepted and is a radical departure from her own society's attitudes and values. Juliet's proposal is nothing short of revolutionary. To re-baptise is to deny the continuity and survival of Montague and Capulet, or to create a new 'group' with a new identity. In Anglicised Ireland, re-baptism implies conquest and subjugation. In the new Verona, re-baptism implies liberation and new-naming. By examining name-changing policies and practices in many settings, it is possible to learn more about the symbiotic relationship between naming and politics. Name changes can serve as indicators of broader social change, as devices for explaining or clarifying patterns of domination and subjugation, and, perhaps, as early-warning signals of potential danger.

Excursions North, Revisited

Underpinning this inquiry into Nunavut and the politics of naming is a continuing examination of representations of Inuit from Outside and from within. Unfashionable though they may be, colonial attitudes die hard. They persist in media representations that are meant to disseminate 'up-to-the-minute' news, and in some of the most 'authoritative' texts. The 11.15 pm ITV news broadcast on 4 October 2002 reached all of Britain. It described the Queen's annual visit to Canada with a perplexing mix of misinformation and half-truths. Viewers saw pictures of what the reporter called 'Baffin Island', where Her Majesty 'was greeted by some of the local Inuit Indians.' Baffin is Canada's largest island, the size of many a small country. Its main community of Iqaluit has the only real airport and is probably where the Queen landed. Since 1999, Iqaluit has been the capital of Nunavut – the new Canadian territory similar to the provinces and larger than most British counties. Nunavut (which the report failed even to mention) covers nearly two million square kilometres – about one-fifth of Canada.

The term 'Inuit Indians' is a bizarre invention. Inuit are the people sometimes called 'Eskimos'; some non-Inuit indigenous people in Canada and the U.S.A. are called 'Indians' – an error dating back to Columbus's arrival in 1492, when he thought he had found India. Those people – who are entirely unrelated to Inuit – are variously referred to as Native Americans, First Nations, indigenous or Aboriginal people, or by one of the hundreds of culturally specific names such as Ojibway, Cree, Tlingit, Lakota, Cherokee. Except for an occasional immigrant to the region, none of these 'Indian' people live in Nunavut. 'Inuit Indians' is something the reporter made up.

A 2003 science article in the *Independent* refers to 'Inuits' – the equivalent of referring to male residents of England as 'Englishmans' (Burne 2003: 8). Any reader would consider 'Englishmans' absurd; any editor would correct the error. In the case of 'Inuit' (which is the plural form – the singular being 'Inuk') the error was missed. Throughout the world, media depictions of the Arctic are steeped in the language of conquest and colonisation. Explorers are quasi-military conquerors who launch 'assaults' on the Pole. Indigenous people are seen as aides, there to increase the 'conquerors'' comforts – ignored or treated as exotic items for study or observation, in need of 'civilisation'. The *Daily Telegraph* sent a team for a brief visit to Holman Island (Uluqsaqtuuq) and published a photo-essay in its magazine supplement, headlined 'Dressed to Kill: Hunting with the Eskimos of Holman Island'. In a letter to the editor which the *Telegraph* declined to publish, Holman Mayor Gary Bristow, Holman Community Corporation Chairman Robert Kuptana and anthropologist Richard Condon wrote: 'thousands of ... readers have had their opinions and attitudes about the Canadian Arctic falsely influenced by individuals with no understanding of even the most basic aspects of Canadian Inuit culture ... (Bristow et al. 1992).

> 'Among hunters there is no code of honour,' the article proclaims ... apparently measuring Inuit hunting against aristocratic English fox hunts. 'The hunter ... is merciless and self-interested, gathering food only for himself and his family' ... The unsuccessful hunter and his family could go hungry only steps away from someone else's well-stocked tent. (Thompson 1992: A3)

The *Telegraph* published photographs of unnamed members of the Holman community. We do not see comparable images of unidentified British people. Two of Holman's most respected elders, Jimmy and Nora Memogama, were rendered anonymous. Some errors were amusing. *Telegraph* readers were told of a 'young white man who stepped off a train to stretch his legs; his frozen body was discovered the following spring' (Bristow et al. 1992). It is possible that, realising the reporter's ignorance and gullibility, someone had a joke at the journalist's expense. No one has ever stepped off a train at Holman. The nearest railhead is more than a thousand miles away, near the Alberta border. The photo-essay is not just an amusing example of journalistic ignorance. It is representative of a disturbing trend in journalistic coverage of the North ... Each year ... Holman is visited by journalists who desire to write or photograph the definitive article about an isolated Inuit community ... the community has no way to ... monitor or comment upon their finished works ... [The] worst harm is not the offence they give to northern residents but the distorted view they present to thousands of readers about northern life and northern people. In an age when Inuit culture is being attacked by numerous animal rights groups, articles like 'Dressed to Kill' ... perpetuate prejudice. (Bristow et al. 1992)

'Authoritative' Sources

Even when conscientious journalists think they are doing their homework, the sources they consult as authoritative are themselves filled with misinformation. The venerable *Oxford Dictionary for Writers and Editors* declares Inuit to be 'Canadian Native American people', their language 'Inupiaq', 'Inuk' to mean [a member of] a Canadian or Greenland Native American people ...' and 'Iñupiat ... [a member of] an Alaskan Native American people, or the language of this people' (Ritter 2000: 172). The *Oxford English Reference Dictionary* defines 'Inuit' (a plural meaning 'the people') as 'an Inupiaq-speaking Eskimo, esp. in Canada' (Pearsall and Trumble 1996: 739). The *Oxford Colour Spelling Dictionary* informs us that the plural of 'Inuit' (which, you will recall, *is* already a plural) is 'Inuk or Inuks' (Waite 1996: 277). Let us unpick the inaccuracies in this maddening mess. Most Iñupiaq-speakers live in Alaska and Siberia. 'Inuit' cannot refer to 'an' anybody because it is a plural. The designation 'Native Americans' refers to indigenous people of the United States, sometimes including Iñupiat and Yup'ik (also called Eskimo or Inuit) of Alaska but not including people from Canada. Inuit live mainly in Arctic and sub-Arctic Canada, Alaska, Greenland and Siberia (Alia 2004a: 56).

Iñupiat constitute only one of the Inuit subcultures. Yup'ik are also Inuit and have their own language. Inuvialuit are Inuit who live in the western Canadian Arctic and have their own language (akin to Inuktitut but quite separate, and written in Roman orthography rather than Inuktitut syllabics). The generic for the Inuit language is Inuktitut, though there are several related languages and dialects. I have heard Inuit jokingly or ironically call themselves 'Inuks', when speaking in English to Qallunaat, anglicising the plural – as when Deborah Evaluardjuk expressed resistance to assimilation by saying, 'We were not going to be turned into white Inuks' (Alia 1995). In reality there is no such thing as this plural in the Inuktitut language, and no Inuit, even jokingly, call themselves 'Inuits'. That is an invention of the British 'scholars' who misinformed Oxford's three publications – and consequently, continue to misinform the public. The correct form is 'Inuk' (one person); 'Inuuk' (two people); Inuit (three or more people).

Structural Violence Theory

Johan Galtung identifies two kinds of violence, 'direct' or 'personal' violence and 'structural' violence. 'Direct violence' is equivalent to the conventional meaning of 'violence', in which someone is injured or killed. There are chilling reminders of the nightmare-meaning that can accompany renaming. In 1938, Jews in Germany were prohibited from changing family names and required to readopt identifiably 'Jewish' names which, in the interest of assimilation, they had 'Europeanised'. The German government restricted Jewish given names to a list of 185 men's names and ninety-one women's names. Similar laws were enacted to restrict Jewish naming in Norway and France. Those events culminated in destruction – not of labels or symbols – but of people.

On the other hand, the pressure to assimilate – applied by a dominant group – is a form of 'structural violence'. The government-sponsored numbering and surnaming of thousands of Canadian Inuit was a potent example. Although the effects of structural violence are often less visible or immediate, it is observably destructive and – as in the case of Kurdish, Jewish, and Armenian people – may often be a pathway leading to direct violence. Galtung emphasises that 'there is no reason to assume that structural violence amounts to less suffering than personal violence' (Galtung 1980: 7). One result of structural violence is what is sometimes called cultural genocide, whose consequences sometimes include waves of suicide. The anthropologist, Eleanor Burke Leacock, considered the high rates of suicide among indigenous peoples, internationally, to be a form of indirect genocide, and thought it ought to be studied and reported in that way (Leacock 1984). In an earlier study, I began to develop the model which has been updated here, in an effort to help clarify these concepts (Table 5.1).

Table 5.1 **A Model for Examining Levels of Violence** (continuum)

Decisions and behaviour of journalists and editors; media representations:

→ → → → → → → → → → → → → → →
← ← ← ← ← ← ← ← ← ← ← ← ← ← ←

Non-violence	*Structural violence*			*Direct violence*
Freedom to name persons and places	Oppressive or repressive structures; *disempowerment; war*	Cultural genocide; *forced or pressured renaming*	Culture-wide suicide or state-sanctioned *murder*	Genocide; legally sanctioned *execution*

Source: Adapted from Alia 2004a: 77

Reclaiming Cultures: "Q Numbers", Decolonisation and Cultural Regeneration

The personal naming stories in the Introduction omitted one of my 'names'. Besides carrying the name of Valerie for my parents' meeting-place, Lee for my ancestor, Leah, and the self-bestowed surname of Alia, I am Q-0170. Like members of subjugated groups the world over, I had to pay for my name. Unlike the experiences of Inuit paying legal fees to correct their Inuktitut names, or of Jews paying fees to European government for 'good' (as opposed to insulting) surnames, my 'Q Number' was administered with tongue in cheek and the fee was donated to charity.

ALL YOU QALLUNAAT, GET REGISTERED!
What do radio host Peter Gzowski, actress Cynthia Dale, blues singer Colin James and former Edmonton Oilers defenceman Randy Gregg have in common? They're all official members of a unique club called the Iqaluit Qallunaat Registry, a fund-raising project started by the Iqaluit Elders Society. It's a gentle parody of the E-number system by which Inuit were once registered by the Canadian government …

Abe Okpik, who was awarded the Order of Canada for organizing Operation [*sic*] Surname, helped Iqaluit's elders create a 'Q' number system to raise money for their organization … they have sold registration certificates and mock Q-number disks, bearing a striking resemblance to the original E-numbers, to Qallunaat … at a cost of $10 … The idea has been a big hit with southern visitors. When Gzowski, Dale, James, Gregg and other southern celebrities passed through Iqaluit last May enroute to Pond Inlet for a celebrity golf tournament to promote literacy, one of the first places they headed for was the Iqaluit Elders Centre where they all enrolled in the Qallunaat Registry. (*Arctic Circle* 1991: 13)

We have seen that traditional Inuit naming makes no reference to titles, gender or hierarchical relations. The system is based on *sauniq* – namesake commemoration so powerful some call it a form of 'reincarnation'. There is no concept of surname and no renaming at marriage. Patrilineal Western surnaming made little sense in this system; it was met with a range of responses, from anger and resistance to polite compliance. My earlier research suggested that the interference some called cultural genocide was substantial. In the mid-1990s, a decade after the research was begun, the evidence suggested a need to revise those findings in the light of (a) new understanding of my earlier findings and (b) developments over the past several years. Between 1994 and 2006, those developments – including an identity and cultural renaissance – have continued to escalate.

There is a metaphor that may be useful for understanding this phenomenon. Medical science has shown that some types of brain damage, formerly thought to be permanent and irreparable, may be subject to recovery. For example, brain tissue is able to regenerate in ways thought impossible before. This depends on the extent and location of the damage, the physical and psychological characteristics of the individual, and the particulars of his or her environment. Dr Pamela Klonoff, clinical director of the Barrow Neurological Institute, says that most 'significant traumatic brain injuries produce a period of memory loss and … confusion' lasting from a few minutes to several months. Brain cells that die are not replaced by new cells, but cells that are damaged but not totally destroyed sometimes recover, and sometimes cells can be trained to take over the function of cells that were lost (Curry 1998; Swiercinsky et al. 1993). I believe that in a comparable way, damaged cultures have considerable powers of regeneration, depending on the nature, location and extent of damage. In the case of the Inuit renaissance, the relevant factors include:

- a general trend towards cultural revival;
- post-Project Surname developments
  - self-government in progress, the development of Nunavut;
  - language retention programmes;
  - cultural relearning;
  - various projects to correct naming errors, restore personal and place names and/or write them into the public record;
- resources particular to the culture;
- Inuit humour;
- 'creative stubbornness' – a survival orientation
  - 'underground naming'
  - strong commitment to family and community.

When threats and perceived threats to cultural continuity are removed, 'underground naming' – the use of private (sometimes secret) names to retain one's culture – moves back above ground. Inuit are restoring pre-Project Surname names or combining them with non-Inuit names and usage – through legal channels or just through daily use. Inuit are naming babies in the old ways – not only traditional *sauniq* names, but names based on the child's response. A young Iqaluit couple told me they had tried many names for their newborn son because he 'was crying all the time', tried a succession of names until he stopped crying. That custom is reported by Inuit across Nunavut, Nunavik and the Northwest Territories and also in the research on Greenland (Nuttall 1992; Søby 1992).

In 1991, with teasing humour, Abe Okpik – now an elder – invented a cross-cultural turnaround between colonised and coloniser, which he named 'the Q number Project'. As we saw in Chapter 2, Inuit were given discs with numbers on one side and the words 'Eskimo Identification Canada' on the other. Each had a prefix – 'W' for 'Western' or 'E' for 'Eastern Arctic'. In the Nunavut region the discs were known as 'E numbers'. Thus, 'Q numbers'. 'Q' stood for *Qallunaat* – non-Inuit people. Q numbers were a playful response to what we have seen was a deeply affecting and contentious, government-administered identification programme. In Iqaluit in 1991, I paid ten Canadian dollars for a red-brown leather disc stamped with a Q number of my own, and henceforth became 'Q-0170'. In creating the Q number Project, Abe Okpik was not just joking. Q numbers were sold to raise funds for the Iqaluit Elders' Centre. The project appealed to Qallunaat residents and visitors, and the proceeds contributed to the physical survival of the community. The money went to elders for their own programmes, and for their work teaching language and culture to younger generations of Nunavut citizens. It also served as a playful way to teach Qallunaat about colonial history, while drawing on Inuit culture to regain control.

Much is being written on cultural appropriation. I do not wish to minimise the importance of this work, but I do want to suggest that we should pay equal attention to the phenomenon of cultural *re*appropriation. Abe Okpik found a creative and constructive way to readdress his own problematic role – as an Inuk hired by Qallunaat to rename other Inuit. A year before devising the Q number Project he told me he was looking for ways to help remedy the problems left by Project Surname (Alia 1984–2006). It included counselling people about how to proceed with legal name changes, encouraging them to keep or return to their original names, and administering Q numbers to former colonisers or their actual or symbolic kin. Susanne Dybbroe reminds us that

> The maintenance of cultural identity is a process related to symbolic control. The demands for self-determination ... and the affirmation of cultural rights mark a clash with Western domination, which in the postwar era has extended to all levels of Inuit and Greenlandic society and culture ... this domination, as in other parts of the world, makes itself also felt in the very fabric of culture; people's perception of self, of the world, their power to think alternatives. The hegemonic process, whereby this has been effected, is part of the lived experience in the Arctic today ... . [control of] Arctic resources ... the false opposition between tradition and modernity ... culture and development.
> ... the surrounding world tries to enforce a heritage turned into a token, whereas Inuit and Greenlanders try to retain its principle. Not the perceived loss of 'culture', but the loss of self-determination in its widest sense, resulting from the process of foreign hegemony, is what threatens Inuit identity today ... [in the] political process ... [Inuit are struggling] for the right to ... a modern, 'authentic' ... self defined, cultural identity. (Dybbroe 1996: 50)

Everywhere, colonised peoples are taking on the colonisers, taking a turn at calling the shots, forging new collaborations. Cultures thought to be dead or dying are experiencing renewal and rebirth. There is a Jekyll and Hyde aspect to this phenomenon. At best, it leads to liberation and cooperation, at worst, to ethnic cleansing. Nearly twenty years ago, Harold Isaacs saw it coming. In *Idols of the Tribe: Group Identity and Political Change* he wrote:

> ... our tribal separatenesses are here to stay ... They are not about to dissolve into any new, larger human order. And a good thing too, some argue, since, as Solzhenitsyn said, these diversities are the wealth of humanity ... On the other hand, with all the beauty goes all the blood. If tribal separateness and its life-giving qualities are here to stay, so are intertribal hostility and the death-dealing consequences ... The underlying issue is still: can existence be made more humane, and if so, how? (Isaacs 1989: 216–17)

Isaacs' precocious questions do not come with answers. I think Inuit are on the right track, using humour along with serious determination, joining jokes with political savvy. If we are lucky, we will all be the richer for it. I see much promise in our pothole-dotted political landscape. Challenging old racism, and new imperialism, peoples formerly labelled 'colonised' or 'coloniser' are working together in new ways. I am more optimistic about the prospects for cooperation and cross-cultural respect than I was at the start of this research.

Conclusion: It's all in the Names ...

Canada has long been portrayed – from inside and from without – as a quintessentially *northern* nation. Imbedded in what some have called the 'idea of North' is the *reality* of North. While the northern 'idea' is often focused on landscape, the northern reality is most centrally concerned with *people* and their relationship to the life-giving and life-challenging land – less the "scape' of visiting painters and poets than the named and located home of its indigenous inhabitants. The North that permeates Canadian literature, identity and culture is a mix of 'idea' and lived experiences of northerners and visitors.

Visitors from Europe, southern Canada and other parts of North America wrote about their northern experiences and carried photographs of Inuit with them when they returned home. Few of them named the people they had photographed – either because they were unable to gather, understand or spell Inuktitut names or because they did not care enough to ask. It is often said that Inuit are the world's most photographed people; especially given their cultural importance, it makes sense that people are working to find and restore their names. In 2000

Nunavut Tunngavik Inc. and the Department of Indian and Northern Affairs developed Nunavut Sivuniksavut, an education programme for young beneficiaries of the Nunavut Land Claim Agreement. Participants study Inuit history, the Nunavut Agreements and current issues, and conduct research (Angus 2000: 1, 2). One project, spearheaded by Nunavut Commissioner Peter Irniq and described in Chapter 3, involves working with elders, using the Internet to extend their range, to find the names of Inuit left anonymous in the archives. This project is more than an exercise to fill in missing history. Putting names on anonymous images is a way of reclaiming the images (and their link to families and communities) for Inuit while sharing them with Qallunaat and recording them for future generations.

The place-name changes herald a new era, in which Aboriginal people have increasing control over the right to name and govern their homelands. Harold Isaacs documented emerging worldwide retribalisation, supporting his case most strongly by citing changes in personal and place names.

> Recent political change has brought name changes to many places ... the Russians have begun to erase Chinese names from the territory of eastern Siberia ... Nine cities and towns and two hundred and fifty rivers and mountains that had retained their Chinese names for more than a century suddenly acquired brand-new Russian names in 1973 ... altered history has led to much renaming ... (Isaacs 1989: 74)

Remie's studies of culture change and religious continuity suggest that Balikci and others may have erred in assuming (as I did at the outset of this study) that cultural demolition was the inevitable result of contact.

> Arviligdjuarmiut traditional religion did not [as Balikci claimed] collapse completely. On the contrary, it remained intact to a considerable extent and was effective in several domains of domestic and social life till at least the early 1960s ... the traditional religion of the Arviligdjuarmiut went, so to speak, 'underground' ... carefully and systematically hidden from the Pelly Bay missionaries. The traditional religion thus developed into a separate universe of discourse to which missionaries had little or no access. (Remie 1983: 53)

Inuit cultural continuity is a reality, documented by Inuit and Qallunaat over several decades. Many people have told me that traditional practices and beliefs are stronger than ever. Contact between cultures never goes in only one direction. While the outward trappings of the dominant culture may prevail, we must question even the notion of 'dominance' in the Arctic, where visitors were in a distinctly weaker position to survive. Qallunaat who arrived in Inuit territory in light European woollens with no hunting skills were certainly not in a position (except in their imaginations) to dominate anyone. Many survived because of Inuit knowledge and skills and willingness to share them. Traditions persisted despite the outward appearance of acculturation. More importantly, 'traditions' (never pure except in the minds of scholars) are in constant flux, and show much evidence of change. Inuit are responding to, and creating cultural and political change, while assuring the continuity of their identities. In Nunavut, the names will never die.

> The survival of the Eskimo people depends on the survival of the language … There are only very few Eskimos, but millions of whites, just like mosquitoes. It is something very special and wonderful to be an Eskimo – they are like the snow geese. If an Eskimo forgets his language and Eskimo ways, he will be nothing but just another mosquito. (Okpik 1962: 28)

> We must teach our children their mother tongue. We must teach them what they are and where they came from. We must teach them the values which have guided our society over thousands of years … It is this spirit we must keep alive so that it may guide us again in new life in a changed world. (Amagoalik 1977: 53)

> When at the end of life we draw our last breath, that is not the end. We awake to consciousness again, we come to life again, and all this is effected through the medium of the soul … . These two, the shore spirit and the shark, were my principal helpers … The song I generally sang when calling them was of few words:

> > Joy, joy, joy, joy!
> > I see a little shore spirit,
> > A little aua,
> > I myself am also aua,
> > The shore spirit's namesake,
> > Joy, joy! (Aua in Petrone 1988: 120–25)

CHRONOLOGY OF KEY EVENTS AND DEVELOPMENTS IN NUNAVUT AND THE CIRCUMPOLAR NORTH

Circa 1005	Norse voyage to Vinland (Greenland) and find Aboriginal people whom the Norse called 'skraelings', who run them out of the region.
1576	Martin Frobisher, looking for a Northwest Passage to the Orient, sails into Frobisher Bay.
1800s	Qallunaat whaling period.
1855	Edwin Watkins of the Church Missionary Society introduces the syllabic writing system that had been developed by James Evans for the Cree, to Inuit in Northern Quebec (Nunavik).
1859	A Moravian missionary visiting Cumberland Sound is 'sorry to see the Eskquimaux wearing European clothes …' (Mayes 1978: 29).
1876	The Reverend Edmund James Peck (Anglican) translates the Gospels into Inuktitut syllabics.
1877	The Northwest Territories Council is created.
1894	Reverend Peck establishes the first permanent mission in the Baffin region at Blacklead Island.
1929	Scheduled air service begins along the Mackenzie Valley.
1930s	The Soviet government administers a surnaming programme to rename Yuit in Siberia.
1930s–40s	Disc numbers are distributed to Inuit in Canada.
1940s	Canada and the U.S.A. build weather stations, signal stations, and air-defence posts in the Canadian Arctic (Crowe 1991: 180).

1941	First Canadian Census to include the North; disc numbers are in regular use by this time.
1944	The Arctic Institute of North America (AINA) is founded jointly by Canadians and Americans.
1950s	Establishment of communities in Inuit Arctic and sub-Arctic Canada; people are encouraged to move off the land.
1950	James Houston introduces soapstone to sculptors at Port Harrison, supported by the Canadian Handicrafts Guild and the federal government.
1950	Inuit are permitted to vote in a Canadian election for the first time. Not all Inuit are included
1951	The Northwest Territories Council now includes elected, as well as appointed, members and starts alternating meetings between Ottawa and the North.
1953	The Department of Northern Affairs and Natural Resources is formed; its Arctic Division is devoted solely to Inuit.
1955	Work begins on the Distant Early Warning Line (known as the DEWline).
1955	Inuit families are moved from Port Harrison, Northern Quebec and Pond Inlet, Baffin Island to new communities in the High Arctic, at Resolute Bay and Grise Fiord.
1957	Abraham (Abe) Okpik, George Koneak, Ayaruak and Shingituk make a 'historic first appearance at the Eskimo Affairs Committee meeting in Ottawa' (Crowe 1991: 203).
1958	The first Inuit community council is formed at Baker Lake; creation of the CBC Northern Service.
1959	Federal government starts cooperatives for Native people.
1959	James Houston introduces printmaking at Cape Dorset (Kinngait).
1962	Inuit in Districts of Keewatin and Franklin vote in a federal election for the first time (Rousselière 1962: 16).
1965	Abraham Okpik is appointed the first Aboriginal member of the Northwest Territories Council.

1967	Elected regional councils start; the first advisory group is in the Keewatin.
1968	The Project Surname process is started.
1969	Jean Chrétien's *White Paper on Indian Policy* promotes assimilation but also sparks Aboriginal communications projects; the Anik satellite system is launched.
1970	Northwest Territories Centennial; Project Surname is celebrated, though not yet completed.
1972	Project Surname is completed.
1973	The Arctic Peoples' Conference is held in Denmark (precursor to ICC).
	Canada launches the Native Communications Programme.
	Inuit Tapirisat of Canada (ITC) initiates a study of Inuit land use and occupancy, showing Inuit have 'aboriginal title' and laying the groundwork for the creation of Nunavut Territory.
1975	The Legislative Assembly of the Northwest Territories becomes fully elected, is run by consensus with no political parties, and has an Aboriginal majority.
1976	ITC proposes creation of Nunavut Territory as part of the proposed 'comprehensive settlement' of Inuit land claims in what at the time is the eastern part of the Northwest Territories.
	Inuvialuit (western Inuit) who live in the region of the Beaufort Sea and Yukon North Slope leave ITC to form a separate organisation and negotiate a land claim Agreement of their own.
	Canada considers a proposal to divide the Northwest Territories into two federal electoral districts: Nunatsiaq and the Western Arctic, a proposal implemented in 1979.
1977	Founding of the Inuit Circumpolar Conference (ICC).
	Labrador Inuit file a claim separate from that of the Inuit of the Nunavut region, involving 72,500 square kilometres of northern Labrador, an area larger than that of Ireland; it is the beginning of a long process that is not entirely resolved until 2006 (see below).

1978	Federally funded 'Project Inukshuk' marks the start of Inuit television on Anik B satellite.
1979	Start of Greenland Home Rule.
1980	The 'Thérrien Report' commissioned by the Canadian Radio Television and Telecommunications Commission (CRTC) highlights preservation of Aboriginal languages and cultures.
	ITC passes a unanimous resolution at its annual general meeting, calling for creation of Nunavut.
1981	The founding of Inuit Broadcasting Corporation (IBC) (the first Aboriginal television network).
1985	Qunngaatalluriktuq (Elise Attagutaluk) presents her names resolution to Pauktuutit, the Inuit Women's Association.
1986	Qunngaatalluriktuq dies; in the coming years her name will be given to many children.
1989	Soviet (Siberian) delegates attend ICC assembly for the first time, at Sisimiut, Greenland, and are given provisional status.
1990	Soviet delegates from Siberia become full members of ICC.
	The first (Russian) Congress of Northern Minorities is held in Moscow, with the support and presence of Mikhail Gorbachev and representatives of ICC.
	Tungavik [also spelled Tunngavik] Federation of Nunavut (TFN) signs an Agreement-in-principle with the federal and territorial governments, toward settlement of the land claims agreement to divide the Northwest Territories.
1991	The Q-Number Project is launched in Iqaluit.
1992	Television Northern Canada (TVNC) begins broadcasting in January.
	TFN and government negotiators set the provisions of a final land claims Agreement, with a plan to conclude a separate Nunavut Political Accord outlining the process for creating Nunavut Territory.
	Voters in the Northwest Territories (including those in what is now Nunavut) vote in a plebiscite, and approve the proposed new boundaries.
	October: signing of the Nunavut Political Accord.

November: Inuit ratify the Nunavut Land Claims Agreement.

1993   Signing of the Nunavut Land Claims Agreement.

Nunavut Land Claims Agreement Act and Nunavut Act are adopted by Parliament and receive Royal Assent.

1995–96   The Nunavut Implementation Commission (NIC) produces two documents, *Footprints in New Snow* and *Footprints II*; '*Footprints II* is used as the blueprint for the foundation of the Government of Nunavut' (Nunavut 2005).

1999   Official celebrations of the launch of Nunavut Territory.

Paul Okalik is elected Nunavut's first Premier.

Launch of Canada's nation-wide Aboriginal People's Television Network (APTN).

2000–02   Peter Irniq helps implement a programme to correct errors resulting from Project Surname.

1999   1 April, official launch of Nunavut Territory and the Government of Nunavut.

2004   The claims of Labrador Inuit are finally resolved, with the ratification on May 26, of the last land claim Agreement involving Inuit in Canada. It provides for self-government – the right of Inuit to pass their own laws and control health, education and justice in the new region of *Nunatsiavut*, 'our beautiful land' covering 72,500 square kilometres and 5,300 Inuit and *Kablunângajuit*, people of mixed Labrador Inuit and European ancestry (Canadian Broadcasting Corporation 2004).

2005   In December, the 5,300 Inuit and Kablunângajuit of Labrador sign a Final Agreement with the Government of Canada, marking the start of Inuit self-government in Nunatsiavut.

GLOSSARY

Amauti, Amautik	Baby-carrying hood in Eastern Arctic woman's parka
Atiq	Name, essence, soul, soul-name
Custom adoption	Inuit-style adoption, in which the child knows and has frequent contact with both the birth parents and the adoptive parents
DEWline	Distant Early Warning System, put in place by the U.S.A. during the Second War and maintained during the Cold War; later abandoned and replaced by the North Warning System
Disc (disk) numbers	Numbered, pressed-fibre discs given to Inuit to be worn as a means of identification
Disc list	The roster of disc numbers in each community; later extended, colloquially, to mean any list of community residents
Inuk	One (Inuit) person
Inuuk	Two (Inuit) people
Inuit	The people (plural form; 'Inuits' is redundant)
Inuktitut	The main Inuit language in Nunavut; closely related to other Inuit languages and dialects in the Canadian Western Arctic, Siberia, Alaska, and Greenland
Inuvialuit	Inuit from the Western Arctic
Kablunângajuit	People of mixed Labrador Inuit and European ancestry, mainly living in northern Labrador (Nunatsiavut) (see also Qallunaat and related spellings of the base word, *Kabluna* – non-Inuit person)

Kamiks	Boots, usually made of sealskin; the design is different for males and females
Nunatsiavut	Inuit northern Labrador
Nunavik	Inuit northern Quebec
Nunavut	The Inuit homeland, in the Canadian Eastern Arctic (means 'Our Land' in Inuktitut)
Outside (Out)	Anywhere south of 55 or 60 degrees latitude
Pauktuutit	The Inuit Women's Association of Canada
Qallunaaq	Non-Inuit (visitor) (Inuktitut for 'people with bushy eyebrows'. Also spelled *Kabloona*; *Kabloonak*; *Kadluna* and variations of these
Qallunaat	Plural form of Qallunaaq, according to *Nunatsiaq News* usage
Sauniq (saunik)	Namesake (literally 'bone'); refers to bone-to-bone relation between the namesake and the recipient of the name

BIBLIOGRAPHY

Aksayook, E., Pitseolak, K. and Kickidemoosie, N. undated. Text to accompany the permanent exhibit at Angmarlik Centre. Pangnirtung, Nunavut, Canada.

Algeo, J. 1985. 'Is a Theory of Names Possible?' *Names*, Vol. 33: 136–44.

Alia, V. 2005. 'Inuit Names: The People Who Love You'. In D.R. Newhouse, C.J. Voyageur and D. Beavon (eds), *Hidden in Plain Sight: Contributions of Aboriginal Peoples to Canadian Identity and Culture*. Toronto: University of Toronto Press, pp. 251–66.

———. 2004a. *Media Ethics and Social Change*. Edinburgh: Edinburgh University Press.

———. 2004b. 'Scattered Voices, Global Vision: Indigenous Peoples and the "New Media Nation"'. In K. Karim (ed.), *The Media of Diaspora*. London: Routledge, pp. 36–50.

———. 1999. *Un/Covering the North: News, Media, and Aboriginal People*. Vancouver: University of British Columbia Press.

———. 1996. 'June 30, 1992. (The morning after my mother died)', *Canadian Woman Studies/les cahiers de la femme*, Vol. 16, No. 4 (Fall): 77.

———. 1995b. Transcript for *Nunavut: Where Names Never Die* (radio documentary). 'Ideas', Toronto: Canadian Broadcasting Corporation (CBC).

———. 1994. *Names, Numbers and Northern Policy: Inuit, Project Surname and the Politics of Identity*. Halifax: Fernwood Books.

———. 1991. 'Aboriginal Perestroika', *Arctic Circle*, (November/December): 23–31.

———. 1989. 'Toward a Politics of Naming', Unpublished Ph.D. dissertation, York University, Canada.

———. 1987. 'Shaping New Medical Care for Inuit', *Up Here*, (June/July): 48–49.

———. 1986/7. 'Naming Themselves: Inuit Regain a Right', *Up Here*, (December/January), 12–23.

———. 1985a. 'Changing Clues for the Development of a Political Onomastics', *Onomastica Canadiana*, Vol. 61, No. 1, (June): 25–34.

———. 1984. *Quest for a Name; the Politics of Naming in Toni Morrison's Song of Solomon*. Ottawa: Hands Across the Border: Canadian and American Women Writers, unpublished paper.

———. 1982. *Literature on Naming: Mary V. Seeman's Work*. Unpublished paper. North York, Ontario: York University, Graduate Programme in Social and Political Thought.

———— (researcher, writer, narrator) and Moss, A. (producer). 1995a. *Nunavut: Where Names Never Die*. Two-hour radio documentary series. *Ideas*. Toronto: Canadian Broadcasting Corporation (CBC).

Alia, V. and Bull, S. 2005. *Media and Ethnic Minorities*. Edinburgh: Edinburgh University Press.

Allport, G. 1961. *Pattern and Growth in Personality*. New York: Holt, Rinehart and Winston.

Amagoalik, J. 1993. 'They Came, They Polluted, They Left', *Nunatsiaq News*, 23 July: 9.

————. 1977. 'Will the Inuit Disappear from the Face of This Earth?' *Inuit Today*, Vol. 6, No. 4, (May): 52–54.

Ames, W. (ed.) 1941. *What Shall We Name the Baby?* New York: Pocket Books.

Ang, I. 1996. *Living Room Wars: Rethinking Media Audiences for a Postmodern World*. London: Routledge.

Angus, M. 2000. 'Inuit Students Naming the Past', *Nunatsiaq News*, 14 January: 1, 2, 24.

Appadurai, A. 1988. 'Putting Hierarchy in Its Place', *Cultural Anthropology*, Vol. 3, No.1: 36–49.

Arctic Circle. 1991. ALL YOU QALLUNAAT, GET REGISTERED! July/August: 13.

Ardener, S. (ed.) 1978. *Defining Females: The Nature of Women in Society*. London: Croom Helm. (Note: includes theory developed by E. and S. Ardener).

———— (ed.) 1977. *Perceiving Women*. London: J.M. Dent. (See note in above reference).

Arigaktuk, A. 1967. *Inuttituut*, (Fall/Winter): 4.

Arnakak, J. 2000. 'Commentary: What is Inuit Qaujimajatuqangit? Using Inuit Family and Kinship Relationships to Apply Inuit Qaujimajatuqangit', *Nunatsiaq News*, 25 August, posted on website.

Attagutaluk, E. 1985. *Resolution #85–15*. Ottawa: Pauktuutit, January.

Austin, J.L. 1962. *How to Do Things with Words*. Cambridge, MA: Harvard University Press.

Badanai, H. 1967. *Minutes of Proceedings and Evidence*, No. 21, Standing Committee on Northern Affairs and National Resources, House of Commons First Session, Twenty-seventh Parliament, 1966–67. Witness: Mr. B.G. Sivertz, former Commissioner of the Northwest Territories. Ottawa: Roger Duhamel, F.R.S.C., Queen's Printer and Controller of Stationery, pp. 903–18.

Balikci, A. 1970. *The Netsilik Eskimo*. Garden City, NY: Natural History Press.

————. 1962. 'Some Acculturative Trends among the Eastern Canadian Eskimos', *Akten des 34. Internationalen Amerkanisten-kongresses*, Wien 1960, pp. 504–13.

Bell, D. 1983. *Daughters of the Dreaming*. Melbourne: McPhee Gribble.

Bell, D.V.J. 1975. *Power, Influence, and Authority: An Essay in Political Linguistics*. New York: Oxford University Press.

Bell, J. 2004. 'Nunavut's Population Nears 30,000', *Nunatsiaq News* online, 18 June.

————. 1993. 'The Real World' Editorial. *Nunatsiaq News*, 16 July: 2.

Berton, P. 1988. *The Arctic Grail: The Quest for the North West Passage and the North Pole, 1818–1909.* Toronto: McClelland & Stewart.

Bildfell, J.A. date unknown. 'Medical Report, Eastern Arctic Expedition'. In A.B. Roberts, 1975. *Eskimo Identification and Disc Numbers: A Brief History.* Department of Indian Affairs, Canada.

Birket-Smith, K. 1965. *The Paths of Culture: a General Ethnology,* (translated from the Danish by K. Fennow) Madison/Milwaukee: University of Wisconsin Press.

Boas, F. 1907. 'The Eskimo of Baffinland and Hudson Bay'. *Bulletin XV.* New York: American Museum of Natural History.

———. 1888. *The Central Eskimos. Sixth Annual Report of the Bureau of Ethnology to the Secretary of the Smithsonian Institution, 1884–1885.* Washington, DC: Smithsonian Institution.

Bolinger, D. 1980. *Language the Loaded Weapon: the Use and Abuse of Language Today.* London: Longman.

Boston Globe. 1973. 'Choose Your Own Relative'. Advertisement. *Boston Globe Sunday Magazine.* 13 November.

Bourdieu, P. 1991. *Language and Symbolic Power,* Cambridge, MA: Harvard University Press.

Briggs, J.L. 1982. 'Living Dangerously: the Contradictory Foundations of Value in Canadian Inuit Society'. In E. Leacock and R. Lee (eds), *Politics and History in Band Societies.* Cambridge: Cambridge University Press.

———. 1979. 'The Creation of Value in Canadian Inuit Society', *International Social Science Journal,* Vol. 31, No. 3.

———. 1970. *Never in Anger: Portrait of an Eskimo Family.* Cambridge, MA: Harvard University Press.

Bristow, G., Condon, R. and Kuptana, R. 1992. Unpublished Letter to the Editor of the *Telegraph Magazine,* sent from Holman Island, Canada.

British Broadcasting Corporation. 1998. 'The Jerusalem Report', *BBC News.* British Broadcasting Corporation, 31 August.

Brody, H. 1987. *Living Arctic: Hunters of the Canadian North.* Vancouver/Toronto: Douglas and McIntyre.

———. 1983. *Maps and Dreams.* Harmondsworth: Penguin.

———. 1975. *The People's Land.* Harmondsworth: Pelican.

——— (volume consultant/ed.). 1973. *Peoples of the Earth: Volume 16: The Arctic.* London: Danbury.

Bronski, M. 2003. 'Love's Labor's Lost: Looking Back at "Pins and Needles," the Play that was Union-made', *Forward* (online version), 11 April.

Burne, J. 2003. 'The Hidden Power to Heal', *Independent Review,* 22 April: 8.

Burgess, M. and Valaskakis, G.G. 1992. *Indian Princesses and Cowgirls: Stereotypes from the Frontier/Princesses Indienne et Cowgirls: Stereotypes de la Frontière.* Montreal: OBORO.

Burling, R. 1965. *Hill Farms and Padi Fields: Life in Mainland Southeast Asia.* Englewood Cliffs, NJ: Prentice-Hall.

Cahill, J.G. 1970. 'Eskimo Can Give Peace Lessons', *Paterson News.* 24 June.

Callaway, H. 1978. '"The Most Essentially Female Function of All": Giving Birth'. In S. Ardener, (ed.) *Defining Females.* London: Croom Helm.

Canada. Department of Indian and Northern Affairs. 1972. *Canada's North: 1970–1980*, Ottawa: Department of Indian and Northern Affairs.

Canada. Undated. *Canada's Geographical Names*. Ottawa: Energy, Mines and Resources Canada.

Canadian Permanent Committee on Geographical Names. 1987. *Native Geographical Names: Resolutions, 1986–87*. Ottawa: Energy, Mines and Resources Canada.

Canadian Press. 1969. 'Eskimo Number System on Way Out'. Winnipeg: *Leader Press*, 24 June, p. 5.

CBC (Canadian Broadasting Corporation). 2005. 'For first time PM invites First Nations leaders to top meeting', CBC News online, Friday, 21 October.

CBC (Canadian Broadcasting Corporation). 2004. 'Nunatsiavut: Our Beautiful Land', *CBC News Online*, 2 July.

Chairman of the Dominion lands Boards. 1933. 'Letter to H.H. Rowatt, Deputy Minister, Department of the Interior, June 26'. In A.B. Roberts, 1975. *Eskimo Identification and Disc Numbers: A Brief History*. Department of Indian and Northern Affairs, Canada, June, p. 3.

Christ, C.P. 1980. *Diving Deep and Surfacing: Woman Writers on Spiritual Quest*. Boston, MA: Beacon Press.

Clifford, J. 1997. *Routes: Travel and Translation in the Late Twentieth Century*. Cambridge, MA: Harvard University Press.

CNN. 2002. '"British Schindler" Gets Knighthood', *CNN News*, 31 December.

CNN. 2002. 'Honor for British Schindler', *CNN News*, 26 September.

Conlogue, R. 2004. 'Putting Names on a Nameless Past', *Globe and Mail*, 22 May: R4.

Contenta, S., Clark, W. and Barnes, A. 1982. 'Abandoned Baby Winning Her Fight', *Toronto Star*, 17 December: 1.

Correll, T.C. 1976. 'Language and Location in Traditional Inuit Societies'. In M.R. Freedman (ed.) *Inuit Land Use and Occupancy Study*, Vol. 2. Ottawa: Department of Indian Affairs and Northern Development, pp. 173–79.

Cowan, E. 1969. 'Eskimos of Canada: Between Conflicting Cultures', *New York Times*, Sunday, 13 April: 22.

Crowe, K. 1991. *A History of the Original Peoples of Northern Canada*, rev. edn. Montreal/Kingston: McGill-Queens University Press.

Curry, A. 1998. 'Love Lost and Found: Amnesia – the Injured Brain'. *Dateline*. New York: NBC News, published online at MSNBC.com.

Curwin, K. 1987. Editorial, *Nunatsiaq News*, 26 January.

Damas, D. 1984. 'Copper Eskimo'. In D. Damas (ed.), *Handbook of North American Indians*, Vol. 5, *Arctic*. Washington DC: Smithsonian Institution, pp. 397–414.

Davies, C.S. and Levitt, J. 1970. *What's in a Name?* London: Routledge and Kegan Paul.

Davis, R. and Zannis, M. 1973. *The Genocide Machine in Canada: The Pacification of the North*. Montreal: Black Rose.

Denmark. 1978. *Greenland Home Rule Act*, No. 577, Section 1, Government of Denmark, November 29.

Dion, K.C. 1983. 'Names, Identity and Self', *Names*, Vol. 31, No. 4 (December): 245–57.

Dorais, L-J. 1997. *Quaqtaq: Modernity and Identity in an Inuit Community*, Toronto/Buffalo/London: University of Toronto Press.

Doucette, W. 1991. Unpublished Letter to *Toronto Star*, in Sivertz (1993). Toronto, 5 August: B 1–7.

Driscoll, B. 1980. *The Inuit Amautik: I Like My Hood To Be Full*. Winnipeg: Winnipeg Art Gallery.

Driver, H. 1969. *Indians of North America*. Chicago, IL: University of Chicago Press.

Dufour, R. 1977. *Les Noms de Personnes Chez les Inuit d'Iglulik*, Thèse de Maîtrise en Anthropologie, Université Laval, Canada.

———. 1975. 'Le Phenomène du Sipiniq Chez les Inuit d'Iglulik', *Recherches Amerindiennes au* Québec, Vol. 3: 65–69.

Dybbroe, S. 1996. 'Questions of Identity and Issues of Self-determination', *Etudes/Inuit/Studies*, Vol. 20, No. 2: 39–53.

Edgar, J. 1989. 'Georgia: the Qallunaaq with One Name', *Nunatsiaq News*, 28 April.

Elliot, J.L. 1971. *Native Peoples*. Scarborough, Ontario: Prentice-Hall Canada.

Embleton, S.M. 1983. 'Are Personal-Name-Derived Place Names Sexist?' *The Ninth Lacus Forum*, 1982. Columbia, SC: Hornbeam.

Epstein, H. 1979. *Children of the Holocaust*. New York: Bantam.

Ernerk (Irniq), P. 1971. *Tukisivksat*, Vol. 1, No. 1, February.

Esfandiary, F.M. 1966. *Identity Card*. New York: Grove Press.

Étienne, M. and Leacock, E. (eds) 1980. *Women and Colonization: Anthropological Perspectives*. New York: Praeger.

Etzel, J.B. 2005. 'Amagoalik, John'. In M. Nuttall (ed.), *Encyclopedia of the Arctic*, Vol. 1, No. 1: 74–75.

Fienup-Riordan, A. 1993. *The Nelson Island Eskimo*. Anchorage: Alaska Pacific University Press.

Foucault, M. 1980. *Power/Knowledge*. New York: Pantheon.

Freedman, M.M.R. 1984. 'The Grise Fiord Project'. In D. Damas (ed.), *Handbook of North American Indians*, Vol. 5. Washington: Smithsonian Institution, pp. 676–82.

Freeman, M.A. 1978. *Life Among the Qallunaat*. Edmonton: Hurtig.

French, A. 1988. 'My Name is Masak'. In P. Petrone, *Northern Voices*. Toronto: University of Toronto Press, p. 203.

Friel, B. 1982. *Translations*. London: Faber and Faber.

Galtung, J. 1980. *The True Worlds: A Transnational Perspective*. New York: The Free Press.

Gilberg, R. 1984. 'Polar Eskimo'. In D. Damas (ed.), *Handbook of North American Indians*, Vol. 5, *Arctic*. Washington DC: Smithsonian Institution, pp. 577–94.

Goffman, E. 1959. *The Presentation of Self in Everyday Life*. New York: Doubleday.

Goodale, J. 1971. *Tiwi Wives: a Study of the Women of Melville Island, North Australia*. Seattle: University of Washington Press.

Gould, G. 1971. *The Idea of North*. Toronto: Canadian Broadcasting Corporation.

Government of the Northwest Territories. 1971. Report of the Territorial Council. Yellowknife: Government of the Northwest Territories.

———. 1971a. *Project Surname: A Summary*. Yellowknife: Government of the Northwest Territories, unpublished manuscript, November.

———. 1970. *Report of the Territorial Council*. Yellowknife: Government of the Northwest Territories.

———. 1969. *Council of the NWT, Transcript: Debates*, 40th Session, 7 Oct. and 39th Session. Yellowknife: Government of the Northwest Territories, 18 June.

———. 1968. *Council of the NWT, Transcript, Debates*, 36th Session, Yellowknife: Government of the Northwest Territories.

Government of Nunavut. 2005. Official website.

Graber, J.A. ('JAG') 1931. Review of 'Mourning Becomes Electra' and letter to the reviewer, *Bulletin*, NY: YMHA, no specific date or page number available.

Grace, S.E. 2001. *Canada and the Idea of North*. Montreal and Kingston, Canada: McGill-Queen's University Press.

Grant, S.D. 1988. *Sovereignty or Security? Government Policy in the Canadian North 1936–1950*. Vancouver: University of British Columbia Press.

Guemple, D.L. 1980. 'Growing Old in Inuit Society'. In V.W. Marshall, *Aging in Canada: Social Perspectives*. Don Mills, Ontario: Fitzhenry & Whiteside, pp. 95–101.

———. 1979. 'Inuit Socialization: A Study of Children as Social Actors in an Eskimo Community'. In K. Ishwaran (ed.), *Childhood and Adolescence in Canada*. Toronto: McGraw-Hill Ryerson, pp. 39–53.

———. 1969. 'The Eskimo Ritual Sponsor: A Problem in the Fusion of Semantic Domains', *Ethnology*, Vol. 8, No. 4 (October): 468–83.

———. 1965. 'Saunik: Name Sharing as a Factor Governing Eskimo Kinship Terms', *Ethnology*, Vol. 4, No. 3: 323–35.

Gunew, S. 2004. *Haunted Nations: The Colonial Dimensions of Multiculturalisms*, London/New York: Routledge.

Hall, S. 1980. 'Race, Articulation and Societies Structured in Dominance'. In UNESCO, *Sociological Theories: Race and Colonialism*. Paris: UNESCO, pp. 305–45.

Hamilton, H. 2003. *The Speckled People*. London and New York: Fourth Estate (HarperCollins).

Hanson, A. 1989. 'Abe Okpik: A Man Who Does For Others'. True Northerners. *Nunatsiaq News*, 10 February: 16–17.

Harper, K. 2001. 'Peck Did Not Create First Syllabic System'. Letters & Opinions, *Nunatsiaq News*. 4 May: 9.

Hart, G.W.M. and Pilling, A.R. 1966. *The Tiwi of North Australia*. New York: Holt, Rinehart and Winston.

Hechter, M. 1986. 'Rational Choice Theory and the Study of Race and Ethnic Relations'. In J. Rex and D. Mason (eds), *Theory of Race and Ethnic Relations*. Cambridge: Cambridge University Press.

———. 1975. *Internal Colonialism: The Celtic Fringe in British National Development, 1536–1966*. Berkeley, CA: University of California Press.

Heller, L. 1983. 'Changing a Name? Trouble's the Game'. *Toronto Star*, 6 January: E1.

Henderson, A. 2005. 'Inuit Qaujimajatuqangit'. In M. Nuttall (ed.), *Encyclopedia of the Arctic*, Vol. 2, 1003–04.

Herbert, R.K. 1996. 'The Dynamics of Personal Names and Naming Practices in Africa'. In E. Eichler et al. (eds), *Name Studies: An International Handbook of Onomastics* 2. Berlin: Walter de Gruyter, pp. 1222–27.

Herbert, W. 1981. *Hunters of the Polar North: the Eskimos*. Amsterdam: Time-Life.

Hickerson, N.P. 1980. *Linguistic Anthropology*. New York: Holt, Rinehart and Winston.

Hickey, G.C. 1964. *Village in Vietnam*. New Haven, CT: Yale University Press.

Hodge, B. 1979. 'Birth and the Community'. In R. Fowler, B. Hodge, G. Kress and T. Trew (eds.), *Language and Control*. London: Routledge and Kegan Paul.

Hodgson, S.M. 1970. *Annual Report of the Commissioner of the Northwest Territories*, R.M. Harvey (ed.) Yellowknife: Department of Information under the authority of the Commissioner of the Northwest Territories.

———. 1969. *Annual Report of the Commissioner of the Northwest Territories*, 38th session; 39th session, Yellowknife: Government of the Northwest Territories.

Holmes, D. 1989. *Dehcho: Mom, We've Been Discovered*. Yellowknife, NWT: Dene Cultural Institute.

———. 1986. 'Toponymist Ready for Flood of Names'. *News/North*, 6 June.

Hook, J.N. 1982. *Family Names: How Our Surnames Came to America*. New York: Macmillan.

Humphrey, C. 1978. 'Women, Taboo and the Suppression of Attention'. In S. Ardener (ed.), *Defining Females*. London: Croom Helm.

Inuit Cultural Institute. 1981. 'The Nunavut Concept: A Proposal for Inuit Self-Determination'. *Ajurnangimmat*, 28–37.

Inuit Tapiriit Kanatami. 2005. *Inuit Sign Historic Partnership Agreement*. Press release, 31 May.

Inuktitut Magazine. 1984. *Report on Avataq Cultural Institute's Names Project*. Ottawa: Department of Indian and Northern Affairs, Fall, pp. 35–36.

Inuttituut. 1967. 'Abe Okpik Meets the Queen'. *Inuttituut* (Summer).

Ipellie, A. 1976. 'Inuit Names', *Inuit Today*, Vol. 5, (June): 44–47.

Irving, J. 1985. *The Cider House Rules*. New York: William Morrow and Company, Inc.

Irqugaqtuq, B. 1977–78. 'The Autobiography of a Pelly Bay Eskimo', *Eskimo Magazine* (Fall–Winter): 22–23.

Isaacs, H.R. 1989. *Idols of the Tribe: Group Identity and Political Change*, Cambridge, MA: Harvard University Press.

Jakobson, R. 1970. *Main Trends in the Science of Language*. New York: Harper and Row.

Janeway, E. 1980. *Powers of the Weak*. New York: A. Knopf.

Jenness, D. 1977 (1932). *The Indians of Canada*. Originally published as Bulletin 65, Anthropological Series No. 15 of the National Museum of Canada. Ottawa: Minister of Supply and Services Canada.

———. 1968. *Eskimo Administration V: Analysis and Reflections*. Technical Paper No. 21. Montreal: Arctic Institute of North America.

————. 1964. *Eskimo Administration II*. Technical Paper No. 14. Canada: Arctic Institute of North America.

Jenness, D. and Macdonald, R. St. J. (eds) (no date). *The Arctic Frontier*. Toronto: University of Toronto Press, pp. 120–29.

Jull, P. 1988. 'Building Nunavut: A Story of Inuit Self Government', *The Northern Review*, No. 1, (Summer): 59–72.

Junghare, Indira Y. 1975. 'Socio-psychological Aspects and Linguistic Analysis of Marathi Names'. *Names*, Vol. 23, 31–43.

Kaganoff, B.C. 1977. *A Dictionary of Jewish Names and their History*. New York: Schocken.

Kahn, M. 1980. *Children of the Jinn*. U.S.A.: Wideview Books.

Kaplan, J. and Bernays, A.1997. *The Language of Names*. New York: Simon & Schuster.

Keesing, R.M. 1975. *Kin Groups and Social Structure*. New York: Holt, Rinehart and Winston.

Kelling, R. 1975. *Language: Mirror, Tool and Weapon*. Chicago, IL: Nelson-Hall.

Kemp, W.B. 1984. 'Baffinland Eskimo'. In D. Damas, *Handbook of North American Indians*, Vol. 5. Washington, DC: Smithsonian Institution, pp. 463–75.

Kent, R. 1935. *Salamina*. New York: Harcourt Brace.

Kilabuk-Bourassa, N. 1985. Pangnirtung: *Tusautit Newsletter*, Year 2, No. 4, 13 December.

Kingston, M.H. 1976. *The Woman Warrior: Memories of a Girlhood among Ghosts*. New York: Holt, Rinehart and Winston.

Kleivan, I. 1984. 'West Greenland before 1950'. In D. Damas, *Handbook of North American Indians*, Washington DC: Smithsonian Institution, pp. 595–621. (Translated from Danish by Charles Jones.)

Koopman, A. 2002. *Zulu Names*. Pietermaritzburg, South Africa: University of Natal Press.

Kramarae, C. 1981. *Women and Men Speaking*. Rowley, MA: Newbury House.

————. 1977. 'Perceptions of Female and Male Speech', *Language and Speech*, Vol. 20, No. 2 (April/June): 151–61.

Kramer (Kramarae), C. 1975. 'Women's Speech: Separate but Unequal'. In B. Thorne and N. Henley (eds), *Language and Sex: Difference and Dominance*. Rowley, MA: Newbury House.

Kramarae, C., Thorne, B. and Henley, N. 1978. 'Perspectives on Language and Communication', *Signs: Journal of Women in Culture and Society*, Vol. 2, No. 3, (Spring): 638–51.

Kramarae, C. and Treichler, P.A. 1988. *Amazons, Bluestockings and Crones: A Feminist Dictionary*. London: Pandora.

Kuchmij, H. 1995. 'The Story of Joe and Elise'. CBC Television, *Man Alive* series. Toronto: Canadian Broadcasting Corporation.

Kurzweil, A. 1980. *From Generation to Generation*. New York: Schocken.

Lahiri, J. 2004. *The Namesake*. London: Flamingo.

Lantis, M. 1984. 'Nunivak Eskimo'. In D. Damas, *Handbook of North American Indians*, Vol. 5 *Arctic*, Washington DC: Smithsonian Institution, pp. 209–23.

Leacock, E.B. 1981. *Myths of Male Dominance: Collected Articles on Women Cross-culturally*. New York: Monthly Review Press.

Leacock, E.B. and Lee, R. (eds) 1982. *Politics and History in Band Societies.* Cambridge: Cambridge University Press.

Leader Press. 1969. Saskatchewan: *The Leader Press,* 24 June: 5.

Lévi-Strauss, C. 1966. *The Savage Mind.* Chicago, IL: University of Chicago Press.

Levy, R.I. 1973. *Tahitians: Mind and Experience in the Society Islands.* Chicago, IL: University of Chicago Press.

Library and Archives Canada. 2005. Project Naming website.

Lyall, E. 1983. *An Arctic Man.* Edmonton: Hurtig.

Macnamara, J. 1982. *Names for Things: a Study of Human Learning.* Cambridge, MA: MIT Press.

Marcus, A.R. 1992. *Out in the Cold: the Legacy of Canada's Inuit Relocation Experiment in the High Arctic.* Copenhagen: International Work Group for Indigenous Affairs.

Marcus, G.E. and Cushman, D. 1982. 'Ethnographies as Texts', *Annual Review of Anthropology,* Vol. 2: 25–69.

Markey, T.L. 1982. 'Crisis and Cognition in Onomastics', *Names,* Vol. 30: 3129–41.

Mayes, R.G. 1978. 'The Creation of a Dependent People: The Inuit of Cumberland Sound, Northwest Territories, 1953–1973'. Unpublished Ph.D. dissertation, Montreal: McGill University Department of Geography.

Miller, C and Swift, K. 1977. *Words and Women: New Language in New Times.* New York: Anchor.

Morrison, T. 1977. *Song of Solomon.* New York: New American Library.

Mueller, C. 1973. *The Politics of Communication.* New York: Oxford University Press.

Müller-Wille, L. 1984. 'The Nameless Arctic: Inuit Put Their Names on the Map', *The Northern Raven,* Vol. 4, No. 2 (New Series), Autumn.

National Library and Archives of Canada. 1946. Ottawa: Government of Canada.

Native Press. 1986. 'Places to Get Their Real Names', *Native Press,* 31 January: 2.

Neethling, B. (S.J.) 2005 *Naming among the Xhosa of South Africa.* Lewiston/ Queenston/Lampeter: The Edwin Mellen Press.

————. 2000. 'An Onomastic Renaissance: African Names to the Fore'. *South African Journal of African Languages,* Vol. 20, No. 3.

————. 1996. 'January to December: Traditional Xhosa Nomenclature'. *Nomina Africana,* Vol. 10, Nos. 1 and 2.

Neill, M. 1981. Introduction to First Edition. In 1984. *Biographies of Inuit Artists,* second edition. Ottawa: Canadian Arctic Producers, pp. 6–8.

Nicolaïsen, W.F.H. 1974. 'Names as Verbal Icons', *Names,* Vol. 22, 104–10.

Nuttall, M. 1992. *Arctic Homeland: Kinship, Community and Development in Northwest Greenland.* Toronto: University of Toronto Press.

Okalik, L. 1993. 'Poetry on Signing of the Nunavut Agreement'. *Nunavut,* Vol. 12, No. 4 (July–August): a14.

Okalik, P. 2001. *What Does Indigenous Self-Government Mean?* Speaking notes, Brisbane, Australia, Government of Nunavut website, Premier Paul Okalik's web page, 13 August.

Okpik, A. 1970. *Project Surname*, Yellowknife: Territorial Secretary, Northwest Territories Centennial. Government of the Northwest Territories.

———. 1962. 'What Does It Mean to Be an Eskimo?' *North*, Vol. 9, No. 2: 28.

Ortner, S.B. and Whitehead, H. (eds) 1981. *Sexual Meanings: The Cultural Construction of Gender and Sexuality.* Cambridge: Cambridge University Press.

Paine, R. 1977. 'The Nursery Game: Colonizers and Colonized in the Canadian Arctic', *Etudes/Inuit Studies*, Vol. 1, No. 1: 5–32.

Paton, A. 1981. *Ah, But Your Land Is Beautiful!* New York: Scribner's.

Pearsall, J. and Trumble, B. (eds) 1996. *The Oxford English Reference Dictionary*, second edition. Oxford: Oxford University Press, p. 739.

Petersen, C. 1983. 'Unnatural Design of Place Names'. *Chicago Tribune*, 14 April.

Petersen, R. 1984. 'The Pan-Eskimo Movement'. In D. Damas (ed.), *Handbook of North American Indians*, Vol. 5, *Arctic*, Washington, DC: Smithsonian Institution, pp. 724–28.

Petrone, P. 1988. *Northern Voices: Inuit Writing in English.* Toronto: University of Toronto Press.

Poole, F.P. 1981. 'Transforming "Natural" Woman: Female Ritual Leaders and Gender Identity among Bimin-Kuskusmin'. In S.B. Ortner and H. Whitehead (eds), *Sexual Meanings: the Cultural Construction of Gender and Sexuality.* Cambridge: Cambridge University Press.

Pratt, M.L. 1992. *Imperial Eyes: Travel Writing and Transculturation.* London: Routledge.

Pryde, D. 1969. 'What They Say', *Arctic Development Digest*. Montreal: Canadian Century Publishers, Vol. 1, No. 4, (December): 29–30.

Pullen, T.C. 1987. *Letter to the Editor of the Globe and Mail.* In K. Curwin, Editorial, *Nunatsiaq News*, 26 January.

Qitsualik, R.A. 2003. 'Playing Cowboys and Inuit'. *Indian Country Today* website, 23 January.

Quigley, M. 1982. 'Language of Conquest, Language of Survival', *Canadian Forum*, November, 14–15.

Rapoport, N. 1980. 'The Woman Who Lost Her Names'. In J.W. Mazow (ed.), *The Woman Who Lost Her Names: Selected Writings by American Jewish Women.* San Francisco, CA: Harper and Row.

Rasmussen, K. 1929. *Intellectual Culture of the Iglulik Eskimos. Report of the Fifth Thule Expedition, 1921–1924*, Vol. 7.

———. 1929b. *Intellectual Culture of the Copper Eskimos. Report of the Fifth Thule Expedition, 1921–1924*, Vol. 9.

Rassky, S.F. 1988. 'What's in a Name? For Indians, Cultural Survival', *New York Times*, 4 August.

Reitz, J.G. 1980. *The Survival of Ethnic Groups.* Toronto: McGraw-Hill Ryerson.

Remie, C.H.W. 1983. 'Culture Change and Religious Continuity among the Arviligdjuarmiut of Pelly Bay, NWT, 1935–1963', *Etudes/Inuit Studies*, Vol. 7, No. 2: 53–77.

Rennick, R. 1969. 'Hitlers and Others Who Changed their Names and a Few Who Did Not'. *Names*, Vol. 17: 199–207.

Richler, M. 1994. 'The Style and Substance of Pierre Trudeau,' *Times Literary Supplement*, 8 April.

Robbe, P. 1981. 'Les Noms de Personne Chez les Amassalimiut', *Etudes/Inuit/Studies*, Vol. 5, No. 1: 45–82.

Ritter, R.M. ed. and compiler. 2000. *The Oxford Dictionary for Writers and Editors*, second edition. Oxford: Oxford University Press, p. 172.

Robert-Lamblin, J. 1981. 'Changement de Sèxe' de Certains Enfants d'Ammassalik (Est Groenland): Un Rééquilibrage du Sèxe Ratio Familial?' *Études/Inuit/Studies*, Vol. 5, No. 1: 117–25.

Roberts, A.B. 1975. *Eskimo Identification and Disc Numbers: A Brief History*. Paper prepared for the Social Development Division, Department of Indian and Northern Affairs, Canada. June.

Robinson, L. 1993. 'Baffin, in Nunavut 1999: In the Words of the People'. *Up Here*, August/September: 14–17.

Rode, Z.R. 1976. 'The Origin of Jewish Family Names', *Names*, Vol. 24: 165–69.

Rostaing, J-P. 1985. 'Native Regional Autonomy: The Initial Experience of the Kativik Regional Government.' *Études/Inuit/Studies*, Vol. 8, No. 2: 3–40.

Roussellière, Father G.M. 1972. 'The New Eskimo Names: A Real Mess', *Eskimo*, New Series, No. 3 (Spring-Summer): 18.

———. 1971. 'Surnames for the Eskimos', *Eskimo*, New Series, No.1 (Spring-Summer): 12–13.

———. 1962. 'The Eskimo Have Voted', *Eskimo*. Vol. 62 (Fall): 16.

Saladin d'Anglure, B. 1980. 'Petit-ventre, L'Enfant-géant du Cosmos Inuit', *L'homme*, Vol. 20: 1.

———. 1978. 'L'Homme (Angut), Le Fils (Irniq) et la Lumière (Qau) ou le Cercle du Pouvoir Masculin Chez les Inuits de l'Arctique Central', *Anthropologica*, Vol. 20, Nos. 1–2: 101–44.

———. 1977. 'Iqallijuq ou les Reminiscences d'une âme-nom Inuit, *Études/Inuit/Studies*, Vol. 1, No. 1: 33–63.

———. 1970. 'Nom et Parente Chez les Esquimaux Tarramiut du Nouveau-Québec (Canada)', *Échanges et Communications, Mélanges Offerts à Claude Lévi-Strauss, Réunis par J. Pouillon et P. Maranda*. Paris-La Haye: Mouton, pp. 1013–39.

Sanavik Cooperative. 1973. Baker Lake 1973 Prints (catalogue).

Satyamurti, C. 2005. 'Immigrants', *Independent on Sunday*, 29 May: 25.

Seenan, G. 2003. 'We'll Fight To Save *Gaelic*, So Long As You Don't Use It', *Guardian*, 31 May: 10.

Sennet, R. 1980. *Authority*. New York: Vintage.

Shakespeare, W. 1940. *The Tragedy of Romeo and Juliet*, edited and with notes by George Lyman Kittredge. Boston, MA: Ginn.

Sherif, M. and Cantril, H. 1947. *The Psychology of Ego-involvements*. Hoboken, NJ: John Wiley & Sons.

Sivertz, B.G. 1993. Letter to the Honourable Bertha Wilson, Royal Commission on Aboriginal Peoples. Subject: Relocation of 87 Inuit in 1953–55. (Open letter copied to public officials, northern scholars, former northern politicians and administrators and major Canadian news media), with enclosures, including letter from W. Doucette (above), 18 May.

Skinner, E.P. (ed.) 1973. *Peoples and Cultures of Africa*. Garden City, NY: Natural History.

Smith, D.G. 1984. 'Mackenzie Delta Eskimo'. In D. Damas (ed.), *Handbook of North American Indians*, Vol. 5, *Arctic*. Washington, DC: Smithsonian Institution, pp. 347–58.

Søby, R.M. 1992. 'Kullorsuaq: Naming Customs'. Unpublished paper.

Spender, D. 1980. *Man Made Language*. London: Routledge and Kegan Paul.

Spitzer, A. 2000. 'Getting the names right – finally', *Nunatsiaq News*, 20 October: 7.

Stefansson, V. 1922. *The Friendly Arctic: The Story of Five Years in Polar Regions*. New York: MacMillan.

Steffens, L. 1931. *The Autobiography of Lincoln Steffens*. New York: Harcourt Brace and Company.

Stein, A. 1993. *Hidden Children: Forgotten Survivors of the Holocaust*. Toronto: Penguin.

Strauss, A. 1982. 'Social Worlds and Legitimation Processes'. *Studies in Symbolic Interaction*, Vol. 4: 171–90.

———. 1978. 'A Social World Perspective', *Studies in Symbolic Interaction*, Vol. 1: 119–28.

Svensson, Tom G. 1985. 'The Sami and the Nation State: Some Comments on the Ethnopolitics in the Northern Fourth World', *Études/Inuit/Studies*, Vol. 8, No. 2: 158–66.

Swiercinsky, D.P., Price, T.L. and Leaf, L.E. 1993. *Traumatic Head Injury*. Kansas City, KS: The Head Injury Association of Kansas and Greater Kansas City, Inc.

Sykes, J.B. (ed.) 1982. *The Concise Oxford English Dictionary of Current English*, seventh edition. Oxford: Oxford University Press, p. 325.

Tester, F.J. and Kulchyski, P. 1994. *Tammarniit (Mistakes): Inuit Relocation in the Eastern Arctic 1939–63*. Vancouver: UBC Press.

Thompson, F. 1992. 'British newspaper article deserves "harsh rebuttal" – Holman Mayor', *News/North*, 2 November, A3, A30.

Toronto Star. 1991. 'Jews Had To Buy Names', 1 August: A7.

Toronto Star. 1987. 'Legal Santa Claus Loves "The Little Greedy Monsters"', 17 December.

Toronto Star. 1987. Photograph, 29 January: A14.

Toronto Star. 1983. '"Please, Judge – Call me God"', 16 March: A16.

Trott, C.G. 2005. *Ilagiit* and *Tuquraqtuq: Inuit Understandings of Kinship and Social Relatedness*. Paper prepared for First Nations, First Thoughts, Centre of Canadian Studies, University of Edinburgh, unpublished paper.

Tukisiviksat. 1971a. 'Yellowknife: Government of the North West Territories', Vol. 1, No. 3, April.

Tukisiviksat. 1971b. Vol. 1, No. 1, February.

Tungavik and Minister of Indian Affairs and Northern Development. 1993. *Part 9: PLACE NAMES, 33.9.1 and 33.9.2, an Agreement Between the Inuit of the Nunavut Settlement Area and Her Majesty the Queen in Right of Canada*. Ottawa: Minister of Indian Affairs and Northern Development.

Tunnuq, M. 1992. 'Recollections and Comments'. *Inuktitut*, No. 75. Ottawa: Inuit Tapirisat of Canada.

Valaskakis, G.G. 1988. 'The Chippewa and the Other: Living the Heritage of Lac du Flambeau', *Cultural Studies*, Vol. 2, No. 3, October.

Vanast, W.J. 1991. 'Hastening the Day of Extinction: Canada, Quebec, and the Medical Care of Ungava's Inuit, 1867–1967', *Études/Inuit/Studies*, Vol. 15, No. 2: 55–84.

Vygotsky, L.S. 1962. *Thought and Language*. Cambridge, MA: MIT Press.

Waite, M. (ed.) 1996. *The Oxford Colour Spelling Dictionary*. Oxford: Clarendon Press, p. 177.

Walz, J. 1970. 'Civilization, Good and Bad, Invades the Canadian North', *New York Times*, 13 March, reprinted in *Paterson News*, June 1972: 8–9.

———. 1969. 'Canada Promotes Nationalism in the Arctic', *New York Times*, 5 May: 14.

Wasserman, H. and Jacobs, S. 2003. *Shifting Selves: Post-apartheid Essays on Mass Media, Culture and Identity*. Kwela, South Africa: Kaapstad.

Weber, B. 2001. 'Inuit Lawyer Wins Name Appeal'. *Edmonton Journal*, 1 December, no page number.

Wertham, F. 1953. *Seduction of the Innocent*. New York: Rinehart.

Weslager, C.A. 1971. 'Name-giving Among the Delaware Indians'. *Names*, Vol. 19: 268–83.

Whitney, W.D. 1979 (1875). *The Life and Growth of Language: an Outline of Linguistic Science*. New York: Dover.

Whorf, B.L. 1972. 'Grammatical Categories'. In F.W. Householder (ed.), 'Syntactic Theory 1', *Structuralist*, Middlesex: Penguin, pp. 103–14.

Williamson, R. 1993. 'Memories of John Kavik 1897–1993', *Inuit Art Quarterly*, Vol. 8, No. 3 (Fall): 46.

———. 1974. *Eskimo Underground: Socio-Cultural Change in the Canadian Central Arctic*. Uppsala, Sweden: Institutionen förallmen ochjamförand etnografi vid Uppsala Universitet.

———. 1968. Motion to the Northwest Territories Council, July, in Roberts, op. cit., p. 28.

Wilson, P.J. 1973. 'Tsimehety Kinship and Descent'. In E.P. Skinner (ed.), *Peoples and Cultures of Africa*. Garden City, New York: Doubleday.

Winter, E. 1968. *And Not to Yield: An Autobiography*. New York: Harcourt, Brace & World.

Winter, E. and Shapiro, H. 1962. *The World of Lincoln Steffens*. New York: Hill and Wang.

Wormsley, W.E. 1980. 'Tradition and Change in Imbonggu: Names and Naming Practices', *Names*, Vol. 28: 183–94.

Zabeeh, F. 1968, *What is in a Name? an Inquiry into the Semantics and Pragmatics of Proper Names*. The Hague: Martinus Nijhoff.

Additional References and Sources

Acoma. 1993. Conversations with members of the Acoma Pueblo in Arizona.

Aglukark, S. and Irschick, C. 1999. 'E186' (song), Nipi Music (SOCAN)/C. Ischick (SOCAN) in Aglukark, S. 1999. *Unsung Heroes* (CD), EMI Music Canada.

Alia, V. 1984–2006. Interviews and conversations with Inuit and Qallunaat in Iqaluit, Pangnirtung, Igloolik and other locations in Nunavut, Greenland, Alaska and southern Canada, Britain and Europe.

———. 1985b. Journal kept during first trip to Baffin Island, Nunavut.

———. 1982–87. Interviews with first, second, and third generation immigrants to Canada.

Anilniliak, Nancy. 1985. Personal communication. Pangnirtung, Nunavut.

Billing, D. 1985. Letter to V. Alia from the Science Advisor of the Northwest Territories, 17 July.

Crowe, K. 1984–96. Personal communications.

Embleton, S.M. 1989. Personal communication. Toronto.

Graber, S.P. 1986. personal communication. Portland, Oregon.

Idlout, L. 2002. *E5–770, My Mother's Name* (CD), Ottawa: Heart Wreck Records.

Immaroitok, B. 1985. Interview with V. Alia. Ottawa: Inuit Tapirisat of Canada.

Irniq (Ernerk), P. 2000. E-mail to Valerie Alia. 11 December.

Jarvie, M. 1984–94. Personal communications concerning family members who were 'hidden children'.

Kramarae, C. 1989. Personal communication.

Leacock, E.B. 1984. Personal Communication.

MacDonald, J. 1993. Letter to V. Alia. Igloolik: Igloolik Research Centre, 27 October.

McDonald, G.C. 2006. E-mail correspondence, 16, 17, 18 January.

Müller-Wille, L. and Weber, L. 1985–2005. Personal communications.

Neill, T.M. 1984–86. Interviews and conversations with V. Alia.

Okpik, A. 1985–95. Interviews and conversations. Iqaluit, Nunavut and Sisimiut, Greenland.

Olsen, C.C. (P.) 1985–98. Personal communications.

Phillips, R.A.J. 1993. Interviewed by V. Alia by telephone from his home in the Gatineau region of Quebec, 9 November.

Restivo, D. (David) 2004. Personal communication.

Schechter, E. 1988–90. Personal communications with V. Alia.

Sivertz, B.G. 1993b. Telephone Conversation with V. Alia, Victoria, British Columbia, 14 December.

Toukmanian, S. 1984. Personal communication.

INDEX